D1068218

Culture, Conflict, and Counterinsurgency

Culture, Conflict, and Counterinsurgency

Edited by Thomas H. Johnson and Barry Scott Zellen

Stanford Security Studies
An Imprint of Stanford University Press
Stanford, California

03/25/14
WW
$45.00

Stanford University Press
Stanford, California

Printed in the United States of America on acid-free, archival-quality paper

Library of Congress Cataloging-in-Publication Data

Culture, conflict, and counterinsurgency / edited by Thomas H. Johnson and Barry Scott Zellen.
    pages cm
  Includes bibliographical references and index.
  ISBN 978-0-8047-8595-2 (cloth : alk. paper)
  1. Afghan War, 2001—Social aspects. 2. Counterinsurgency—Afghanistan.
3. Military intelligence—Afghanistan. 4. Afghanistan—Social life and customs.
5. Counterinsurgency. 6. Military intelligence. 7. Culture. I. Johnson, Thomas H., editor of compilation. II. Zellen, Barry Scott, editor of compilation.
  DS371.412.C85 2014
  958.104'71—dc23
                                                                                    2013021447
ISBN 978-0-8047-8921-9 (electronic)

Special discounts for bulk quantities of Stanford Security Studies are available to corporations, professional associations, and other organizations. For details and discount information, contact the special sales department of Stanford University Press. Tel: (650) 736-1782, Fax: (650) 736-1784

Typeset by Thompson Type in 10/14 Minion

CONTENTS

NOTES ON CONTRIBUTORS

Thomas Barfield is an anthropologist who conducted ethnographic fieldwork with nomads in northern Afghanistan in the mid-1970s as well as shorter periods of research in Xinjiang, China, and post-Soviet Uzbekistan. He is author of *The Central Asian Arabs of Afghanistan* (1981) and *The Perilous Frontier: Nomadic Empires and China* (1989) and coauthor of *Afghanistan: An Atlas of Indigenous Domestic Architecture* (1991). Currently Professor of Anthropology at Boston University, Barfield is also President of the American Institute for Afghanistan Studies. Since 2001 his research has focused on problems of law and political development in contemporary Afghanistan. In 2007 Barfield received a Guggenheim Fellowship for his most recent book, *Afghanistan: A Cultural and Political History* (Princeton, 2010).

LT Robert "Jake" Bebber is an Information Warfare officer in the U.S. Navy. He is currently serving on the staff of the Commander of the United States Seventh Fleet, headquartered in Yokosuka, Japan, and embarked on the USS *Blue Ridge*. From December 2007 to November 2008, LT Bebber was the Information Operations Officer for Joint Provincial Reconstruction Team Khost in Khost, Afghanistan. LT Bebber received his PhD in Public Policy in 2007 from the University of Central Florida in Orlando. LT Bebber is supported by his wife Dana and lives in Yokosuka, Japan. He is currently Lieutenant in the U.S. Navy.

Colonel Michael R. Fenzel is a native of Chicago, Illinois. He holds a BA in Economics from Johns Hopkins University, an MPA from Harvard University, and an MA in National Security and Strategic Studies from the U.S. Naval War College and is a PhD Candidate in National Security Studies at the Naval Postgraduate School. Colonel Fenzel has served as a strategist and policy analyst for the U.S. Army Chief of Staff, as a Director for Transnational Threats and Director for Combating Terrorism at the National Security Council (NSC) on the White House staff (2000–2001). Mike has taken part in seven contingency deployments over the last twenty-five years, including the parachute assault into Iraq in March 2003 and two extended deployments to Afghanistan between 2004 and 2008, where he served as the Deputy Director for Military Operations, Deputy Brigade Commander for 1st Brigade, 82nd Airborne Division, in Regional Command East, and Battalion Task Force Commander in Eastern Paktika along the border with Pakistan. He has most recently commanded the 2nd Brigade of the 1st Armored Division (2010) and 3rd Brigade of the 82nd Airborne Division since early 2012. Colonel Fenzel is a White House Fellow, Life Member on the Council on Foreign Relations, and Douglas MacArthur Leadership Award winner and has also been awarded for valor twice in combat.

Alexei Gavriel is an applied anthropologist conducting research on the integration of sociocultural knowledge into contemporary military operational planning and intelligence. He serves as Afghanistan Program Manager for Glevum Associates' Media Evaluation Project, which examines client-funded media content and reports on its impact on Afghan individuals and society through determining whether a target audience is being reached and if the primary messages of the media are understood. He has conducted ethnographic research in a variety of remote locations among indigenous reindeer herders in the Russian tundra, Roma-Gypsy ghetto dwellers in Eastern Slovakia, and nationalist-separatists in the former Yugoslavia.

Professor Thomas H. Johnson is a faculty member of the National Security Affairs Department at the Naval Postgraduate School as well the Director of the Program for Culture & Conflict Studies. Under his direction, the CCS program coordinates research activities on Afghanistan and other countries of South and Central Asia as well as the Middle East. At NPS, Professor Johnson teaches courses on Afghanistan, Central Asia, terrorism, and insurgencies/

counterinsurgencies. He also regularly contributes to the Regional Security Education Program and the Leadership Development and Education for Security and Peace Program at NPS, where he briefs deploying troops. Johnson has taught at the University of Southern California and the Foreign Service Institute and frequently lectures at Service Academies. Before joining the faculty of the Naval Postgraduate School, he served on the faculty of George Mason University. For two decades, Professor Johnson has conducted research and written on Afghanistan and South Asia. He is a member of the Afghanistan Editorial Board of the National Security Archive. His publications have appeared in the *American Political Science Review, International Security, Foreign Policy, Military Review, Journal of Politics, Orbis: A Journal of World Affairs, Central Asian Survey, China and Eurasian Forum Quarterly, Small Wars and Insurgencies, Strategic Insights, The Brown Journal of World Affairs, Strategic Review, Politikon: South African Journal of Political Science,* and the *Journal of Modern African Studies,* as well as numerous scholarly edited volumes and texts. His commentaries have appeared in numerous media outlets to recently include the *Atlantic Monthly, Washington Post, Wall Street Journal, Newsweek, Christian Science Monitor, Newsday, Baltimore Sun, Chicago Tribune, San Francisco Chronicle, The Telegraph, Folha de S. Paulo,* and on PBS the Jim Leher NewsHour, CNN's Christiane Amanpour Show, TVO's *Agenda,* BBC's Channel One, NPR's *All Things Considered,* Press TV, CNN Radio, and the Voice of America. He spent much of summers 2008 through 2010 in Afghanistan conducting field research for a book manuscript on the culture and implications of the Taliban as expressed through their narratives, especially in the form of *shabnamah* or "night letters," poetry, chants, and other artifacts. In 2010, he served as the Counterinsurgency Advisor to the Commander of Task Force Kandahar.

Brig. (retd.) Feroz Hassan Khan is a Lecturer in the Department of National Security Affairs, Naval Postgraduate School, Monterey, California. He served in the Pakistan Army for thirty years, with his last assignment as Director in the Pakistan Strategic Plans Division. Khan has represented Pakistan in bilateral and multilateral negotiations on security, arms control, and nonproliferation issues and has published in reputed journals, newspapers, and book publications. He is the author of *Eating Grass: The Making of the Pakistani Bomb* (Stanford University Press, 2012).

Steffen Merten is a sociocultural dynamics researcher and analyst living and working throughout Asia on issues related to human terrain mapping and countering violent extremism. Merten's core interests also focus on new ways of applying technologies for the collection and analysis of sociocultural information for global security applications, with a specific concentration on modeling Middle Eastern tribal systems and understanding information environments through data visualization. He is currently Lead Analyst at Kestrel Technology Group, LLC.

Major Nathan Springer is an active duty armor officer with multiple combat tours in Iraq and Afghanistan. Following his troop command in northeastern Konar and eastern Nuristan Province, Afghanistan (OEF 07-08), he obtained an MA in Security Studies, National Security Affairs, at the Naval Postgraduate School. He then served as the Chief of Operations at the U.S. Army and Marine Corps Counterinsurgency Center. Subsequently, he graduated from the Art of War Scholars program at the Command and General Staff College in June 2011. He then served as the Executive Officer for the 3rd Squadron, 4th U.S. Cavalry Regiment, 3rd Brigade, 25th Infantry Division in Nangarhar, Afghanistan, in support of OEF 11-12. Currently, MAJ Springer serves as the Executive Officer for the 3rd Brigade Combat Team, 25th Infantry Division. He is currently Brigade XO, 3rd Brigade, 25th Infantry Division, Schofield Barracks, Hawaii.

Marc W. D. Tyrrell's research focus is on the practical and philosophical grounds of how sense making is possible. He has written and presented internationally in the fields of Organizational Management, Culture and Conflict, Job Search and Recruiting Technology, and Religious Movements. He holds a BA in Religion and Sociology, an MA in Canadian Studies, and a PhD in Sociology (Social Anthropology).

Barry Scott Zellen is an author, editor, and theorist specializing in geostrategic and polar issues. He lived and worked in the Arctic from 1988 to 2000, where he managed several indigenous language media properties affiliated with the Northern Native Broadcast Access Program (NNBAP). He is presently a Senior Research Fellow at the Anchorage-based Institute of the North and a Member of the Board of the Arctic Research Consortium of the United States (ARCUS). His published books include *Breaking the Ice: From Land Claims to*

Tribal Sovereignty in the Arctic (Lexington Books, 2008); *Arctic Doom, Arctic Boom: The Geopolitics of Climate Change in the Arctic* (Praeger Security International, 2009); *On Thin Ice: The Inuit, the State and the Challenge of Arctic Sovereignty* (Lexington Books, 2009); *The Realist Tradition in International Relations: Foundations of Western Order* (4 volumes) (Praeger Security International, 2011); *State of Doom: Bernard Brodie, the Bomb, and the Birth of the Bipolar World* (Continuum Books, 2011); *The Art of War in an Asymmetric World: Strategy for the Post-Cold War World* (Continuum Books, 2012); *State of Recovery: The Quest to Restore American Security After 9/11* (Bloomsbury Academic, 2013); and *The Fast-Changing Arctic: Rethinking Arctic Security for a Warmer World* (editor; University of Calgary Press, 2013).

INTRODUCTION

Thomas H. Johnson and Barry Scott Zellen

A DIVERSE MIXTURE OF WAR FIGHTERS, cultural experts, anthropologists, government officials, and strategic analysts first convened in March 2009 at the U.S. Naval Postgraduate School in Monterey, California, to discuss the impact culture has on both conflict behavior and counterinsurgency environments. The Naval Postgraduate School's Program for Culture and Conflict Studies hosted this "enlightening conference aimed at exploring the importance of culture and its role in conflicts around the globe," which marked the starting point for our two-year study of culture, conflict, and counterinsurgency.[1] As part of this study, experts have provided their analysis of cultural dynamics in a variety of conflict environments and historical contexts. These studies focus not only on the current war zones of Afghanistan, Pakistan's northwest frontier, and Iraq but also on past hot spots like Ireland and Vietnam and one very cold spot: the circumpolar Arctic region. As we reported in 2009, "Understanding the importance of culture in conflict has prompted many government agencies and the military to attempt to create specialists dedicated to the analysis of human terrain dimensions of the battle space," several of whom presented analyses at our conference. "International experts in modeling techniques provided additional insight into their methodology and the application of cultural modeling by using insurgent movements in Iraq and Afghanistan as case studies."[2]

The key objectives of this project were to assess and debate the following questions: Is cultural understanding important, or is it merely a fad of the day? Where and how is culture important in a national security and foreign policy context? What frameworks and narratives should be used to analyze culture? How are cultural phenomena and information best used by the military? What are the challenges of cultural data collection and application? What constitutes cultural data? What assumptions need to be made explicit concerning such data? What has been the impact of cultural understanding on our recent counterinsurgencies? Does it take intimate cultural information and knowledge to counter an insurgency? What are we good at here, and where do we fail miserably?

Among the many fascinating presentations and discussions at our original 2009 conference, a number of participants have agreed to share their ideas and insights on the nexus of culture, conflict, and counterinsurgency and to elaborate on them in the form of chapters in this book. This group includes academic experts in fields as diverse as military history and cultural anthropology, as well as military service personnel and defense planners who have practiced the art of counterinsurgency in Iraq and Afghanistan as well as past battle spaces like Vietnam. Their insights provide us with the essential ingredients required to prevent, quite simply, the tragic repetition of history. By sharing their insights from the field, and from history, they can help enlighten our strategy and tactics in the proverbial War on Terror and help prevent our being drawn into a largely self-imposed quagmire resulting from the unwillingness not only to learn from history but also to adapt to the specific cultural context of the current fight. We clearly saw this in the early stages after our invasion of Iraq, and it has been a continuing problem haunting our efforts in Afghanistan. Indeed, as suggested in the following pages, Afghanistan might well be the poster child for a military intervention plagued by misunderstanding a country's history, culture, and environment. But at the same time, it serves as a valuable reminder of the enduring salience of cultural understanding and the continuing strategic and diplomatic value of cultural knowledge.

A PATH TO VICTORY: NAVIGATING THE NEXUS OF CULTURE AND CONFLICT

By better understanding the cultural foundations of these protracted conflicts that still rage across Afghanistan and neighboring Pakistan, reorienting our efforts to rebuild Afghanistan from the bottom up, so that the institutions we nurture are compatible with the enduring cultural topography of the conflict zone, and shifting our strategy from an attritional engagement where time is on our opponent's side to a smarter war plan that similarly embraces the cultural dimensions of the conflict, a meaningful and enduring victory may still be achieved in part. Just as Vietnam was doomed not by any inherent tactical or strategic realities to be a military failure for the United States and its allies but instead by the choices made (or sometimes not made) in the course of the fight, Afghanistan need not become Obama's—or contemporary America's—Vietnam. But without significant course change reflecting cultural nuances, Afghanistan may yet ultimately become America's Vietnam.

The chapters of this book are organized into two separate sections. Part I is on "Culture and Conflict: From Theory to Methodology," and Part II is on "Culture and Conflict: From Methodology to Practice; Lessons from Afghanistan." Part I examines the nexus of culture, conflict, and strategic intervention and asks the following questions: *Where and how is culture important in a national security and foreign policy context? Is cultural understanding important, or is it merely a fad of the day?* After making the case that it is indeed important, one might argue essential for victory on the War on Terror, we proceed to answer the subsequent questions: *What constitutes cultural data? What assumptions need to be made explicit concerning such data? What frameworks should be used to analyze culture? And lastly, what are the challenges of cultural data collection and application?*

Part II addresses how cultural phenomena and information can best be used by the military and addresses the following questions: *What has been the impact of cultural understanding on our recent counterinsurgencies? Does it take intimate cultural information/knowledge to effectively counter an insurgency? And, ultimately, what are we good at here, and where must we improve things?* It concludes that it does indeed take intimate cultural information and knowledge to counter the insurgencies that have erupted ever since kinetic operations in Operation Enduring Freedom achieved their early successes. The authors contributing to Part II of this work consider the impacts of cultural understanding on our counterinsurgency efforts in Afghanistan and reflect on lessons learned, including the use of cultural knowledge in doctrine and training, in policy formation, and in the context of future conflicts around the world.

PART I: CULTURE AND CONFLICT:
FROM THEORY TO METHODOLOGY

Alexei Gavriel, a member of the Canadian Forces, was deployed on Operation Athena in Kandahar, Afghanistan, as an intelligence analyst. He "propose[s] to demystify the practices of anthropology by integrating its unique concepts and collection methodologies into two formal intelligence disciplines, cultural intelligence and ethnographic intelligence."[3] Gavriel is both a war fighter and an applied anthropologist conducting research on the integration of sociocultural knowledge into contemporary military operational planning and intelligence. He argues that "[s]everal misunderstandings and misconceptions regarding cultural intelligence exist. Cultural intelligence is not the uncovering of a hidden or secret code that allows the user unrestricted control over a population, just as there are no secret handshakes or passwords. These misconceptions likely stem from further misconceptions about what 'culture' is. Cultural intelligence is an intelligence discipline that analyzes cultural knowledge to assess or interpret the impact it has on the operating environment, adversary, and operational planning considerations. It has strategic-, operational-, and tactical-level implications."[4]

Professor Marc Tyrell from the Institute of Interdisciplinary Studies (IIS) at Carleton University in Ottawa examines the "applied use of evolutionary theory in modeling culture and cultural conflicts. Over the past 150 years in the social sciences, evolutionary theory has been misapplied, misunderstood, hijacked by megalomaniacs, and attacked by people who have no concept of what a theory is. Throughout the time that it has been in intellectual play, however, it has proven to be one of the most robust theoretical explanation we have for change over time."[5] As Tyrell recounts, "There have been a lot of changes, refinements, and arguments about evolutionary theory since Darwin's day, and we now have a much better, albeit much more complex, idea of how it works and, perhaps more important, what parts of it can and should be applied outside the area of biology."[6] Tyrell "outline[s] the possible applications of Darwinian evolutionary theory to 'culture,'" looking at Mosul, where "we can see that many of the existing institutional barriers to change had been removed during the occupation. This, however, meant that people [have] defaulted 'back' to their real source of security and governance—the tribe and neotribe. Attempts to impose a governance structure totally at odds with that default value were doomed to fail. However, reconstructing the battle space by looking at the reality and by sharing the 'authorship' [would allow] for the co-construction of a narrative that would be acceptable for both sides. This narrative, in turn, is a symbolic structure that, with time, could embed itself back into Iraqi culture, gaining emotional connotations among the population by lived experience."[7]

Moreover, "There are certain implications of the cultural coding system being partially communicative ([that is], stored outside the individual). In cultural evolution, for example, the coding system is much more subject to mutation, both initially and on a[n ongoing] day-to-day basis. Furthermore, cultural evolution is inherently partially Lamarkian, that is, the inheritance of acquired characteristics. These 'inherited' cultural codes may be very strongly embedded in the neurological structures of the brain as a result of early childhood learning—a 'learning' that is often stored in narratives."[8] Tyrell asks: "Can a Darwinian evolutionary theory of culture be predictive without falling into either the determinist or teleological fallacies it has in the past?"[9] It probably can be, he concludes, but "with only a limited time horizon. In any given work space at particular points in time, there are only a limited number of options available to compete effectively. Which option(s) that will be chosen by a relevant group will be constrained by their closeness to existing cultural narratives in both form and lived reality. Perhaps this explains why Muslim sympathy for al-Qaeda was so high in the 1980s ([when it was seen to be] opposing an invader) and plummeted after the September 11 attacks ([when it was seen to be attacking] civilians)."[10]

Steffen Merten is a human terrain researcher specializing in Middle Eastern tribal systems and a former social network analysis researcher at the Naval Postgraduate School Core Lab. He served with Operation Iraqi Freedom from 2003 to 2004 and is currently developing an integrated methodology for modeling tribal systems. In his chapter, he outlines ways that data fusion may be achieved and how it can dramatically enhance the analytical capabilities of cultural analysts, especially in tribal social systems. By using visual analytics theory and technology to conduct the labor-intensive aspects of data fusion, and accepting the theoretical justification of fusion among the geospatial, relational, and temporal data dimensions, the field of cultural analysis seems poised to make a major contribution to counterinsurgency (COIN) doctrine. The software developers racing to fill this technological need include I2, Access Pro, and a company called Palantir Technologies, which has proven especially well suited for data fusion during the author's ongoing analysis of the Omani tribal system and is discussed in detail by Hartunian and Germann (2008).

However, Merten cautions that these software advances must be accompanied by two caveats: First, that, no matter how powerful or versatile the technology, a deep understanding of the social system will always depend on "expert opinion familiar with the culture, indoctrination procedures, and institutional foundations" that lend significance to relationships, as well as the skill, intuition, and innovation of the analyst/collector. Second, we must also refrain from attempting to reinvent the wheel by tapping existing sources of social data ranging from deployed company intelligence officers to civil affairs teams operating outside the combat zone. While the need for effective human terrain analysis seems especially acute in the combat zone, as one colleague described it, "Building these models in the war zone is like trying to build a bike while running beside it." Just as we have accumulated a wealth of geospatial data for use in any future deployment throughout the globe, we must have the strategic foresight to match and fuse this information with its relational context. By harnessing technology to fuse geospatial, relational, and temporal data in a meaningful way, we may drastically enhance the field of cultural analysis and further empower the war fighter in his or her mission of defeating contemporary and future insurgency.

PART TWO: CULTURE AND CONFLICT: FROM METHODOLOGY TO PRACTICE; LESSONS FROM AFGHANISTAN

Starting out the second part of this work, Professor Thomas Barfield of Boston University and president of the American Institute for Afghanistan Studies "examine[s] the role culture, customs, and justice play in the diverse landscape of Afghanistan. One of the initial problems with cultural studies, argues Barfield, is the mere definition of the word *culture*, a definition that varies wildly within different fields of study. Economists and political scientists discard many of the all-encompassing 'kitchen sink' definitions of culture—the very same definitions anthropologists adhere to. What we really want to know are the linkages and interdependencies [among] society, economy, [and] politics, and the only way to get a handle on th[ose] is to approach [them] in a holistic fashion. Discovering what habits exist in a given society, how one sees the world, how one interacts in the world: That's culture, it is learned behavior. This, however, requires an open mind, and it is precisely one reason why many anthropologists prefer to work alone rather than in teams wearing uniforms and carrying guns. The way people express their world is through their language; it is really a linguistic process, and it is important to look at it like that and not study [other people's] world[s] through translation. European states and America [have] all endorsed a centralized state government for places like Afghanistan because without it they cannot understand how law and order can exist. But, in fact, what we see in a place like Afghanistan [is that] we have social order in places with weak or nonexistent states. Why is that? Because at the local level there is a cultural code of conduct, an evaluation of behavior that allows people to be evaluated without the need for government intervention or oversight. Of course the biggest example of this is *Pashtunwali*" (the way of the Pashtun), "a legal code that explains what's right [and] what's wrong; but it is also a standard behavior, more precisely, a standard of autonomy. The important thing to remember is [that], from an outsiders' view, particularly a military outsiders' view, [one is] immersed in this local system. The question is what the interaction is; it's not state to state, it is individual to individual. Here the whole question of understanding what motivates people is not ideological; it's not necessarily [about] economic motives; it could be larger cultural motives. When asking why culture matters in a context such as this, Professor Barfield believes it is understanding the world you are interacting with. With so many people now in Afghanistan, it becomes a significantly important question that has political, policy, and strategic ramifications."[11]

In the next chapter, Thomas H. Johnson examines the social and political roles of religious figures in southern Afghanistan in an attempt to develop a more nuanced understanding of the present insurgency. Islamic groups and Afghan mullahs play a critical role in politics in southern Afghanistan; the Taliban, Deobandis, Sufis, and Tablighi Jamaat are the most important religious groups and influences there. Religion and politics are blurred as religious authorities frequently shift between religious and political roles. The West has had a tendency to misunderstand the relevance and implications of these roles. Jihad is an important feature of Islamic life in southern Afghanistan. Large numbers of southern insurgents are fighting in support of jihad and the implementation of sharia (Islamic law). Several predominant religious figures and influences tend to advocate jihad. The West has underestimated the role of jihad in the present Taliban movement. The ulema council in southern Afghanistan represents a sector of the clergy that has remained relatively unradicalized by war. Insurgents and jihadists have frequently assassinated members of this council because it offers legitimate opposition to the Taliban's radicalization of young madrasah students and unemployed villagers. The political activities of two Islamic groups that represent a large number of rural and poor Afghans are misunderstood. Some Sufi groups in

Kandahar have allied with insurgents since 2003 and have promoted rural resistance to secular authority. The Tablighi Jamaat, though avowedly apolitical and detached from the insurgency, has a relationship with the mujahedeen who regularly attend this group's meetings. These issues have important policy implications. Political and military strategies aimed at countering the Taliban insurgency while ignoring the Taliban jihad are ill founded and will probably not succeed. Currently there is very little contact between NATO or the International Security Assistance Force (ISAF) and the ulema of southern Afghanistan. Rather than stereotype all religious leaders and institutions as militantly fundamentalist, policies that incorporate certain religious groups into civil society should be considered. And there is a critical need to fix the corrupt justice system in Afghanistan. A central component of the Taliban's strategy to win the trust and confidence of the Afghan population is based on the role of Taliban mullahs as arbitrators of individual and community disputes. This shadow justice system is proving very popular.

Feroz Hassan Khan, a retired brigadier general in the Pakistan Army and currently on the faculty of the Department of National Security Affairs at the Naval Postgraduate School, discusses Pakistan's turbulent history, noting that, "[f]or most of its existence, Pakistan has been dominated by a view that it faces an existential threat from India. Pakistan's leadership has viewed national security almost exclusively through this prism at the expense of economic, political, judicial, and social demands."[12] Khan argues that Pakistan today "continues to find itself at a crossroads with a growing strategic threat from India's emerging force doctrines, internal security threats to the viability of the state, and a massing insurgency within the disputed tribal borderlands on the west. Facing threats on multiple fronts, Pakistan must meet the challenge to reorient its military forces to face them all—but how? In October 2008, a joint session of parliament unanimously passed a resolution calling extremism, militancy, and terrorism [grave dangers] to the stability of the nation-state. The leaders underscored that cross-border attacks would not occur on other countries and [that] all foreign fighters would be dispelled. Still, Pakistan has not been able to strike a precise balance between the asymmetric problems it faces of internal extremism and external conventional threats."[13] Khan argues that "three factors help explain Pakistan's [hesitation about] shifting toward a counterinsurgency-focused military. First, India's evolving force posture threatens a near-term conventional conflict that could threaten the very existence of the state. Pakistan has always sought to maintain a viable defense against conventional and nuclear attack from India, and only with meaningful international assurances will Pakistan shift its force posture away from India. Second, [there is] a persistent and significant deficit of trust that exists with the United States that compels reluctance on Pakistan's part. Unilateral impatience and verbal arm twisting on the part of the U[nited] S[tates] towards Pakistan does not build sufficient confidence between the two nations, particularly while Pakistan is attempting to achieve a balanced relationship between the civilian and military apparatus. Third, the unpopularity of the 'War on Terror' and operations in Afghanistan and drone operations in Pakistan [have] created a domestic legitimacy problem for civilian leaders in Pakistan. Cooperation with the United States is politically damaging for politicians as they attempt to cater to both their diplomatic partners and a restless domestic population. Each reason alone cannot fully explain the failure of Pakistan to evolve towards a more nuanced counterinsurgency strategy, but together they help provide a clearer framework for why Pakistan's military remains conventionally focused."[14]

At the time Colonel Michael R. Fenzel, a PhD candidate at the Naval Postgraduate School, wrote his chapter, he was designated to take command of the 2nd Heavy Brigade Combat Team, 1st Armored Division, at Fort Bliss, Texas, in July 2010. In his previous assignment, he had commanded 1-503rd Airborne Battalion, 173rd Airborne Brigade, in Vicenza, Italy, and subsequently commanded Task Force Eagle through Operation Enduring Freedom IX in Afghanistan. He served as a deputy brigade commander in Afghanistan for the 1st Brigade of the 82d Airborne Division in Regional Command East (2005–2006). A year later, he returned to Paktika Province for fifteen months as the commander of 1st Battalion (Airborne), 503rd Infantry Regiment, which became Task Force Eagle, responsible for the border districts of Eastern Paktika and 400 kilometers of border frontage with Pakistan. In his chapter, he observes that historically the rural population in modern Afghanistan has rejected all large-scale reforms attempted by a central government. Unfortunately, change acceptable to the tribes will simply not come from the center. Establishing security in this war-torn land is achievable only if we focus our efforts and resources at the district level, where the subtribes are culturally dominant. Nowhere in Afghanistan is this more pressing than along the border of Pakistan's Federally Administered Tribal Areas (FATA). It is commonly accepted that the Taliban, al-Qaeda, and other foreign fighters use the FATA as a safe haven from which to plan, resource, stage, and launch attacks in the border districts and deeper into Afghanistan's interior. Since 2006, the number of foreign insurgents involved in the border fight has substantially increased, which strengthens the insurgency and decreases security. The struggle to secure this area has become the front line in the counterinsurgency fight and the coalition's most important strategic task. If we can establish security and stabilize the border provinces and districts in southern and eastern Afghanistan, Fenzel believes the accompanying momentum may guide the rest of the country to a sustainable peace. The problem is that the insurgents are most effective in these rural areas, and limited troop levels make a confounding proposition on a wider scale. He thus proposes a fundamental shift in the way we think about fighting the counterinsurgency in Afghanistan. To set the conditions for success, we need to engage tribal leaders and establish a district-level security architecture in which the district governor is the key leader elected by the *shura*. In conjunction, he adds, we need a bottom-up focus that places the coalition maneuver company commander where he can work closely with the district governor. Next, we need to redistribute critical assets now located at the provincial level down to the district level. Afghan security forces should be redistributed to districts and rural areas, and we should dismantle entities like the provincial reconstruction teams and reassign those assets to the maneuver battalions for use in the maneuver companies at the district level. Finally, he concluded, we need to integrate native Afghan intellectual capital into our maneuver company operations to improve cultural engagement and provide expertise in critical development skills.

ENS Bebber is an information warfare officer at Navy Information Operations Command, Maryland, and served as the information operations officer at Joint Provincial Reconstruction Team Khost in 2008. Information operations (IO) traditionally suffer from a lack of available metrics by which planners can assess their environment and measure the effectiveness of their programs. This often places IO practitioners at a distinct disadvantage when attempting to gain the confidence of unit commanders, who are tasked with allocating scarce battlefield resources and who are often skeptical of information operations as a whole. This project was an attempt to develop an information operations environmental assessment tool that can be used and replicated at the unit level (battalion or less) for use by planners to establish an initial benchmark (where am I?) and measure progress toward achieving the IO program goals and objectives (where do I want to go?). The provincial reconstruction team in Khost province, Afghanistan, needed a tool by which the leadership could benchmark current conditions and evaluate the information environment under which the population lived. It was believed that such a tool could provide clues as to whether our IO (and overall provincial reconstruction team, or PRT) efforts were having the intended effect.

And, in our final chapter, Major Nathan R. Springer, chief of operations at the U.S. Army/Marine Corps Counterinsurgency Center, examines what he believes to be a successful implementation of population-centric counterinsurgency strategy in northeastern Afghanistan through the lens of his experiences executing it in his area of operation as an Army troop commander from May 2007 to January 2008 and as the Squadron Fires Effects Coordination Cell (FECC) officer in charge. He recounts how his unit, the 1st Squadron, 91st Cavalry, 173rd ABCT, arrived at the decision to apply a population-centric strategy. He outlines the differences between an enemy-centric and a population-centric focus, the transition points between the two strategies and within the population centric strategy, and implementation of the population-centric strategy by line of operation. Finally, he describes the battlefield calculus in terms of the time, patience, and personal relationships required to at once empower the traditional Afghan leadership.

KNOWING THE ENEMY

Throughout the history of warfare, commanders have constantly stressed the importance of knowing the enemy and taking these lessons to heart; the United States spends substantial amounts of money on intelligence gathering during both war and peacetime. So, while knowing the enemy is an important factor in modern conventional warfare, knowing the country and the culture of its population is even more important in a counterinsurgency environment. We have seen the results that stem from a lack of cultural training of our deployed soldiers. Incidents like the Abu Ghraib prison scandal in Iraq and the burning of dead Taliban bodies in Afghanistan were signs of the dehumanization of the enemy that resulted from cultural ignorance. Cultural understanding results in the foresight needed to prevent civil affairs disasters. Extensive knowledge of the Muslim culture is vital to the missions in Iraq and Afghanistan because Islam is a total way of life in both countries.[15]

In addition to Islam, soldiers must understand the secular cultural differences of the people with whom they are interacting. The Afghan Pashtun tribal code of *Pashtunwali*, for example, is an extremely important factor in parts of Afghanistan in defining the relations among Afghans as well as others. An in-depth knowledge of *Pashtunwali* by the U.S. military would allow for the assessment of specific tactics and procedures in the context of the Afghan culture and society where they are being employed. Operations executed with a blatant lack of cultural knowledge can result in a variety of negative consequences, as we have seen throughout our engagements in Iraq and Afghanistan. While the U.S. military does conduct cultural training of its personnel before deployments, most of this training is inadequate and almost exclusively on Islam at the expense of country-specific customs like *Pashtunwali*.

U.S. military personnel are in contact with the local populace everyday in Afghanistan and other countries in which they are deployed. For its first month or so in country, a unit will conduct routine patrols to determine the lay of the land and gain a basic understanding of the area of operations. As time goes by, the unit will eventually learn which neighborhoods and villages are friendly to U.S. forces, where influential people live, which neighborhoods carry a greater likelihood of enemy contact, and so on. Unfortunately, by the time a unit has fully grasped its environment, their deployment is near its end and the next unit is ready to take over and restart the whole process of learning to understand the area. Important relationships within the local population that took great time and effort to build are weakened once the new unit arrives. While an outgoing commander might share his experience and tribal contacts with the incoming commander to establish a context for the new unit, a lot of the information is lost in transition. In other words, a unit might achieve relative success in an area over its six- to twelve-month deployment, but the process is dramatically slowed down or even reversed once a new unit arrives. Therefore, each unit must be fully prepared to maximize its time in country, or it will achieve minimal progress in reconstruction and security by the time the replacements arrive.

The U.S. military places most of its emphasis on training for combat operations, as it should. In fact, many would argue that too much emphasis on cultural training could take away from the level of combat readiness of each individual soldier.[16] Although this mind-set embraces the fear of sending U.S. soldiers into harm's way without proper military training, its focus is misguided. A conventional war is very straightforward and basically comes down to killing the enemy before he kills you. Training in basic marksmanship and war-fighting skills is the main focus because victory over the clearly defined and identifiable enemy is of the greatest importance. Yet, in a counterinsurgency, the opinion and beliefs of the population are even more important than the body count of enemy insurgents. Unfortunately, U.S. troops still associate victory with enemy body counts and decisive victories. For example, soldiers will seldom run around a patrol base bragging about how many schools they visited during the day in support of the reconstruction effort. The commendations and captive audiences are usually reserved for stories of killing the enemy. U.S. troops go through strenuous training that prepares them for the worst-case scenario in a combat zone. So it is difficult to arrive in hostile territory and place that aggressive mentality off to the side to concentrate on the hearts and minds of the population, but that is exactly what they must do. U.S. military personnel are placed in an extremely contradictory combat zone where they are handing out school supplies to children at one moment and then fighting for their lives the next. The ensuing mental strain cannot be taken lightly, but it is a necessary evil. Our troops obviously have the training required to protect themselves, which is why our army is able to defend itself more effectively than any other military in the world, but that only allows for short-term victories. To achieve long-term success, American soldiers must have the knowledge to peacefully engage the local population and gain their support.

The cultural training conducted by the U.S. Army has improved since the initial invasions of Afghanistan and Iraq, but there is still much more room for improvement. If they had time, most army units would start operation-specific training a little over one year prior to a deployment. Current operational deployment tempo would not allow for this kind of timeline, but that is the best-case scenario. Among other things, Afghan training usually consists of mock face-to-face Pashto or Dari. Senior company leaders usually receive more advanced training because they are the ones expected to lead most of the patrols once in Afghanistan. In terms of tactical operations in Afghanistan, the contrast between the enemy body count and popular support is important and represents divergent perspectives in a counterinsurgency. A focus on the number of dead insurgents implies that the conflict is winnable by killing as many of the enemy as possible. Alternatively, a focus on popular support means the "hearts and minds" or, better put, "trust and confidence" of the local population are targeted. A military is typically more proficient at killing the enemy, so it is difficult to shift gears and concentrate on interaction with the populace. Situations occur on patrols when soldiers must determine how their actions will influence the civilian population around them and then make a quick, well-informed decision. Increasingly common events like the

Taliban using villages for cover in Afghanistan must be met with the proper response from U.S. soldiers. When the priority is placed on enemy body count instead of gaining popular support, then the high risk of collateral damage is accepted as well. For example, if a U.S. patrol takes fire from a mosque and then kill the enemy while destroying the mosque in the process, then the destruction of the mosque was necessary for an increased enemy body count. A focus on popular support would mean that another tactic would be used that might involve greater risk to U.S. soldiers but would leave the mosque intact and possibly improve relations with the Afghans who use the mosque. A tactic that has become too common for U.S. soldiers in Afghanistan is to immediately escalate to air power when Taliban militants put up a strong defense inside a village. This usually results in civilian casualties and loses the support of the Afghan population. In each of the situations mentioned, the typical military response is to place unit security above all other factors regardless of any religious or cultural implications. In contrast, a greater focus on religious and cultural training allows the soldier to view situations through multiple perspectives rather than only that of the U.S. military. From basic training to the arrival at his or her first unit, a soldier is taught to view the world through a military perspective, but it is time to evolve the training to actually coincide with the counterinsurgent warfare in Afghanistan.

The United States already has a tarnished reputation in parts of the Middle East, and the actions of the military can be used to improve relations on the local level. U.S. ground troops who leave the safety of the forward operating base (FOB) put their lives at risk to provide security for the indigenous civilian population. However, these actions alone will not amount to anything if the population does not see tangible results. Trust and friendship are gained after consistent acts of selfless service and good will to the Afghan people. Soldiers must demonstrate that they sincerely care for the well-being and safety of the populace to build common bonds. Once this is accomplished, the number of local nationals willing to come forward and give information on the location of improvised explosive devices (IEDs) and enemy ambushes and offer basic support should increase. The intelligence produced by the civilian population inevitably saves the lives of both American and local security forces. In other words, the rewards for showing respect and dignity toward religion and culture are beyond measure. However, while good relations with the civilian population are a force multiplier, any bad relations can have devastating consequences for a unit. When incidents like Abu Ghraib occur on the tactical level, they have negative results on the overall political and military strategies as well. Units on the ground that had nothing to do with the atrocities are seen as guilty by association and must strive to regain the trust of the population in their respective areas. In turn, commanders must not only worry about the reputation of their own unit, but they must also execute damage control for the irresponsible actions of other units. Every soldier, sailor, marine, and airman represents the United States, and their actions will either feed negative stereotypes or develop positive views among the Iraqi and Afghan populations.

The predeployment tactical training that the U.S. Army currently provides for its soldiers is above standard for the purpose of force protection and combat-oriented operations. Furthermore, the training required for soldiers to kill and capture insurgents is excellent, and the evidence lies with the constantly rising body count of the enemy. Training was taken one step further as soldiers were taught how to interact with the civilian population in Iraq and Afghanistan. However, despite all the media attention concerning Islam since 9/11, the U.S. Army has failed to recognize the true importance of religion and how understanding Muslim beliefs is a key to interacting within many cultures. Part of the problem is the military culture of combat arms that promotes the belief that any training not oriented toward combat is pointless. The ultimate glory in the current military culture, as in the past, is achieved by finding and destroying the enemy, not building worthwhile relationships with the civilian population. The current training allows U.S. soldiers to basically maintain the status quo in countries such as Afghanistan.

Providing effective across-the-board cultural training for a massive organization like the U.S. Army is a daunting task because there are so many deployable units, and the operations tempo is extremely high at this time. There are several important societal norms like *Pashtunwali* and tribal affiliation that are extremely important to soldiers on deployments to Afghanistan. In an ideal world, all those concepts would be taught to deploying soldiers. However, the reality is that Army units place a greater priority on training and maintaining their war-fighting skills because that is the seemingly main job of the military. While using Islam as the basis of cultural training may not address other important factors of Afghanistan, it is a way of finding middle ground with the U.S. military culture. There are some lessons that soldiers will have to learn on the ground while under fire, but their training must enable them to minimize those situations. In the end, soldiers would finally be

equipped with the tools necessary to properly interact with the civilian populace and achieve more than maintenance of the status quo.

It is to this important task that we now turn in the pages ahead.

NOTES

1. Coeditor Thomas H. Johnson is founder and director of the Program for Culture and Conflict Studies at the Naval Postgraduate School. We kindly thank Sarah
Kauffmann, Matthew DuPee, and Matthew Dearing for their contributions to this
introduction, through their excellent presentation summaries and abstracts as presented in their jointly-authored 2009 conference report on the CCS website. See
Sara Kaufmann, Matt DuPée, and Matt Dearing, "Conference on Culture, Cultural
Modeling, Counterinsurgency and Conflict Behavior," *The Culture and Conflict Review*, April 1, 2009; available at www.nps.edu/Programs/CCS/WebJournal/Article
.aspx?ArticleID=31.

2. Ibid.

3. Ibid.

4. Ibid.

5. Ibid.

6. Ibid.

7. Ibid.

8. Ibid.

9. Ibid.

10. Ibid.

11. Ibid.

12. Ibid.

13. Ibid.

14. Ibid.

15. John L. Esposito, *What Everyone Needs to Know about Islam* (New York: Oxford University Press, 2002), 151.

16. Nina M. Serafino, "Peacekeeping and Related Stability Operations: Issues of
U.S. Military Involvement," in *CRS Issue Brief for Congress* (Washington DC: The Library of Congress, June 25, 2005), 12.

Part I

CULTURE AND CONFLICT

From Theory to Methodology

1 INCORPORATING CULTURAL INTELLIGENCE INTO JOINT INTELLIGENCE

Cultural Intelligence and Ethnographic
Intelligence Theory

Alexei J. D. Gavriel

> *What we need is cultural intelligence. What makes them tick?*
> *Who makes the decisions? What is it about their society that's*
> *so remarkably different in their values, in the way they think,*
> *compared to my values and the way I think in my western,*
> *white-man mentality?. . . What you need to know isn't what*
> *our intel apparatus is geared to collect for you.*
>
> **—General Anthony C. Zinni[1]**

CONTEMPORARY THEATERS OF OPERATION, such as Afghanistan and Iraq, have defined the requirement for a reformation in intelligence focus that incorporates sociocultural knowledge to meet the challenges presented by changing adversaries and operational environments. Although the defense community has become intimately familiar with the integral importance of cultural knowledge to current operations, there has been limited depth thereafter to understand what sociocultural knowledge is and where it comes from, and as a consequence it has struggled to unambiguously define what cultural intelligence is and express a sort of mysticism over how academics, such as anthropologists, come about producing this knowledge. The intent of this chapter is to demystify the practices of anthropology by integrating its unique concepts and collection methodologies into two formal intelligence disciplines, cultural intelligence (CULINT) and ethnographic intelligence (ETHINT), and incorporate their use into existing joint intelligence infrastructure.

CULTURAL INTELLIGENCE

Misconceptions and Reality

In the movie *The Beast* (1988), the main character, a Soviet soldier named Constantine Koverchenko, takes a personal interest in the local Afghan culture. Fellow soldier Samad, a Muslim serving in the Soviet Army, explains to Koverchenko the Afghan Pashtun people's code of honor. This code, known as

Pashtunwali, is explained as having three main obligations: *Melmastia, Badal,* and *Nanawateh.* The first, *Melmastia,* is the obligation to show hospitality to visitors. The second, *Badal,* is the obligation to seek justice and revenge. Last is *Nanawateh,* the obligation to provide asylum or sanctuary to anyone who asks, even if that person is an enemy. Later in the movie, Koverchenko is captured by the Mujahideen, who intend to kill him under the obligation of *Badal* for the destruction the Soviets had caused to their village. However, when Koverchenko utters the word *"Nanawateh,"* the Mujahideen are forced to stop and provide him with sanctuary.

This example illustrates the largest misconception of cultural intelligence: that cultural intelligence is the uncovering of a hidden or secret code of a foreign society and that the mastering of this code allows unrestricted control over a population. This misconception likely originates from further misconceptions about culture in general.

Culture consists of shared patterns of ideas and behaviors; however, variation will exist in any group as individual members retain a degree of agency to make personal decisions. Although culture is shared, there is no single Afghan point of view as there is no single American point of view. Understanding a social group's culture, however, allows an understanding of why members act in the manner that they do and how they think and perceive the world around them:

> Culture might also be considered as an "operational code" that is valid for an entire group of people. Culture conditions the individual's range of action and ideas, including what to do and not to do, how to do or not do it, and whom to do it with or not do it with. Culture also includes under what circumstances the "rules" shift or change. Culture influences how people make judgements about what is right and wrong, assesses what is important and unimportant, categorizes things, and deals with things that do not fit into existing categories. Cultural rules are flexible in practice. For example, the kinship system of a certain Amazonian Indian tribe requires that individuals marry a cousin. However, the definition of cousin is often changed to make people eligible for marriage.[2]

While we must remind ourselves of the principles of culture, we need not doubt that, in operational environments with such complex human terrain as Iraq and Afghanistan, the large role culture plays in both of these societies has an impact on ongoing counterinsurgency operations.

Cultural intelligence (CULINT) is an intelligence functional discipline that analyzes cultural knowledge to assess or interpret how it impacts, influences, and affects the operational environment, adversary, and operational planning considerations.[3] CULINT does not produce cultural knowledge but rather seeks to understand the effects of culture and the human terrain. Cultural knowledge can be used to assess the effectiveness of adversary and coalition information operations, assess local reaction or fallout from coalition potential courses of action, and understand how local social organization can have an impact on operations, how local dynamics may fuel conflict, or even how local values and perceptions shape the local actors' views of coalition forces and operations. This is what cultural intelligence is in reality. The use of secret handshakes or code words that, when used by an outsider, force the natives to make one their king is a reality confined to Hollywood.

Levels of Cultural Knowledge

Cultural knowledge initially establishes a level of basic intelligence that can be used to "set the scene at the outset of operations and to meet intelligence requirements dealing with unchanging facts" of the operational environment.[4] However, a level of sufficient knowledge about a social group's culture to support intelligence analysis, such as cultural relativism, is not something that can be developed overnight. For this reason there are three progressive levels of cultural knowledge: cultural awareness, cultural understanding, and, finally, cultural intelligence.[5]

A level of cultural awareness is achieved when the "what" can be answered about what makes the social group's culture different from our own. This incorporates a very basic understanding of the social group's religion, language, history, economy, and a basic customary understanding of the necessary "do's and don'ts"—a level of comprehension typical of any tourist visiting a foreign country.

A level of *cultural understanding* is achieved when the "why" can be answered. Cultural understanding involves understanding a social group's perceptions, attitudes, mind-set, and beliefs that stem from the group's values and behaviors. Whereas a level of cultural awareness allows recognition of a group's religion, a level of cultural understanding provides comprehension of the embeddedness of religion in everyday life and to what extent religion shapes the values, perceptions, and actions of group members.

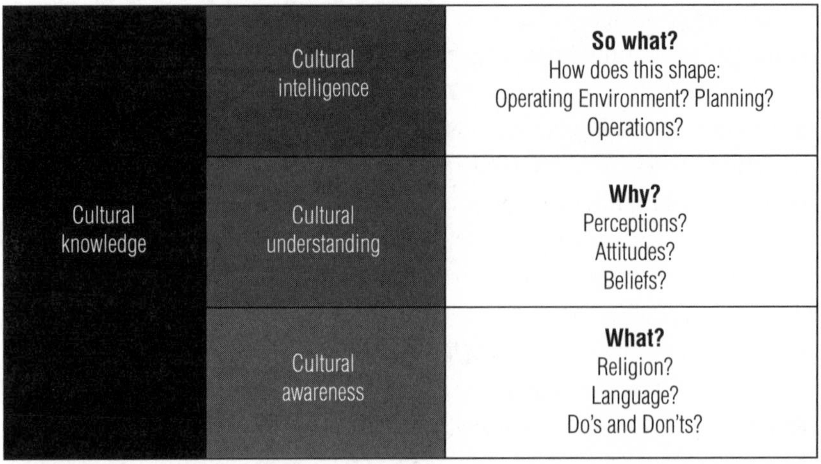

	Cultural intelligence	**So what?** How does this shape: Operating Environment? Planning? Operations?
Cultural knowledge	Cultural understanding	**Why?** Perceptions? Attitudes? Beliefs?
	Cultural awareness	**What?** Religion? Language? Do's and Don'ts?

Figure 1.1. Cultural intelligence: Levels of cultural knowledge.

SOURCE: Marine Corps Intelligence Activity (MCIA), "Cultural Intelligence: Global Scope, Operationally Focussed," Quantico, VA: Marine Corps Intelligence Activity, 2007.

A level of *cultural intelligence* is achieved when this understanding can be comprehended to answer the "so what?" of how cultural aspects shape the operational environment and affect or impact operations, the adversary, or planning considerations. At this level, cultural knowledge provides not only *basic intelligence* but also *current* and *estimative intelligence* (see Figure 1.1).

Support to Levels of Operation

Cultural knowledge is additionally useful at all levels of operation from the strategic level in the "formation of policy and military plans at national and international levels" to the planning and conduct of campaigns and operations at the operational and tactical levels.[6]

Strategic intelligence can be supported through the development of a comprehensive understanding of the social structures, ideologies, and narratives insurgents use to organize their networks and mobilize segments of the population.

Effective cultural intelligence preparation of the operational environment could aid operational intelligence in understanding the various factions and groups that occupy the commander's area of responsibility and additionally what social factors may be fueling elements of the conflict. Civil–military cooperation (CIMIC) organizations can benefit from an understanding of how indigenous values are represented in dispute resolution. Psychological operations (PSYOPS) units would also benefit from cultural knowledge in the development of information operation campaigns that would speak to locals in a manner they would be receptive to.

Indoctrinating soldiers with cultural knowledge during predeployment training can benefit operations at the tactical level by making soldiers more interculturally effective in conveying proper respect to indigenous customs, thus minimizing the possibility of turning potential friends into enemies through cultural insensitivity—especially in this "strategic corporal" era of war fighting.

In contrast, an absence of this knowledge can have grievous consequences as noted by the former human terrain system (HTS) senior social scientist Dr. Montgomery McFate: "Misunderstanding culture at a strategic level can produce policies that exacerbate an insurgency; a lack of cultural knowledge at an operational level can lead to negative public opinion; and ignorance of culture at a tactical level endangers both civilians and troops."[7]

Defeating Ethnocentric Bias in Intelligence Analysis

Perspective, or the requirement to "think like the adversary," is the first principle of joint intelligence.[8] Perspective requires intelligence analysts to seek to understand an adversary's thought process and continuously develop and refine their ability to think like the adversary. Joint intelligence doctrine directly states that the joint force commander (JFC) should direct the J2 intelligence staff to assess all proposed actions from the perspective of how an adversary will likely perceive these actions and what the adversary's probable responses would be. "Understanding how an adversary will adapt to the environment, conceptualize the situation, consider options, and react to our actions" are all integral intelligence requirements that are inhibited by ethnocentrism if intelligence staffs do not possess enough knowledge about a culture to understand the world from the adversary's perspective.[9]

Virtually all intelligence assessments are made from an ethnocentric viewpoint as the assessed courses of action of adversarial forces are based on our own beliefs of how these forces might act. These beliefs stem from our own logic, values, and ideas—our cultural programing—and are in essence an assessment of what our course of action would be given the same circumstance. All of our assessments have an ethnocentric bias as we do not understand the values and beliefs of the cultures we operate among and therefore base our assessments on the standard of another culture, in this case our own. An eth-nocentric bias can, however, be overcome through cultural relativism.

A level of cultural relativism, or understanding a culture in terms of its own values and beliefs, must be achieved to overcome ethnocentric bias in intelligence analysis and provide intelligence staffs with the necessary per-spective outlined by joint intelligence doctrine. "The ability to think like an adversary is predicated on a detailed understanding of the adversary's goals, motivations, objectives, strategy, intentions, capabilities, methods of opera-tion, vulnerabilities, and sense of value and loss," most of which is further predicated on a detailed understanding of an adversary's culture.[10]

This comprehensive level of understanding, available only through a cul-turally relative, nonethnocentric perspective, is outlined in joint intelligence doctrine as being:

> . . . essential to: recognizing challenges to our national security interests; es-tablishing security policy; when appropriate, formulating clear, relevant, and attainable military objectives and strategy; determining, planning, and con-ducting operations that will help attain [national] policy objectives; and iden-tifying the adversary's strategic and operational COGs [centers of gravity].[11]

Cultural Information Credibility and Source Reliability

The credibility of information and the reliability of its source are of the up-most importance in military intelligence. Sociocultural knowledge is devel-oped through the process of ethnography. Cultural information can be found from a variety of other sources; however, just as a CNN report would not be considered a valid source of HUMINT data, Wikipedia and the like are not valid sources of ethnographic data, as in both cases the collector has no ability to assess the credibility or reliability of the information and its source.

The perils of incomplete or inaccurate cultural knowledge can be far worse than the complete absence of cultural knowledge. McFate highlights such an example during the Abu Ghraib prison fiasco where a 1973 study on Arab cul-ture and psychology, *The Arab Mind*, was allegedly used to understand Arab psychological vulnerabilities regarding sexual shame and humiliation.[12] The study outlines that the social segregation between the sexes in Arab society has made sex a mental preoccupation, and it was allegedly thought that this could be leveraged by taking sexually humiliating photographs of the pris-oners, which in turn could be used to blackmail them into becoming infor-mants. The presumption that the prisoners would do anything to prevent the dissemination of these images completely overlooked the broader context of Iraqi society and the importance of *Al-sharaf*, the obligation to "uphold one's masculine honor," which requires its restoration through the appeasement of blood. The result of the complete misuse of this data "demonstrates the folly of using decontextualized culture as the basis of policy."[13]

All information derived from a human collection instrument has a high-risk margin of error. In the case of HUMINT, specialized collectors are trained to minimize this error as much as possible. The case is no different for ETHINT, which employs specific collection methodologies and concepts that serve not only to minimize the risk associated with collector error but also to minimize the effects of partial, incomplete, or noncontextualized cultural data. Intelligence estimates and assessments based off of CULINT have the potential to have large repercussions, which requires a need to limit this margin of error by using reliable sources of cultural information, such as ethnographic intelligence.

ETHNOGRAPHIC INTELLIGENCE

What Is Ethnographic Intelligence?

Ethnographic intelligence (ETHINT) is an intelligence collection discipline that produces sociocultural knowledge through the use of specialized ethnographic collection methodologies and analytical processes that are guided by anthropological concepts.

Information versus Intelligence

NATO standardization doctrine defines *information* as "unprocessed data of every description which may be used in the production of intelligence" and *intelligence* simply as "the product resulting from the processing of information."[14] In this context, *ethnographic information* is data that have been collected through ethnographic collection methodologies that are unprocessed. These data later become intelligence when they are processed into a product. Processing occurs to ensure the data's validity and that they are free from bias contamination, meaning that they remain sterile of the collector's own cultural biases. Ethnographic information that is valid is holistic in scope, contextualized, triangulated with other data, and integrated to form definitive patterns. This process is what transforms ethnographic information into ethnographic intelligence and is the fundamental difference that uniquely separates ETHINT from other intelligence collection disciplines.

Scientific Method, Data Limitations, and Predictive Power

Ethnography uses a scientific method known as *grounded theory* in which theories about what is going on in a social group are developed from collected data, or from the "ground up."[15] This differs from traditional scientific methods, which formulate a hypothesis and then test it. In ethnography, preconceived, deductive hypotheses are discouraged. Instead, inductive hypotheses as to "what is going on in the social group" are formulated from empirical observations over time that form definitive patterns and subsequently safeguards presupposed conclusions from bending data to suit.

Ethnography takes place in the field, rather than a laboratory, and subsequently the researcher cannot control, manipulate, or re-create the influences that affect the group's environment. As such, systematic observation in the natural, or "real-world," setting captures the perspectives and behaviors of a social group at a particular point in *time and space*. This "time and space" disclaimer does not mean that the information will become "untrue" at a certain expiration date but rather that ethnographic data are true (accurate) to the time and surroundings in which they were collected, as the group's culture will inevitably change and adapt over time. While this poses an issue for the replicability of findings, because it would be impossible to go back in time to recreate the exact environment in which data were collected, it does not hinder its predictive power.

The process of ethnography produces sufficient knowledge to develop a level of *cultural predictability* by capturing the patterned behaviors and ideas that are shared by a community. It must be recalled, however, that although culture is shared it is not a binding law that all members unfailing abide and that individuals possess their own agency to manipulate outcomes in their favor. Therefore, understanding a society's culture will not provide 100 percent predictability of the actions of all members of a social group but rather a general level of predictability of the social whole and how their shared beliefs and ideas may shape their perceptions, actions, or reactions in the future.

Ethnographic Collection

Intelligence collection requires specialized assets, whether human or technical, to obtain and process data into an intelligible form where it can be used by all-source intelligence analysts. Capability is the primary factor considered in the selection of a source or agency to procure certain types of data as the collection asset "must have the appropriate sensor system or processing capability" to carry out the task.[16]

Ethnography uses the researcher as the primary tool of data collection, which requires the ethnographer to be trained in specialized collection methodologies and use anthropological concepts as a lens through which to collect information. As such, ethnographic research methodologies and data collection techniques are designed specifically to avoid bias and ensure the accuracy of data immediately on the onset of their collection. Collection is also profoundly guided by anthropological theories, which not only serve to regulate the quality of collected data but also to expand on and uncover additional cultural information that may lie below the surface of what has been collected.

Other intelligence collection disciplines, such as HUMINT and IMINT, also require and train specialized operators and/or analysts to collect and interpret information for the production of intelligence. Similar to the way HUMINT requires personnel specially trained in interrogation and source handling operations, ETHINT requires specialist personnel trained in ethnographic collection to produce cultural knowledge. This measure is not only to ensure capability of the collection asset but also to ensure that the asset is suitable to safeguard against data corruption. Whereas HUMINT is concerned with falling victim to the adversary's deception plan, ETHINT is concerned with falling victim to "ethnocentric behavior—the imposition of one's cultural values and standards, with the assumption that one is superior to the other—[which] is a fatal error in ethnography" as it compromises the emic perspective sought in the research endeavor.[17]

Collection is an integral stage in the conduct of ethnographic research due to the high risk of an ethnocentric collector bias contaminating data, which would subsequently contaminate and invalidate all further processing. Herein lies the peril of the fine line between an empirical observation and a value-based judgment, which warrants an appropriate asset to ensure that any nuance of the latter is vetted. Unlike the analysis of all-source intelligence, where information can be evaluated for credibility and analyzed for deception during processing, ethnographic data must be collected without any error on the part of the collector as the analysis of data is blinded or enlightened only by the lens of the collector. In this context, the analyst is privy only to what the collector sees, and if the collector does not see something, neither will the analyst. If a collector is not a trained ethnographer and inadvertently reports something that is out of context or from a biased perspective, without being on the ground, an analyst would have no frame of reference to vet this information. This issue, however, is resolved in ethnography by the fact that the collector and analyst are usually the same person.

ETHINT as Source and Agency

Collection in joint intelligence doctrine is defined as "the exploitation of sources by collection agencies and the delivery of the information obtained to the appropriate processing unit for use in the production of intelligence."[18] In terms of ETHINT, a source, or "person from whom, or thing from which, information can be obtained," would be considered the methodologies used to study members of a social group.[19]

The term *source* in HUMINT would be used to describe a person who could act as an informant to provide information. Because culture is shared, a group is required for study, as no one individual member can be considered an authority for the entire group. This requirement does not imply that key informants cannot be used. In fact, key informants are developed to provide insight into certain issues or aspects of the culture. Their use, however, is incorporated into the knowledge acquired through the researcher's observation of the entire group. The term *source* in ETHINT is better understood as it would be in IMINT, where a source is a technical means, such as a satellite, that can be used to collect information, in this case in the form of imagery. It would prove extremely difficult to sit an individual down and have that person inform you what about his or her culture makes that individual, and how he or she interprets the world, different from you and how you perceive things. For this reason, a source in ETHINT is best understood as a "technical means," or more accurately as proven ethnographic methodologies, which can provide information about a social group's culture.[20]

The exploitation, or utilization, of sources in ETHINT is conducted by an agency, or "an organization or individual engaged in collecting and/or processing information."[21] An ETHINT agency would consist of either an individual ethnographer or of a group of ethnographic researchers of varying educational qualifications. An ETHINT collection team would be best understood as "an agency, in addition to having a collection capacity, [that] also possesses some degree of processing power and therefore produces intelligence."[22] Processing, like collection, in ETHINT is deeply founded in anthropological concepts and theoretical paradigms that regulate the validity of information and change raw data into an intelligible form—cultural knowledge—that can be used by analysts in the production of all-source intelligence.

Primary Sources: Direct-Access Ethnography

Fieldwork is the basis of ethnographical research as it allows the researcher to see how individuals react given real-world incentives and constraints and avoids the artificial, or idealized, responses typical of research conducted in a controlled environment. As such, primary ethnographic fieldwork methodologies require intrusion, or *direct access*, into the social group under study and interaction with community members to collect data.

Participant observation is the chief fieldwork data-collection methodology and involves the total immersion in a culture under study to be resocialized into the practices of that community. Most ethnographic endeavors have traditionally required the researcher to live among the social group from periods of six months to two years; however, some applied ethnographic research is often restricted to periods shorter than three months to meet specific research objectives. Living in a foreign community for a long period of time enables the fieldworker to see the explicit and tacit aspects of individuals' day-to-day lives expressed in their ideas, values, and patterned behavior. "The longer an individual stays in a community, building rapport, and the deeper the probe into individual lives, the greater the probability of his or her learning about the sacred subtle [or tacit] elements of the culture: how people pray, how they feel about each other, and how they reinforce their own cultural practices to maintain the integrity of their system," which often remain outside of a person's awareness or consciousness.[23] The duration of immersive study is also fundamental to understanding the true underlying mechanisms of a society as, over time, members forget their "company behavior" and present a more natural and less idealized image of the community. Participant observation requires the researcher to actually participate in the daily lives of community members. Thus, to be a participant observer researching a baseball team, the researcher would be required to play baseball with the team. External observation of the baseball team would be considered *nonparticipant observation*, and although it is also an acceptable form of research, it must be understood as separate from participant observation. As the primary data-collection method, participant observation sets the stage for the use of additional collection methods.[24]

Ethnographic interviewing allows ethnographers to explain what they observe and experience and place it into a larger context. Structured *formal interviews* are used in ethnographic interviewing; however, *informal interviews*, casual conversations with an implicit research agenda, are more common as they allow insight into what individuals think and how their perceptions compare with those of other community members while minimizing the risk of researcher-influenced responses typical of structured interviews and surveys. *Key actor* or *informant interviewing* is an exceptionally effective and efficient source of data and analysis. Key actors can take any form, from formal or informal leaders in the community to "cultural brokers" straddling two cultures, allowing them a special vantage point and objectivity about their own group. Although no individual is a perfect representative of an entire group, more articulate or culturally sensitive individuals can "provide detailed historical data, knowledge about contemporary interpersonal relationships (including conflicts), and a wealth of information about the nuances of everyday life."[25] The researcher is particularly interested in basic features of the culture—knowledge that is elementary to the key actor, however, "such naive questions . . . often lead to global explanations of how a culture works . . . [and can] point out the difference between the key actor and a respondent."[26] Over-reliance on a single informant must be cautioned, of course, as multiple actors are required to provide an accurate and more holistic view of the culture. This requirement for multiple sources is similar to that in HUMINT collection; however, in the case of HUMINT, multiple sources are used to corroborate a single truth, whereas ETHINT seeks to uncover the multisided perspectives of a certain issue.[27]

Surveying is used in ethnographic research to "determine variation in attitudes, knowledge, perceptions, demographic information, and behavior of [the] study population."[28] Surveying is effective in obtaining limited information from a large group of people and provides quantifiable answers to close-ended questions. Surveys are, however, susceptible to misinterpretations and misrepresentations as "many people present an idealized image on questionnaires, answering as they think they should to conform to a certain image."[29] Subsequently, surveys are usually developed to explore specific concerns after an ethnographer has already achieved an effective grasp on the larger situation.[30]

Elicitation methods, such as asking community members to rank order people in their community to understand a community's social hierarchy, are effective in obtaining data on the ways that individuals categorize and organize their understanding of cultural domains. Elicitation is effective for use with individuals or during *focus group interviews*, which involve an interviewer-led discussion among a selection of individuals belonging to a particular group or subgroup under study. Similar to surveys, focus group interviews are conducted after a researcher has established a good grasp on the community, as they allow the researcher to evaluate and provide further insight into themes or patterns that have begun to emerge from the collected data.[31]

Other ethnographic methodologies include the study of *roxemics,* or "the analysis of socially defined distance between people," and *kinesics*, or the study of body language.[32] More advanced ethnographic research practices include *spatial mapping*, which obtains data on "the ways in which cultural data vary across spatial units" by observing the locations of events, institutions, and other material culture, and *network research*, which investigates "patterns of relationships and exchanges among individuals, groups, and other social units" to "understand [the] diffusion of behavior and information through a network."[33]

Secondary Sources: Indirect Access Ethnography

Although ethnographic fieldwork methodologies require intrusive human interaction to be conducted, a variety of other unobtrusive measures are available to supplement interactive methods of data collection and analysis through *indirect access* to a society via means of their "cultural artifacts," such as their literature, communications, or other products. In addition to sources traditionally available to ethnographers, military intelligence, surveillance and reconaissance (ISR) capabilities can increase an ethnographer's ability to use unobtrusive measures and additionally allow a researcher to observe and extract cultural data from restrictive communities and groups, such as insurgent or adversarial networks, of which a researcher would not typically be able to gain access or intrusion.

Ethnographers conduct content analysis on secondary text sources, often referred to as *open-source intelligence (OSINT)*, to elicit themes or content from written data. A society's *literature*, including folktales, poetry, and cultural narratives, is often expressive about the underlying values that drive behavior. It is important to both literate and nonliterate societies as it is often used to transmit critical cultural values from one generation to the next. "A cultural narrative is a story recounted in the form of a casually linked set of events that explains an event in a group's history that expresses the values, character, or self-identity of the group. Narratives are means through which ideologies are expressed and absorbed by members of a society."[34] Examining the literature of a society can help identify a society's core values, how their perceptions organize and interpret events, and also how the group could be mobilized using culturally defining narratives.[35]

A social group's *historical information* is useful for more than simply producing a literature review on a group's origin. While understanding the origin of Afghanistan's Pashtun people is a useful contribution to basic intelligence and general situational awareness, historical analysis of the Pashtuns during Soviet occupation can yield information about underlying tribal conflicts exacerbated during this era. A similar situation exists in studying the former Yugoslavia. Researching the historical origins of Serbs, Croatians, and Bosnians is an effective contribution to understanding what makes each social group unique. Analyzing the role of each of these groups during World War II, when their differences were exacerbated, however, would have provided insightful information concerning the nature of the 1990 civil conflict and the degree of hatred that fueled it.

Imagery intelligence (IMINT) is "intelligence derived from imagery acquired by photographic, radar, electro-optical, infra-red, thermal, and multi-spectral sensors, which can be ground based, sea borne, or carried by overhead platforms."[36] The bulk of IMINT is "derived from sources such as satellites, aircraft, and UAVs," some of which can provide real-time streaming video surveillance of areas and targets of interest.[37] IMINT offers a level of nonparticipant (external) observation unavailable in orthodox ethnographic practices and is equipped with certain analytical techniques, such as geographical profiling and behavior pattern analysis, that serve to monitor the behavior, activities, or other changing information of human populations. This can yield invaluable ethnographic data about the routine of a community under study without disturbing or influencing the environment. Understanding the routine pattern of life of a group of Baluch nomads in the southern Registan desert in Afghanistan, for example, is key to understanding the difference between one of these groups and a group of traffickers or smugglers. Traditional IMINT analysis can provide basic information on the locations and use of buildings and even about the community's economy and different modes of production. Proxemics can also be studied via IMINT down to the level of social interaction between individuals, especially in rural societies, such as Afghanistan, where a lot of social activity takes place out of doors. IMINT has the capability to observe an outdoor *shura* being conducted by village elders, and subsequently analysts on the other end can study its routine conduct and even the socially defined space and seating arrangements of the participants. IMINT, for ethnographic purposes, can easily be developed as a key tool to effectively prepare an ethnographer with sufficient preliminary cultural information about a community before even physically setting foot within it.

Communications intelligence (COMINT) is defined as "intelligence derived from electromagnetic communications and communications systems by those who are not the intended recipients of the information."[38] COMINT obtains information "through the interception of communications and data links. Such information may be collected in verbal form by the recipient of broadcast radio messages [or] by the interception of point-to-point communications such as telephones."[39] Information obtained through COMINT provides unobtrusive observation and a form of one-sided interaction with members of a social group. While this type of data may be more difficult to procure, as the researcher cannot participate to elicit further information, it eliminates a key issue in ethnographic research that the observer only ever sees the social group "with the ethnographer present" and not in a completely natural setting. Overhearing conversations in any setting allows for insight into what people say and how they express their ideas and concerns. A nonparticipant observer in this case would be able to see, for example, how group members adjudicate disputes within the group or what causes the conflict. Something as simple as gossip about other group members or leaders could be evidence of how the group attributes respect to certain personal characteristics of various individuals. More advanced methodologies such as *discourse analysis*, unique to linguistic anthropology, are equipped to use communication to study cultural cognitive structures through identifying schemas, or reoccurring patterned themes, that occur in people's speech that package, motivate, and guide a cultural actor's cognition.[40] Written and electronic communications are also used in traditional ethnographic research. For example, in the study of a corporate organization or an office, "mission statements and annual reports provide the organization's purpose or stated purpose and indicate the image that the organization wishes to present to the outside world. Internal evaluation reports indicate areas of concern. Budgets tell a great deal about organizational values."[41] In addition, "electronic mail is often less inhibited than general correspondence and thus quite revealing about office interrelationships, turf, and various power struggles."[42]

Human intelligence (HUMINT), a "category of intelligence derived from information collected and provided by human sources," involves a range of operations that include debriefings of friendly forces, source operations, and interrogation operations.[43] HUMINT sources, which include informants in adversarial networks and captured enemy personnel (detainees), can also be valuable sources to an ethnographer researching adversarial culture. HUMINT sources offer interaction, but not intrusion, with members of a restricted community that an ethnographer would not typically have access to. It does not allow intrusion based on the fact that the sources can not be observed in their natural setting. Due to this limitation, there is a higher likelihood that cultural information obtained from informants or detainees could be idealized. This representation of the cultural data—idealized descriptions or life histories—can still provide a basis for further analysis of the value informed behavior and perceptions of group members. Adversarial group members who defect or seek amnesty and reconciliation can also serve as cultural brokers, as many of these individuals would likely understand adversarial ideologies as well as the competing ideas that made them defect from the group.

Processing of Ethnographic Information

Processing in ethnographic intelligence, much like collection, is deeply founded in anthropological concepts and theories that serve to prevent the contamination of data and evaluate its validity and also provide the researcher a lens to discern details and patterns that could otherwise go unnoticed. These concepts guide the processing of ethnographic data from the onset of their postcollection evaluation, to their analysis, and finally when they are integrated with all other data resulting from the study.

Evaluation   *Evaluation* in intelligence is defined as "a step in the processing stage of the intelligence cycle constituting appraisal of an item of information in respect of the reliability of the source and credibility of the information."[44]

Information credibility is concerned with the quality of information and the extent to which its accuracy can be trusted. In ETHINT, this is done at and by the source to ensure the validity of collected information through examining it for *veracity*, or conformity to facts; *objectivity*, or that it is not influenced by (collector) bias in representing facts; and *perspicacity*, or the applicability of insights to other data.[45] For ethnographic information to be valid, it must be collected from a nonjudgmental orientation, either emic or etic in perspective, contextualized, and holistic.

Any person conducting ethnographic research will inevitably be a product of his or her own culture with his or her own personal beliefs, biases, and preferences. Having a *nonjudgmental orientation* requires the collector to suspend any personal valuation about the practices of a culture to prevent the data from being contaminated by inappropriate and unnecessary value judgments about what the researcher observes. This is "similar to suspending disbelief while one watches a movie or reads a book—one accepts what may be an obviously illogical or unbelievable set of circumstances to allow the author to unravel a riveting story," and it is the primary safeguard against ethnocentric bias.[46]

Ethnographic data espouse either an *emic* (insider's) or *etic* (observer's) perspective on collection. "Most ethnographers start collecting data from the emic perspective and then try to make sense of what they have collected in terms of both the native's view and their own scientific [etic] analysis."[47] Although both offer imperative perspectives to the research endeavor, data must be clearly demarcated as to which view they represent—similar to how HUMINT distinguishes "source comment" from "analyst comment" in the text of reports.

Ethnography views all elements under study as existing in a context. *Context* refers to the surrounding circumstances—actions of others, the natural environment, economic factors—that affect or influence a group's ideas or actions. Contextualizing ethnographic data involves implementing observations into a larger perspective of the context in which learned and patterned ways of behaving and thinking occur.[48]

Ethnographic data require a holistic outlook "to gain a comprehensive and complete picture of a social group" by realizing the interrelationships that exist between various systems and subsystems within a community.[49] Ensuring a *holistic orientation* forces the researcher to see beyond the immediate data and understand the multilayered and interrelated context of the cultural scene.

Source reliability is concerned with the extent to which a source can be trusted to consistently report accurate information. Ethnographic collection requires intrusion into a social group, and although the ethnographer, a trained collection asset, is the source of ETHINT, this intrusion has direct implications on the resulting data with respect to the ethnographer's *access and rapport* and *duration of fieldwork and depth of embed.*

The examination of a researcher's *access* in a community is integral to understanding whose truth is being told and notably whose truth is not being told. A researcher's access may be wide in some areas of a community but limited or blocked in others by virtue of a researcher's gender, age, social status, or even his or her previous association with other community members. Access is closely linked with *rapport*, which concerns the amount of trust a researcher has developed with informants and the resulting level of truth he or she is privy to. This is also affected by the "role of the ethnographer among the people studied (such as social scientist, missionary, government official)" as this can influence the responses, or "truths," offered by informants who may be interested to see if they can gain something (aid, cash, political voice) or adversely fear consequence (taxes, legal penalties, loss of face).[50]

The *duration of fieldwork and depth of embed* of a researcher in the community are direct variables of the reliability of ethnographic information.[51] For this reason, ETHINT can be seen as existing along a similar spectrum as HUMINT collection methodologies, which range from the most overt, such as debriefings and tactical questioning, to the more covert, such as source and agent handling, with the presumption that the quality of information increases as methods move down the spectrum, closing the gap between the collector and the source of the information.[52] For the ETHINT spectrum, the deeper the embed, the more time in the field, the more reliable the source becomes.

Analysis   Analysis in intelligence is defined as "a step in the processing stage of the intelligence cycle in which information is subjected to review in order to identify significant facts for subsequent interpretation."[53] The analysis of ethnographic data is equipped with anthropological paradigms that provide a theoretical framework to help explain findings and allow events to be viewed in a new light to see previously unnoticed detail. These paradigms are used "when they help us understand the phenomena in question, and often need to adapt existing theories or adopt new theoretical ideas of our own to help us make sense of what is going on around us. A theory is only useful in as much as it helps us make sense of the world around us, so we apply theories to our data to see if they help us make sense of what we have heard and seen, using the bits that help, discarding those that do not."[54] In this context, anthropological paradigms serve as lenses to examine data to see more than what they offer at face value. Such lenses include functionalist, ecological, transactional, cognitive, interpretivism, and globalization paradigms, as described in the following paragraphs.

The *functionalist paradigm* accentuates the functions of customs and/or social institutions in how they relate to one another or to the greater social system.[55] The *ecological paradigm*, which could be argued as a subsidiary of functionalism, examines how human society or culture is shaped by and interacts with the natural environment.[56] The *transactionalist paradigm*, much as its name describes, emphasizes the transactions that occur among individuals and uses these as the basis of social analysis.[57] The *cognitive paradigm*, on the other hand, is interested in the relationships between cultural categories and structures of processes of thought.[58] The *interpretivism paradigm* is captivated by the interpretation of culture, especially in respect of the symbols and rituals of a society.[59] The *globalization paradigm* focuses on the contact between societies, especially concerning the movement of populations, skills, technology, and ideas.[60]

Integration   Integration in intelligence is defined as "a step in the processing stage of the intelligence cycle whereby analyzed information or intelligence is selected and combined into a pattern in the course of the production of further intelligence."[61] Ethnographic information is integrated with existing data through triangulation and the development of patterns. *Triangulation* is at the heart of verifying the validity of data in ethnographic research by comparing different sources to test the quality of the collected information. Triangulation also allows the researcher to learn about new dimensions of a particular issue that allow the researcher to ultimately put the entire situation into perspective. This improves both the quality of data and the accuracy of ethnographic findings. *Pattern development* is conducted by searching for routine patterns of thought and behavior among the massive accumulation of collected data and observations. Although many variations exist within a society, there will be significant patterns among the practices and beliefs of community members. The development of patterns in ethnography both reinforces the reliability of ethnographic findings and serves as a benchmark indicating when ethnographic investigation has neared completion—when the continuous inquiry of informants yields the same and repeating data.

Incorporation into Joint Intelligence Process   CULINT and ETHINT are not new constructs but rather intelligence disciplines forgotten over forty years of Cold War with a known, symmetric, and predictable adversary. Its reintegration, however, requires a paradigm shift on the part of joint intelligence doctrine, which presently focuses too much on the adversary and pays little attention to other elements of the operational environment that affect the commander's mission. Echoed by LCdr John P. Coles in a related article, "intelligence doctrine must stress that knowledge of all foreign peoples in a joint operations area is a fundamental of joint warfare; it is not limited to 'knowledge of the enemy.'"[62] This diversification has even been reflected in a shift in nomenclature to the term *operational environment* over the previous *battle space*; however, further doctrinal definitions must continue to evolve, beginning with "what intelligence provides Joint Force Commanders" as offered by LCdr Coles (addition indicated in brackets):

> Intelligence provides knowledge of the enemy, potential enemy and local foreign populations to JFCs. [In combat situations] intelligence tells JFCs what their adversaries or potential adversaries are doing, what they are capable of doing, and what they may do in the future. In combat, intelligence assists JFCs and their staffs in visualizing the battlespace and in achieving information superiority. Intelligence also contributes to information superiority by attempting to discern the adversary's probable intent and future course of action. In peacetime operations, transition operations or other MOOTW, intelligence provides the JFC true cultural knowledge of local populations, their leaders and coalition partners. This knowledge will help the JFC and his staff design the best courses of action for the given mission.[63]

This improved definition more accurately articulates the diverse requirements for cultural knowledge and will aid commanders during the planning and direction stage of the joint intelligence process in defining cultural information and intelligence requirements.

ETHINT can be incorporated into the joint intelligence process in the "collection" and "processing and exploitation" stages. During the collection stage, ethnographic information is collected through ethnographic collection methodologies. This information is then processed to develop an understanding of what is going on in the social group. During the processing and exploitation stage, raw cultural data are transformed into an intelligible form—cultural knowledge. "An example of processing and exploitation occurs when the technical parameters (frequency, pulse repetition frequency, and bandwidth) detected by an electronic intelligence (ELINT) collection system are compared and associated with known parameters of a particular radar system. Rather than having to deal with raw ELINT data, the analyst is provided with the essential fact—the identity of the radar."[64]

The same model exists in ETHINT. Rather than having to deal with bits of raw cultural data that may or may not represent the entire social group, the analysts are provided with evaluated, processed, and analyzed cultural knowledge. It is not up to an all-source cell to develop cultural knowledge and figure out what is going on in the social group. The all-source cell requires to be fed cultural knowledge to make sense of how it affects and influences the operational environment and planning considerations. "Whereas collection, processing, and exploitation are primarily performed by specialists from one of the major intelligence disciplines, analysis and production is done primarily by all-source analysts that fuse together information from all intelligence disciplines."[65] As an agency, an ethnographic collection team is required to collect and process its own data. This is an important separation of ETHINT from CULINT (see Figure 1.2 and Table 1.1). It is also a convenient separation between those who would be qualified and required to produce cultural knowledge, personnel trained in ethnographic collection, and those who could apply its use in a military context, intelligence analysts or subject

Planning and direction		Intelligence and information requirements are defined by the commander and intelligence staffs.
Collection		Ethnographic collection methodologies are used to cultivate ethnographic information.
Processing and exploitation	ETHINT	Ethnographic information is processed into an ineligible form, cultural knowledge, for use by intelligence analysts.
Analysis and production	CULINT	Sociocultural knowledge is analyzed, interpreted with other intelligence, and produced into products to support the commander's mission.
Dissemination and integration		Intelligence is delivered to and used by consumer.
Evaluation and feedback		Intelligence personnel at all levels assess how well each of the various types of intelligence operations are being performed.

Figure 1.2. Joint intelligence: The incorporation of CULINT and ETHINT into the joint intelligence process.

Table 1.1. Joint intelligence: A comparison of CULINT and ETHINT.

Intelligence types	Cultural intelligence (CULINT)	Ethnographic intelligence (ETHINT)
Intelligence function	Focus discipline	Collection discipline
Definition	"An intelligence discipline that analyzes cultural knowledge to assess or interpret how it impacts, influences, and affects the operating environment, adversary, and operational planning considerations."	"An intelligence collection discipline that produces sociocultural knowledge through the use of specialized ethnographic collection methodologies and analytical processes that are guided by anthropological concepts."
Collection sources	Ethnographic information	Ethnographic collection methodologies
Analytical focus	How does the social group's culture affect the operating environment?	What is going on in the social group?

matter experts. This also alleviates the issue of unprocessed ethnographic information being used out of its context. Comparable to HUMINT or SIGINT, information is not released to all-source cells in its raw form until it has been processed into a product by the collection agency to avoid the peril of its potential misunderstanding or misuse.

CULINT assumes the analytical focus of "how does the social group's culture affect the operational environment?" During the analysis and production stage, cultural knowledge is analyzed, integrated with other intelligence, and developed into products to support the commander's mission. Although CULINT will likely produce separate and specific products and assessments, it will also be a contributor to the production of all-source intelligence. All-source cells, which are responsible for the fusion of information from all intelligence disciplines, will then integrate, evaluate, analyze, and interpret all available information from the various collection disciplines to create products to satisfy the commander's priority information requirements (PIR) and requests for information (RFI).

CONCLUSION

The academic discipline of anthropology, with its conceptual paradigms and proven collection methodologies, is the appropriate authority to regulate the creation of intelligence disciplines that focus on procuring, understanding, and interpreting information about human culture. CULINT, as an intelligence functional discipline, is not vague briefings on religion, customs, and "do's and don'ts": "It provides understanding of not only how other groups act but why. It gives the commander as well as the soldier the knowledge to anticipate reactions to selected courses of action."[66] ETHINT, as an intelligence collection discipline, is far more than charting tribal group locations and village demographics for the creation of maps and pie charts for use in intelligence briefings. Ethnographic collection methodologies allow the researcher to

> . . . learn about the intricacies of a subgroup or community [and] to describe it in all its richness and complexity. In the process of studying these details, they typically discover underlying forces that make the system tick. These cultural elements are values or beliefs that can unite or divide a group but that are commonly shared focal points. An awareness of what role these abstract elements play in a given culture can give the researcher a clearer picture of how the culture works.[67]

Together, CULINT and ETHINT allow military commanders, intelligence staffs, and soldiers an emic understanding of a foreign culture—what makes them tick, what their perceptions and behaviors are that make them unique, and what underlying values and structures influence and drive how they make decisions. As outlined in U.S. MOOTW doctrine: "It is only through an understanding of the values by which people define themselves, that an intervener can establish himself a perception of legitimacy"; such a perception which is required to be a victor in counterinsurgency operations.[68]

NOTES

1. Anthony Zinni, *Non-Traditional Military Missions: Their Nature, and the Need for Cultural Awareness and Flexible Thinking* (Quantico, VA: U.S. Marine Corps War College, 1998), 267.

2. Department of Defense, Field Manual 3-24: Counterinsurgency (Washington, DC: Headquarters Department of the Army, 2006), 3-7.

3. Joint intelligence doctrine differentiates between intelligence "functional disciplines" and "collection disciplines." Intelligence "functional disciplines," such as CULINT, "cover subject-focused aspects of intelligence production," whereas "collection disciplines" are "the means or systems used to observe, sense, and recored or convey information of conditions, situations and events" (DND, 2003: 2–17, 2–15).

4. NATO (North Atlantic Treaty Organization), AAP-6: NATO Glossary of Terms and Definitions (Brussels: NATO Standardization Agency, 2008), 2-B-2.

5. MCIA (Marine Corps Intelligence Activity), Cultural Intelligence: Global Scope, Operationally Focused (Quantico, VA: Marine Corps Intelligence Activity, 2007).

6. Department of National Defence, Joint Intelligence Doctrine B-GL-005-200/FP-000 (Ottawa: Government of Canada, 2003), 2-1.

7. Montgomery McFate, "Does Culture Matter? The Military Utility of Cultural Knowledge," Joint Forces Quarterly 28 (2005), 43.

8. Department of Defense, Joint Publication 2-0: Joint Intelligence (Washington, DC: Joint Chiefs of Staff, 2007), II-1.

9. Ibid.

10. Ibid., II-2.

11. Ibid. On the subject of defeating ethnocentric bias, one can take a lesson from WWII: Analysis in military intelligence tends to adhere to Western economic and political science theories of culture and 'the rational man.' Consequently, this foundation inevitably biases how analysts interpret premises and build assessments. Benedict noted that in 1946 "it was important to answer a multitude of questions about our enemy, Japan"; Ruth F. Benedict, The Chrysanthemum and the Sword: Patterns of Japanese Culture (Boston: Houghton Mifflin, 1946), 4:

> Whether the issue was military or diplomatic, whether it was raised by questions of high policy or of leaflets to be dropped behind the Japanese front lines, every insight was important. In the all-out war Japan was fighting we had to know, not just the aims and motives of those in power in Tokyo, not just the long history of Japan, not just economic and military statistics; we had to know what their government could count on from the people. We had to try to understand Japanese habits of thought and emotion and the patterns into which these habits fell. We had to know the sanctions behind these actions and opinions. (Benedict, 4–5)

Most importantly, in regards to intelligence analysis, she furthered: "We had to put aside for the moment the premises on which we act as Americans and to keep ourselves as far as possible from leaping to the easy conclusion that what we would do in a given situation was what they would do" (Benedict, 5).

12. Raphael Patai, The Arab Mind (New York: Charles Scribners and Sons, 1973).

13. Montgomery McFate, "Anthropology and Counterinsurgency: The Strange Story of Their Curious Relationship," Military Review (March–April 2005), 37.

14. NATO, 2008, 2-I-4, 2-I-6.

15. Barney G. Glaser and Anselm L. Strauss, The Discovery of Grounded Theory (Chicago: Aldine, 1967).

16. Department of National Defence, 2003, 2–7.

17. David M. Fetterman, Ethnography: Step by Step, 2nd ed. (Thousand Oaks, CA: Sage, 1998), 23.

18. NATO, 2008, 2-S-6.

19. Ibid., 2-S-6.

20. Anthropologist Ruth Benedict describes this issue as a "matter of spectacles":

In any matter of spectacles, we do not expect the man who wears them to know the formula for the lenses, and neither can we expect nations to analyze their own outlook upon the world. When we want to know about spectacles, we train an oculist and expect him to be able to write out the formula for any lenses we bring him. Some day no doubt we shall recognize that it is the job of the social scientist to do this for the nations of the contemporary world.

Benedict, 1946, 14.

21. NATO, 2008, 2-A-5.

22. Department of National Defence, 2003, 2–6.

23. Fetterman, 1998, 17.

24. H. Russell Bernard, *Research Methods in Anthropology: Qualitative and Qualitative Approaches*, 2nd ed. (Thousand Oaks, CA: Sage, 1994); Kathleen M. Dewalt and Billie R. Dewalt, *Participant Observation: A Guide for Fieldworkers* (Walnut Creek, CA: AltaMira, 2002); Fetterman, 1998; and Martyn Hammersley and Paul Atkinson, *Ethnography: Principles in Practice*, 3rd ed. (New York: Routledge, 2007).

25. Fetterman, 1998, 48.

26. Ibid.

27. Bernard, 1994; Fetterman, 1998; and Stephan J. Schensul, Jean J. Schensul, and Margaret D. LeCompte, *Essential Ethnographic Methods: Observations, Interviews, and Questionnaires*, 7 vols., volume 2 (Lanham, MD: AltaMira, 1999).

28. Margaret LeCompte and Jean J. Schensul, *Designing and Conducting Ethnographic Research*, 7 vols., volume 1 (Lanham, MD: AltaMira, 1999), 128.

29. Fetterman, 1998, 54.

30. Bernard, 1994, and Schensul, Schensul, and LeCompte, 1999.

31. Jean J. Schensul, Margaret D. LeCompte, Bonnie K. Nastasi, and Stephen P. Borgatti, *Enhanced Ethnographic Methods: Audiovisual Techniques, Focused Group Interviews, and Elicitation Techniques*, 7 vols., volume 3 (Lanham, MD: AltaMira, 1999).

32. Fetterman, 1998, 59.

33. Jean J. Schensul, Margaret LeCompte, Robert Trotter, and Merrill Singer, *Mapping Social Networks, Spatial Data, and Hidden Populations*, 7 vols., volume 4 (Lanham, MD: AltaMira, 1999), 129–130.

34. Department of Defense, 2006, 3–8.

35. Department of Defense, 2006; Jane A. Hill, "Finding Culture in Narrative," in N. Quinn, ed., *Finding Culture in Talk: A Collection of Methods* (New York: Palgrave, 2005); and Holly F. Mathews, "Uncovering Cultural Models of Gender from Accounts

of Folktales," in N. Quinn, ed., *Finding Culture in Talk: A Collection of Methods* (New York: Palgrave, 2005).

36. Department of National Defence, 2003, 2–16.

37. Ibid.

38. NATO, 2008, 2-C-11.

39. Department of National Defence, 2003, 2–16.

40. Naomi Quinn, "How to Reconstruct Shemas People Share, from What They Say," in N. Quinn, ed., *Finding Culture in Talk: A Collection of Methods* (New York: Palgrave, 2005).

41. Fetterman, 1998, 58.

42. Ibid., 59.

43. NATO, 2008, 2-H-4.

44. NATO, 2008, 2-E-6.

45. Alex Stewart, *The Ethnographer's Method* (Thousand Oaks, CA: Sage, 1998).

46. Fetterman, 1998, 23.

47. Ibid., 22.

48. LeCompte and Schensul, 1999b, 18.

49. Fetterman, 1998, 19.

50. Raoul Naroll, *Data Quality Control—A New Research Technique: Prolegomena to a Cross-Cultural Study of Culture Stress* (New York: Free Press of Glencoe, 1962).

51. Ibid.

52. Department of Defense, Field Manual 2-22.3: Human Intelligence Collector Operations (Washington, DC: Department of the Army, 2006).

53. NATO, 2008, 2-A-14.

54. Karen O'Reilly, *Ethnographic Methods* (New York: Routledge, 2005), 1999.

55. Bronislaw Malinowski, *Argonauts of the Western Pacific* (New York: E. P. Dutton, 1922); and A. R. Radcliffe-Brown, *The Andaman Islanders* (New York: Free Press, 1922).

56. Julian Steward, *Theory of Culture Change: The Methodology of Multilinear Evolution* (Urbana: University of Illinois Press, 1955); Roy A. Rappaport, *Pigs for Ancestors* (New Haven, CT: Yale University, 1968); and Marvin Harris, "The Cultural Ecology of India's Sacred Cattle," *Current Anthropology* 7 (1976): 51–66.

57. Fredrik Barth, *Models of Social Organization,* Occasional Paper no. 23 (London: Royal Anthropological Institute of Great Britain and Ireland, 1966).

58. Stephen Tyler, *Cognitive Anthropology* (New York: Holt, Rinehart, and Winston, 1969).

59. Clifford Geertz, *The Interpretation of Cultures* (New York: Basic Books, 1973).

60. Ulf Hannerz, *Transnational Connections: Culture, People, Places* (New York: Routledge, 1996).

61. NATO, 2008, 2-I-6.

62. John P. Coles, "Incorporating Cultural Intelligence Into Joint Doctrine," *Joint Information Operations Centre* 7-13 (2006), 10.

63. Ibid.

64. Department of Defense, 2007, I-15.

65. Ibid.

66. Coles, 2006, 7.

67. Fetterman, 1998, 18.

68. Department of Defense, *Joint Publication 3-07: Joint Doctrine for Military Operations Other than War* (Washington, DC: Joint Chiefs of Staff, 1995), IV-2.

2 THE USE OF EVOLUTIONARY THEORY IN MODELING CULTURE AND CULTURAL CONFLICT

Marc W. D. Tyrrell

THIS CHAPTER PRESENTS A MODEL of one potential Darwinian theory of cultural evolution. It is divided into two main sections.[1] The first draws on the theoretical work from numerous sources to construct an evolutionary model of culture. The primary focus is on defining the necessary units of analysis for such a theory, namely the coding system and the work spaces in which natural selection can take place. The second part of the chapter presents a very cursory examination of the environmental factors that serve to construct the workspaces of "warfare." Two short case examples—one from Mosul 2006–2007 and the other from a jihadi blog—are presented as illustrations of the model.

The story of the relationship between evolutionary theory and cultural modeling is fascinating. Over the past 150 years in the social sciences, evolutionary theory has been misapplied, misunderstood, hijacked by megalomaniacs, and attacked by people who have no concept of what a theory is. Throughout the period that it has been in intellectual play, however, it has proven to be the most robust theoretical explanation for change over time.

Since Darwin's day, there have been many refinements and arguments about evolutionary theory, and we now have a much better, albeit much more complex, idea of how it works and, perhaps more importantly, what parts of it can and should be applied outside the area of biology. This chapter outlines one possible application of Darwinian evolutionary theory to "culture." The chapter itself is divided into two main sections. The first builds a very tentative Darwinian model of cultural evolution, while the second applies this model to the specific concept of "warfare."

EVOLUTIONARY "CULTURE"?

Evolutionary theory is composed of three main subtheories:

1   Natural selection: How does competition operate, and how do groups operate within their environments?
2   Mutation (or change): How does a pattern of information, such as a genetic code, change?
3   Inheritance: How does a member of a population acquire a pattern of information?

I use the phrase "pattern of information" for a very specific reason. In 1997, William Calvin wrote what I consider to be a brilliant article called "The Six Essentials? Minimal Requirements for the Darwinian Bootstrapping of Quality."[2] In this article, Calvin laid out six minimal qualifications for any system to be considered as "Darwinian":

1   There must be a pattern involved.
2   The pattern must be copied somehow.
3   Variant patterns must sometimes be produced by chance.
4   The pattern and its variant must compete with one another for occupation of a limited work space.
5   The competition is biased by a multifaceted environment.
6   New variants always preferentially occur around the more successful of the current patterns.

One of the basic points that Calvin notes in the article is that selection pressures—"competition"—operate on patterns of information. In biology, the classic "pattern of information" is DNA sequences using a quaternary coding system. But there is no inherent restriction of either the coding sequence composition of a "pattern of information" or the scope of the theory; it may include *any* pattern of information governed by the six minimal requirements, and this specifically includes the rather complex patterns of information that go into making up what we call "culture."

Anthropologists use the term *culture* with two completely different connotations.[3] The first meaning concerns the ability of humans to generate symbolic and material "interfaces" and extensions (artefacts, organizations, belief systems, and the like) between themselves and their environments. The second meaning refers to the specific, historically situated interface and extensional structures of a particular group—a meaning often referred to as "the culture of . . . [a specific group]." Both definitions refer back to patterns: the ability, within certain biological limits *to* pattern "reality," as well as specific patternings of reality.

One of the primary reasons for the misapplication of evolutionary theory in the social sciences comes from a very simple fact: We frequently got the unit of analysis, the "coding of the pattern," wrong. The earliest attempt at defining a unit of analysis was in 1889 by Sir E. B. Tyler, who chose institutions as his unit of analysis.[4] Tyler's choice was, in many ways, a good one. Unfortunately, he lacked both a sufficient supporting theory to go from the individual to the group and a way of reconciling his data across cultures. These problems allowed critics such as Sir Francis Galton and Herbert Spencer to hijack evolutionary theory for their own ends.

In addition to the problems with selecting the right unit of analysis and reconciling data, there was one other major problem: the metaphysical and teleological assumptions rampant in Western civilization during the late nineteenth century. For Herbert Spencer, the appropriate application of evolutionary theory was self-evident: Some cultures were "better" than others; larger, more advanced, more complex, and, therefore, more *evolved*. Spencer, who coined the term *survival of the fittest*, argued that the dominance of the Western nations was clear proof that those same nations had progressed further toward some ultimate goal or end point. This is a teleological assumption rooted in Christian theology, which has no part in Darwinian evolutionary theory; it did, however, serve as an excellent justification for the colonial practices of the West.

Sir Francis Galton, not to be outdone by Spencer, took his analysis one step further. If the Western nations were more evolved than other nations, this was because the Western *races* were more advanced. If this is so, he reasoned, then the goal of society must include the improvement of the "race" through both selective breeding programs (for example, eugenics programs) and racial culling (for example, mandatory sterilization programs). Galton's ideas were later merged with the earlier ravings of Arthur de Gobineau and became the theoretical basis for the Nazi racial purity laws of 1935 with consequences we all know.

The reactions of most social scientists to the misuse of evolutionary theory, especially after World War II, was to abandon it completely. While this has started to change over the past thirty years, there is still a general distrust of evolutionary theory within the social sciences, a distrust that has moved most social sciences completely away from the very concept of "science," especially within anthropology.[5]

RECONSTRUCTING A SCIENCE OF CULTURE

> *Whether we consider a very simple or primitive culture or an extremely complex and developed one, we are confronted by a vast apparatus, partly material, partly human and partly spiritual, by which man is able to cope with the concrete, specific problems that face him. These problems arise out of the fact that man has a body subject to various organic needs, and that he lives in an environment which is his best friend, in that it provides the raw materials of man's handiwork, and also his dangerous enemy, in that it harbors many hostile forces.*[6]
>
> **—Bronislaw Malinowski,** *A Scientific Theory of Culture*

Even as evolutionary theory was being rejected inside anthropology, there were several concerted efforts to construct a science of culture using Darwinian assumptions, most notably by Bronislaw Malinowski.[7] Malinowski attempted to provide the "missing theory" that plagued Tyler.

Malinowski started his major theoretical work with one basic assumption, on which he built his entire model: "that the theory of culture must take its stand on biological fact. . . . They [humans] are subject to elemental conditions which have to be fulfilled so that individuals may survive, the race continue and organisms one and all be maintained in working order."[8] This short quotation foreshadows the three major areas of his inquiry: individual survival, racial continuance,[9] and organism maintenance.

Malinowski argued that there were three main types of "needs," each of which derived from a different source. He starts with basic physiological "instincts" and argues that these produce a universal list of processes, or "vital sequences," that all cultures must address. These vital sequences, when considered at the general level of both a group and an individual, give rise to specific "basic needs" that must be met by all cultures.[10]

Each "basic need" is met by a "cultural response" (see Table 2.1). These cultural responses are organized patterns of behavior that have evolved in response to that basic need and within a particular environment.[11] Many of these cultural responses are systematized, "named," and given a social existence— they are a society's "institutions." Within these "institutions," Malinowski noted two types of regularities: (1) a regularity of components or elements[12]

Table 2.1. Malinowski's basic needs and cultural responses.

Basic needs	Cultural responses
Metabolism	Commissariat
Reproduction	Kinship
Bodily Comforts	Shelter
Safety	Protection
Movement	Activities
Growth	Training
Health	Hygiene

SOURCE: Malinowski 1944, 91.

and (2) a regularity in functional type across cultures. These "institutions," in turn, produce a secondary environment and have their own "derived needs" or "imperatives" relating to the survival of the institution.[13] Although this model is useful, it also can be matched in many nonhuman species.

For Malinowski, what sets human cultures apart from nonhuman is the process of symbolization involved in the creation of "integrative imperatives"—a third environment that is primarily symbolic. As Malinowski notes, "Symbolism, in its essential nature, is the modification of the original organism which allows the transformation of a physiological drive into a cultural value."[14] This symbolization must allow for the transmission of cultural knowledge ("the full knowledge of tribal tradition"), coupled with the ability to link emotional states to this knowledge (that is, the production of "values").

Malinowski argued that all cultural organizations (institutions) appear as specific ways to meet particular needs and/or desires that, in turn, produce a series of secondary or derived needs that stem from the operation and maintenance of various institutions.[15] On top of these, there is also a series of what he termed "integrative imperatives"; symbol systems designed to maintain group cohesion (economics, social control, education, political organization).[16] For Malinowski, the institution was the primary interface between individuals and their environments. Institutions embody the composite answers (material, perceptual, and organizational) of a culture to particular needs, problems, and desires.

WHAT IS THE "CODE"?

While Malinowski's theory provides the link between individual and group across the species, it stops short of actually identifying the coding structures of a culture. Evolutionary theory is, after all, very simple, and it requires that there be an equally simple coding system, something analogous, at the cultural level, to DNA. Several theoreticians have attempted to come up with such an analog at the cultural level (for example, Richard Dawkins with his concept of the "meme"), but these attempts have, by and large, been unsatisfactory. Where we have found some limited success, or at least promising potential, is in two areas.

First, the area of evolutionary psychology (broadly construed) has proven to be quite productive in developing insights into how human consciousness and culture have evolved in the past and into some of the constraints that exist on human biological mechanisms (for example, neural circuitry, the operation of neuronal plasticity, "mental modules," and so on) The second area is much less developed, and deals, very loosely, with symbology; it doesn't even have a name as yet, so I will just refer to it as "evolutionary symbology."[17] The basic idea, however, is quite simple and derives exactly from Malinowski's observations on symbolism. To find a coding system for culture that is subject to Darwinian evolutionary mechanisms, that system must be composed of a minimum of two distinct parts: one biological and one communicative.

One potential basic biological code has been formulated by Alan Fiske in his relational models theory.[18] Fiske, arguing from both biological and cultural data, proposes that there are just five forms of social relationships necessary to define the relational component of all cultures:

- *Communal sharing*: a general "what is mine is yours" and vice versa;
- *Authority ranking*: an ordered hierarchical system;
- *Equality matching*: all forms of reciprocity;
- *Market pricing*: a limited one-time exchange; and
- *The null set*: no relationship.

The core of "culture," for Fiske, then, becomes the rules held by a group of people about when to deploy each form of relationship, while the skin of culture is the selection among variant genres of expressing that relationship. Each form of social relationship, then, is a "pattern of information" that is subject to a Darwinian form of natural selection within its immediate environment.

While the evidence for this system of coding is somewhat compelling, there are some problems with assuming that it can operate by itself. In particular, there is the problem of "culture lag" or, in other words, using a form of relationship that no longer exceeds current selection criteria.[19] Once we add in a communicative component, however, this limitation is accounted for. To make this clear, I will need to talk about how symbols operate.

Symbols are composed of two parts: a "sign" and a collection of emotional connotations (what Korzybski called the semantic reaction[20]). The "sign" component of a symbol points towards some "thing" (the "signified"),[21] while the emotional connotation refers to the emotional reactions of *individuals* toward both the sign and the signified. Although symbols almost always have a generally accepted "meaning" or "value," at the level of a culture, this "value" is always a frequency distribution of individually held emotional connotations.

We often hear that "culture is learned," and that is quite true. What is "learned," however, is to associate particular signs both with what they signify and with emotional connotations (including values on relational forms). These symbols are associated with other symbols to form networks that reinforce each other at the individual level by interlocking emotional connotations. These individually internalized symbolic networks are also located externally to each individual, within the culture's institutions. This "collective knowledge" can be described as a "map" of the institution's "territory."[22]

I have been using the relatively neutral term *emotional connotation*, and this may, in some ways, be misleading. The emotions evoked by symbols can be both powerful and subconscious, and there is a very good reason for this. "Culture," understood as the collective "knowledge" or "wisdom" of a group, is all about survival of the group, *not* the individual,[23] even though specific culturally "programmed" responses may also lead to individual survival. Indeed, the human ability to accept cultural programming is, in all probability, an evolutionary survival trait. Consider the following scenario from our remote past:

> Date: Janury 24, 1,256,692 BCE, 10:03 am (GMT +2)
>
> Location: The savannah in what will be Kenya
>
> A hunting/foraging party of six Australopithecines moves in open skirmish order across the savannah, weapons held at the ready. They are tough and well trained and have the highest technology in the world (Acheulian hand axes; MK XXII). The point man spots a stalk of grass moving against the wind and calls out to his squad mates, all of whom immediately run away looking for a tree to climb yelling about demons. The point man, disdaining such rank superstition, cautiously approaches the grass stalk, weapon at the ready. His tension builds as his squad mates yell at him, but, showing the spirit that makes

Australopithecines the rulers of the world, he goes forward—at which point, the "demon" grass reveals itself to be a lion's tail, and he turns into an excellent imitation of steak tartare. As his squad mates note around the campfire the next night, chatting up the women, "sometimes a grass stalk is just a grass stalk, but . . ."

Such a scenario may, at first glance, sound rather silly, but it does capture a core problem with culture: If reactions that lead to survival do not operate at an almost "instinctual" level, then people just will not survive, and the group will die out. In most cases, people get their basic cultural patterns as children, a time when our neural structures are the most malleable.

This early childhood programming operates to establish basic orientations to the world that, in general, carry on throughout our lives, although specifics can, and do, change. Often this childhood programming takes place in the form of "stories" (including myths and fables) that establish broad narratives situating various actions and situations as symbolic and graphically inculcating emotional reactions.[24] This same genre of "programming," "storytelling" broadly speaking, appears in all areas of human life regardless of age and may be encoded in any form, including text, paintings, architecture, dance, music, and so on. This "external-to-the-individual" code storage is another hallmark of culture as requiring a communicative code.

While the major contours of our culture are established during childhood, these same symbolic networks may well act to allow and/or encourage change under certain environmental conditions. In addition, we all undergo constant subtle (and not-so-subtle) reinforcements and/or disproofs of our cultural beliefs during our day-to-day lives that, gradually, change how we perceive the world, splitting it gradually into our "cultural values"—what should be—and our personal perceptions of what is.[25]

WORK SPACES, ENVIRONMENTS, AND COMPETITION

> 1. *The pattern and its variant must compete with one another for occupation of a limited work space.*
> 2. *The competition is biased by a multifaceted environment.*
> —William H. Calvin, *The Cerebral Code*[26]

In biological evolution, a "work space" is an ecological niche—a subset of a particular environment—in which competition between species and variants of species takes place. In cultural evolution, the work space is not quite as easily identified. Historically, at least inside anthropology, the levels of cultural analysis used most often are community, organization, ethnic group, nation, or culture area; comparative studies have been done at all of these levels and, also, at the level of the planetary population.[27]

With the exception of the planetary population, however, none of these levels provide hard barriers that stop interaction across them. This means that we have to come up with a general definition of a work space that will cover all of these levels. For an initial operating definition, I use the following: a cultural work space is a perceived, named, and communicated subset of the total operational environment[28] that has a loose correspondence (real or imagined) to a real, biological need.

Possibly the simplest way to use such a definition is to stretch Malinowski's definition of an "institution" to include both actual and potential institutions and ontologies. This allows us to create some fairly simple guidelines for defining workspaces based on four criteria:

1   The presence of resources that are valued by actors;
2   The degree ontological similarity among actors at the environmental level;[29]
3   The degree of institutional similarity among actors within an environment; and
4   Whether there is any recognized force that can and/or will limit competition.[30]

It should go without saying that some resources must be present that are valued by two or more actors for there to be a work space within which competition can take place.

If the ontologies of various actors competing for specific resources in an environment are dissimilar enough, this may be the cause of competition between them. For example, Andrew Abbott has clearly shown how competing analogies and metaphors shift ontologies among professional groups, causing competition between them for control over the practice of professional knowledge.[31] Competition of this type is frequently *definitional* in that it centers on gaining control over a resource base by redefining people's perceptions. In military terms, this would include situations where the "conventions of war" are disregarded, ranging from the military revolutions of Marius, William the Silent, Napoleon, and Mao to classic, population-centric insurgency/counterinsurgency campaigns.

When there is a high degree of ontological similarity, competition takes place in the form of institutional efficiencies. This is similar to the classic conceptualization of natural selection with gradual change taking place over time. Competition centers around "perfecting" existing understandings of and operations within that work space. In military terms, this would refer to situations where combatants are governed by various "conventions" and generally fight within those conventions.

The final limiting factor is crucial because it acts as a way of enforcing minimal standards of competition as a way of avoiding group dissolution. Indeed, if Sahlins[32] is correct, then one of the key roles played by culture is as a mitigation against, or "channeling of," the potential forms of conflict/competition. But, for that to happen, there must be a mutually recognized "external" force accepted by all actors in the work space.

Culturally (and interculturally) defined ontologies may also set the "rules of the game" as played within a particular work space, along with specific responses for using nondefined "tactics" (that is, for stepping outside predefined potential actions). These "rules of the game," although setting the parameters for actions, also serve to link back in to the individual through a process that psychologist Mihalyi Csikzentmihalyi terms "flow."[33]

In my earlier work, I started to use the term *game* to describe the type of homeostatically stable and culturally recognized forms of interaction bounded by cultural ontologies.[34] In part, the choice to use *games* stemmed from Victor Turner's observations about the nature of the relationship between "play" and "work" in preindustrial societies.[35] The major reason, however, was that Csikzentmihalyi provided a compelling argument that humans have an evolved psychological mechanism that reinforces our desire to play "games" by trading off anxiety and enjoyment, with the "flow experience" as the optimal psychological experience of engaging in a "game."[36]

According to Csikzentmihalyi, "flow" acts as a "natural high" (endorphin rush) that is quite addictive. But, because the ability to access that "natural high" is controlled by specific "rules" (it has to be predictable), it actually serves to condition individuals to "play" by the rules, thereby acting as a positive reinforcement for following cultural rules. Breaking the rules, on the other hand, tends to evoke a negative reinforcement (for example, guilt, shame, disgruntlement, and so on) unless the individual is able to restructure his or her own internal emotional reactions.[37]

A DARWINIAN MODEL OF CULTURAL EVOLUTION

So far, the inclusion of an evolutionary symbology allows us to produce working definitions for the first three requirements of a Darwinian theory:

- There must be a pattern involved.
- The pattern must be copied somehow.
- Variant patterns must sometimes be produced by chance.

The "pattern" involved is a "symbol," symbol "cluster," or "constellation,"[38] or, depending on the particular work space, a "game." Pattern copying takes place in four main ways,[39] all of which are, broadly speaking, communicative acts:

1 Initial "learning"
2 Experiential "learning"
3 Personal "recollection" and
4 Group "recollection"

Initial learning refers to the first time a person "learns" something and, as part of that learning, adopts a relational stance with that action and/or thing. *Experiential learning* refers to changes in relational stance and emotional connotations as a result of day-to-day living and/or breach experiences.[40] Personal *recollection* refers to the reflexive act of an individual reconstructing his or her interpretation of a particular symbol,[41] while group recollection refers to collective reinterpretations of a particular symbol.[42]

Variant patterns are constantly being produced by *chance*: This can occur by innovation, mistake, and/or miscommunication.

The adoption of a Malinowskian framework[43] allows us to identify the next two requirements for a Darwinian model of culture:

1 The pattern and its variant must compete with one another for occupation of a limited work space.
2 The competition is biased by a multifaceted environment.

In particular, a cultural work space is a perceived, named, and communicated subset of the total operational environment that has a loose correspondence (real or imagined) to a real biological need. The primary definers of competition and conflict are:

1 The degree of ontological similarity among actors at the environmental level, and
2 The degree of institutional similarity among actors within an environment.

Although the presence of resources and/or external forces acts as conditions shaping how competition takes place, the environment itself is inherently multifaceted due to inequalities in resources, ontologies, technological "extensions," and actors' perceptions. Competition within work spaces is frequently perceived by individuals as operating according to "rules" and has both positive and negative reinforcement characteristics that act as a form of experiential learning.

TOWARD A CONSIDERATION OF WARFARE

As with any symbol, "warfare" is polysemic (that is, it has multiple meanings and connotations). For the Western world, at least since the Peace of Westphalia, the general "rules of the game" have been established by general "agreement," and these rules include both when the "game" may be "played" and the general form of acceptable game tactics.[44] Wars fought within these general rules are "conventional," at least in the sense that the conventions that compose the game rules are generally accepted by most of the players.[45]

Conflicts that (a) do *not* accept this general ontology are "unconventional" and (b) include "battle spaces" (work spaces in which and through which conflict takes place that are unconventional) beyond the "rules" are, by definition, "asymmetric." Thus, for example, al-Qaeda accepts a definition of media and symbol system *regardless of geographic boundaries* as a primary "battle space," while Coalition Forces use the concept of bounded geography as the primary battle space. This is a classic example of an asymmetric conflict; it is "asymmetric" because the players are using different work spaces and different game rules or, in other words, there is a fundamental, ontological disagreement.

In the next section of the chapter, I will outline some very broad changes in the topologies of battle spaces brought about as a result of changes in ontological perceptions, technologies, and resources.[46]

BROAD TOPOLOGIES OF BATTLE SPACES

In a recent article, Raphaël Baeriswyl, drawing heavily on the work of Jacquees Baud,[47] argues that there are six distinct "battle spaces": topographic space (land, sea), airspace, electromagnetic space, cyberspace, infospace, and human space.[48] Each of these battle spaces has emerged as technological advances has shifted the options as to where conflict may take place. While I find Baeriswyl's idea interesting and useful, it is, however, too limited.[49] The concept of linked battle spaces, however, is useful because it matches shifts in work space definition.

In general, a battle space may be defined as any work space in which and/ or through which combat takes place. Within any battle space, humans will attempt to extend both their senses and their physicality via technology and, as a corollary of this extension, will change the nature of the accessible battle space available. As an early example of this, a spear extends the "reach" of an individual beyond his or her physical reach, while a spear thrower extends the range at which a spear can hit a target. Each of these technological extensions changes the cognized battle space and changes the selection criteria operating in that battle space.

PERCEPTUAL BATTLE SPACE TOPOLOGIES:
A QUICK HISTORICAL ROMP

If Sahlins[50] is correct, then the original use of intrahuman conceptualizations of conflict was to limit and control intra- and intergroup conflict: a Stone Age Mutually Assured Destruction scheme where an increasing number of members of kinship and parakinship networks would be brought into a general conflict. In many cases, there was also some mechanism for the various groups to stop fighting. In the early law codes, for example, this tended to be some such concept as "blood price."[51]

The creation of centralized, magazine, or "theocratic" states marked a shift in both the mechanisms of violent conflict containment and the perception of battlespaces. Rather than a centralizing effort of a tribal confederation (for example, the Old Hittite Empire), we see a centralization around a deity and the personification/incarnation of that deity. In the Sumerian city-states (and probably the Mayan as well), this led to an extreme, hypertrophied concept of battle spaces, where the primary battle space was the realm of the gods.[52]

Later, as the powers of the god(s) declined and were partially replaced by "kings," we start to see the development of standing armies and the beginnings of what we would now call "conventional warfare."[53] This "new" form concentrated on what Baud would call "topographic space," that is, the "physical" (actually perceptual) world, although the realm of the gods was not excluded (consider, by way of example, the use of oracles/prayers before battle). This "dual order" (topographic and let's call it "spiritual") persisted for quite some time until, I would argue, the Peace of Westphalia.

The Peace of Westphalia (1648) and its precursor, the Peace of Augsburg (1555), established a new precedent in the perception of battle spaces by the curious expedient of separating conflict in the secular realm (topographic space) from conflict in the sacred realm (spiritual space). This was done by the curious expedient of recognizing the principle of *cuis regio, eius religio* (literally "whose region, his religion;" albeit limited to Calvinism, Lutheranism, and Roman Catholicism). According to this new convention, there would be a "free exercise of religion" (cf. articles 28, 46, 49) and "warfare" would be separated from the spiritual realm (cf. articles 65 and 123).[54]

In many ways, the Peace of Westphalia established a selection vector that has led to modern "conventional" warfare and, in so doing, has de facto eliminated from consideration a broad range of battle spaces that used to be in the "spiritual realm" until they could be secularized. This secularization started to appear in the late eighteenth century with ideological revolutions (for example, the American Revolution, the French Revolution) and achieved full-blown "secular" status with the wars of national liberation under the (supposedly) secular banner of Marxism. The "spiritual" battle space had, by the Cold War, been reintegrated into warfare under the term *ideology* rather than *religion* and, more recently, with Afghanistan and Iraq, as a "religious" war (at least in the perceptions of some participants).

TECHNOLOGICAL BATTLE SPACE TOPOLOGIES: ANOTHER FAST ROMP

Throughout most of the past 5,000 years or so, warfare involved a shifting interaction between three primary factors: offensive kinetic technologies, defensive kinetic technologies, and mobility. Both offensive and defensive kinetic technologies centered around the application or dispersion of force at a particular point in physical space (such as a human, a wall, or the like), while mobility has been concerned with movement through physical space. Thus, for example, we see an "arms race" in the eleventh through the sixteenth centuries between armor and weaponry and between siege weapons and fortifications. Within the interplay of these three factors, we also see progressive codification of rules both in the sense of tactics (for example, the Strategikon of Maurice[55]), in the sense of ideals (for example, the development of the code of chivalry) and in the sense of military factors influencing social organization (such as the development of feudalism).

Although technological extensions shifted the selection criteria operating in topographical battlespace, we don't see the introduction of "new" battle spaces in the *physical* world until the mid-eighteenth or early nineteenth century with the development of underwater vehicles, aircraft (balloons), steam engines, newspapers, and semaphore telegraphs. The first three of these are extensions into component parts of physical (topographic) space that were (relatively) easily predicted and assimilated. The development of telegraphs and newspapers, however, changed the face of warfare forever by (a) extending the perceptions of people who were not involved directly in the conflict and (b) opening a new battle space—today we would call it "the media."

Newspapers, at least in the form of a technological extension of the old idea of a news crier and also "yellow dog journalism," have actually been around since the late fifteenth or early sixteenth century.[56] But, when they were coupled with the telegraph (first semaphore, later electric), they allowed for the manipulation of rumor (also known as "public perception") at a distance. This opened a new battle space—Baud's and Baeriswyl's "infospace." It isn't that the space did not "exist" beforehand so much as that "infospace" was now centralized into a much smaller, manipulable environment. Infospace warfare was no longer a battle space composed of books written in a specialized language (Latin) and read by a limited number of people; now it was a battle space contained in a limited number of newspapers available in the local language and read by the general public. The vector started by the melding of newspapers and the telegraph has continued and developed into the World Wide Web—a battle space where the constructed "image" is everything because it is abstracted from any physical sensation of what it purports to represent.

By the mid-twentieth century, another technological extension was starting to spawn a new battle space. This was an extension of "thought" (actually, the processual application of "knowledge") in the form of "computers." By the mid-1980s, computers had become a new battle space behind and parallel to infospace, not because of their ability to convey person-to-person information but because of their ability to communicate automated device to automated device information in such areas as just-in-time inventory systems. By 2000, "cyberspace" had emerged as a highly complex battle space that supports most of the infrastructure of modern states, businesses, and individuals in a manner analogous to canals in Sumeria, grassy plains for steppes nomads, and watering holes/oases for desert nomads.

The spread of infospace, especially via the media of radio, movies, and, later, television, melded in with an old technology, rhetoric, to produce a complex and messy battle space with an intersocial part (public diplomacy) and an intrasocial part (social theater). One of the most striking observations about this battle space is that it is strongly analogous to both the public ritual and public diplomacy of the sixteenth and fifteenth centuries BCE in the Near East.

RESOURCE BATTLE SPACE TOPOLOGIES

In the West, the resources being fought over from, say, the fall of the Western Empire up until the Peace of Westphalia were, in general, control over land and population. After the Peace of Westphalia, these were still involved but, increasingly, there were also "new" strategic resources being fought over: coal, iron, oil, and the like; the raw materials necessary to sustain the growing industrialization of the Western economies. The cost of sustaining such colonial empires, however, grew increasingly burdensome after World War II, in part as a result of the constantly increasing cost of "keeping up with the Joneses" in the mechanized arms race; a lesson the British learned well, and the French less so. In effect, the former colonial powers (minus the United States and Soviet Empire) realized that it was far cheaper to buy the resources they needed than it was to maintain their empires (easier, too).

This period of decolonization was, in many ways, disastrous for the ex-colonies. In some instances, such as Singapore, they did quite well and adapted themselves to their new status as recognized players in the post-Westphalian model, while in other cases (such as Zimbabwe) the new rulers were psychopaths who destroyed "their" nations. Most ex-colonies placed somewhere in between these two extremes but, on the whole, were still locked into the economic (and political) systems of the remaining superpowers and ex-colonial powers.

The Cold War period saw the development of a new "convention" in warfare: warfare by proxy, where the proxies involved were almost always factions inside ex-colonies. The goal of the conflicts was to gain influence and, sometimes, control over specific resources without overtly and legally taking control of the territory, a move that, it was believed, could well lead to a direct nuclear exchange. Possessing, or being perceived as possessing, nuclear weapons came to be the minimal requirement for being a "serious player," a view that we still see today with North Korea and Iran.

So, in warfare, we have a vectored game space, where the vector was defined by increasing mechanization and the ability to launch devastating, possibly nuclear, strikes at an opponent. The goal was to gain influence over resources rather than control over territory, and an entire conventional social theater was created (the United Nations) to support the conventional, self-imposed rules of the game space. But this game space, as with all nonhomeostatic game spaces, contained the seeds of its own downfall. The most obvious is the vector requiring extensive mechanized forces.

This requirement for extensive high-technology mechanized forces prohibited many players from entering the game space unless they could either secure an ally that would act as a counterpoise or else develop new tactics that would nullify the overt effects of such a modern force. The vast majority of the so-called Wars of National Liberation relied on having an external ally who was a "real" player. The classic Maoist Three Phase War relied not only on an external ally but, also, on the existence of the UN social theater as a means of applying international pressure to keep the actions of the superpowers and ex-colonial powers limited. This Maoist model was, in its own way, another successful adaptation to the Cold War game space, at least as successful as many of the models opposed to it. But, like the concepts of "conventional warfare" of the same time period, the goal was the same—control over a proxy government that would give the controlling power preferential access to their physical resources.

One of the key "discoveries" of the Maoist model was that you don't have to have actual control over a resource to deny it to your opponents, hence raising the cost of their opposition. Indeed, it is actually fairly easy to raise popular discontent against an outside group that is trying to get preferential access to "your" resources. What is crucial is melding and channeling that discontent into a specific interpretive framework and focusing it.[57] This is where the Maoist Three Phase War excelled; it provided both an operational guide and, at the same time, an interpretive framework to contextualize and focus actions. And, like all strict religious systems, it failed once the game space conditions changed.

What the Maoist model did, however, was convince a number of people with the importance of an interpretive framework for the practice of warfare. And, as the requirements to become a player tightened, the value of controlling the interpretive framework moved away from the Maoist motivational model toward one where controlling the framework was more important than territory or resources. By controlling the framework, you can choose which game spaces will be in play for a given conflict, and, if your group is going to prosper, you will choose game spaces where you can compete better than your opponents.

How do you control an interpretive framework? The simplest way to do so is to provide a target person or group with an explanation of why things are happening to them and what they can do about it. This explanation must be communicated, and it will compete with other explanations in the minds of the target audience. Throughout most of the twentieth century, the majority of communicative media were "broadcast," that is, controllable through a limited number of venues. This is one of the reasons why the totalitarian states of the twentieth century created government media monopolies. But what happens when the de facto monopolies break down and communications become popularized?

Consider the case of the development of a simple printing press: It led to massive social movements and the overthrow of the Roman Catholic monopoly on legitimate religion. In the case of cheap, popular pamphleteering, it led to the overthrow of British rule in the thirteen colonies and, also, to the overthrow of the Russian democratic movement. And, most recently, the development and deployment of cheap and simple audio and video communications (cell phones, YouTube, and the like) has led to the rapid, nongeographically limited, spread of *irhabi* ideologies (among other things).

It is important to remember that the goal of warfare for many of the current groups is control over the interpretive framework of a population, *not* actual physical control over the geographic area, which, they believe, will flow inevitably from control over the framework and massive military costs for their opponents. For many of these groups, kinetic operations, "violence," is merely a means to an end that is shaped not by the logic of violence but, rather, by the logic of communications, a lesson learned from Vietnam where the insurgents lost almost all of the battles but won the war.

TWO SPECIFIC CASES

Mosul, 2006–2007

In December 2008, Major Robert Thornton, Dr. John Fishel, and I published a case study dealing with the American Security Force advising effort in Mosul between 2006 and 2007.[58] One central observation, arising from the interviews, was the nature of the ontological conflict between the Iraqi Forces (both Iraqi Army, or IA, and Iraqi Police, or IP), and the American Forces involved in stabilization efforts.[59] Of particular note were the varying (mis) understandings surrounding the concept/symbol of "governance."[60]

One of the more intriguing statements in this regard comes from James Knight, the head of the Provincial Reconstruction Team (PRT) in Mosul:

> Well, that's one of the weaknesses in Iraq, there was no structure in place, and certainly nothing supported the central and provincial level. There was no institutional structure for this to occur; it had to have been on the personal level. As you know, the governor's effectiveness entirely on his personal relationships and leadership; it had nothing to do with what was mandated in terms of the Provincial Powers Law, which still hasn't been passed I understand, or the other structure that it was clearly anticipated would be in place by the time they had done their three years.[61]

Dr. Knight exemplifies a central problematic in current stabilization efforts: the attempt to *impose* an ontology on a particular population. Such an effort can work—anthropologists usually use the term *cultural genocide* to refer to the process—but the likelihood of its working short of massive physical force is very low.

Let me pull this apart a bit and show how this is a case of competing ontologies. First, Iraq has a fairly loose "national culture" (that is, the "nation" is not synonymous with an ethnic group and has not had hundreds of years to develop as have some other multicultural states such as Switzerland, Belgium, and Canada). The "default" source of governance in Iraq, where "governance" is understood as an institution providing for individual safety (a Malinowskian basic need), is either the tribe or the organization (as a form of neotribalism).[62] Any attempts to socially engineer a governance structure in Iraq had to start from the preexisting tribal and neotribal bases and not from some ideological assumption in the "inherent" validity of a liberal democracy.[63]

Second, government, in the sense of modern liberal democratic structures, has often been used merely as social theater for the global arena. They are the "socially acceptable" forms of ruling and, as long as the forms are followed, there has been very little consistent pressure to eliminate the reality of tribal and neotribal interactions,[64] which are dominated by "Big Man Politics." *As a symbol*, reinforced in day-to-day living, "governance" has tended to mean "his/my tribe/faction" rather than any supposedly "neutral" political arena.

The third factor is somewhat shadowy. For many in the West, there is a belief that function follows form: a "build a democracy under a rule of law and they will all be like us" myth. Let's call this the "Field of Dreams" fallacy. The lived reality is quite different because it is evident to many in the Middle East (and elsewhere) that the United States will *not* always accept local democratic self-determination. What if a local population *chooses* a governance structure that is both ontologically and symbolically repugnant to the United States?[65] Will there be another regime change invasion in Iraq?[66]

So we have the following:

- A multifaceted environment: Iraq as the focus and the wider global community feeding into it.
- A work space: "Governance" understood as an institution providing for individual safety and predictability.

Various competing patterns, including

- Kinship systems
- Religious organizations
- "Modern" governance structures

Now, these competing patterns may *appear* to be mutually exclusive, but they do not have to be.[67] Because symbols contain a communicative as well as emotional component, it is quite possible for communications to act as a way of causing changes in the patterns themselves. Indeed, such a communicative exchange of pattern information is one of the two primary mechanisms by which pattern information changes (that is, Calvin's third requirement that "variant patterns must sometimes be produced by chance"[68]).

In the case of Mosul, such a change ("mutation" if you will) is apparent in some of the things Col. Mark Brackney had to say. First of all, he was primarily focused on the "reality" of governance rather than any ideal of governance:

> The real key here that would be absolutely essential is, number one, what is the government like in that province? How does the provincial council work? How do the district councils work? What are the mayors' jobs? What's their separation of powers? How does that work and who are the people in their area? Who are the sub-district mayors? Who are the district mayors? Who are the council members? Why are they there? How do they get elected? That's number one.[69]

Second, modern forms of governance use a complex, formalized series of assessment procedures both for reasons of "efficiency" and as a form of social theater.[70] Indeed, the entire modern conceptualization of governance is based on a bureaucratic system where the office is more important than the holder of the office. Note that this is the exact inversion of kinship-based systems of governance where the person holding the office is more important than the office itself. The same signs are apparent—person and office—but the emotional connotations are inverted in the symbol.

By focusing on the current *reality*, that is, both the people *and* the offices, Col. Brackney opened up the possibility of pattern change. This was further reinforced when he abandoned one of the key "rituals" of modern governance:

> There were some formal assessment tools that had come down through both the embassy office and the division that they would . . . I'm trying to think what the name was of the actual assessment tool, and I've got that image but it escapes me right now, but anyway, it was a very long form with all kinds of bubble charts about—is it red, green, or yellow in different areas from how many educators were online, how many kids were in school to the quality of the services, was there X amount of electricity, and sewage treatments; and was the governor in place for more than six months, and did he have an actual council? There were all kinds of metrics that way, but there was kind of the underlying metric we had, which was how we were doing in a few key areas. Number one is, "are we seeing an impact, and are we seeing some democratic processes actually taking place within the provincial council and government?"[71]

Again, by concentrating on the reality and, more importantly, by throwing out inappropriate "tools," Col. Brackney was able to focus in on small-scale, immediate culture change. In essence, he was constructing a different interpretive schema for "what is" as a way to point toward "what should be." While the end result of this is unknown (it will be years before we know), the potential for a stable change is much greater because the initial impetus to change was rooted in a reinterpretation of experienced reality.[72]

This highlights a very interesting, and important, point, namely that if you wish to create an increased chance of favorable mutations in a culture, then such efforts (a) must be focused on the immediate reality of the situation and (b) must also be focused on communications.

A "Kinder, Gentler" Jihad

A March 16, 2009, posting on the *irhabi* website revolution.thabaat.net urges bloggers to adopt a "new" stance: "neutrality."[73] In his introduction, the anonymous author notes that:

> Today, there has been quite an influx of blogs in the jihadi media world, with a new one appearing nearly every week or so. When visiting these sites, they quickly become boring, but at the same time, there is no doubt that the one behind it is spreading the haqq and obtaining his rewards. Nevertheless, there is a large gap in the Jihadi reporting and the Intellectual framework of educating Muslims on current events. . . .
>
> My proposition may be seen as non-traditional and modern, but the objective here is to be effective.

His delineation of blogging characteristics is quite intriguing and shows a very solid insight into the use of the new media as a battle space:

> The primary purpose. Firstly, the purpose of the blog should be to serve the global jihad effort; in short, this effort is to gather all of our resources in changing how people look at modern day jihad.

Note carefully that the exact aim is to change how people perceive modern-day jihad. In effect, all of his strategies are aimed at changing the emotional connotations associated with "jihad." In his next point, he argues for the use of "neutral" language, concluding his argument with the following:

> What makes people like Michael Scheuer and William McCants highly respected by the Mujahideen and their supporters? It's because of two major characteristics that is [sic] found in their writings:
>
> a. Neutrality
> b. Thorough (or nearly thorough) research
>
> Similarly, what makes people like Abu Mus'ab al-Suri so respected amongst the Crusaders and their supporters are the same two qualities. *The point here is not to seek respect; rather, it is to widen the pool of people that actually read your works and are effected [sic] by it in one way or another.* [emphasis added]

This final point is crucial: The blogger is arguing for an increase in communications density with the express aim of reaching a wider audience and changing its perceptions. By using "neutral language" and presenting thorough research, the blogger will automatically create in that audience a willingness to listen. But the act of listening (reading) is aimed at producing changes in the emotional connotations of "modern-day jihad," in effect shifting it from "unacceptable" to "acceptable" or "neutral." The goal may well not be "conversion" but, rather, the neutralization of a potential opponent.

Let me note one other point: Who are the potential audience? It is certainly not made up of those without an Internet connection! The intended audience is both the diasporic Muslim community and, at the same time, the non-Muslim world.

Will it work? At the minimum, I fully expect that several *irhabi* bloggers will adopt this stance, simply because (a) the author is respected and (b) arguments from efficiency are part of the generally accepted culture of Islam.[74] Second, there is already extensive "antiwar" and "anti-imperialist" support in the Western world, especially among groups that have little knowledge of either history or combat; so any new blogs constructed along these lines are quite likely to be picked up. Third, this strategy has an excellent chance of overcoming one of the main symbolic problems suffered by the *irhabi* inside the Muslim community: a perception that they have little scholarly depth.

Looked at in a Darwinian framework, this type of strategy was highly predictable.[75] Consider the following:

A multifaceted environment: the global (Internet-connected) population

A work space: "Warfare [as political action]" understood as an institution providing for group safety/security.

Two main competing interpretive patterns, "jihadi" as:
- "Terrorist" (*irhabi*), or
- "Freedom fighter" (in self-defence)

The "mutation": shifts perceptions by appealing to neutrality, rationality and research.

The key problem, from the *irhabi* side, was the general perception of them as being "terrorists" even within Islam. As a revitalization movement,[76] al-Qaeda and their fellow travelers had to construct fairly rigid in-group/out-group boundaries. After their initial successes against the Soviets in Afghanistan, they no longer had a key out-group to oppose. Their subsequent decision to focus on the United States as that key out-group increased their isolation from much of the Islamic world. Unlike Afghanistan, al-Qaeda could not point to an invasion of Muslim lands by "infidels," thereby removing one of the key supports for jihad.[77] They are left with an "adapt or die" situation in which they must reclaim their status as "freedom fighters," or they will risk expulsion from the Umma.

CONCLUSIONS

While far from complete, I would suggest that the preliminary model presented in this chapter offers us the opportunity to develop a proper, Darwinian evolutionary theory of culture that has at least some predictive value.

For example, in the first case, Mosul and governance, we can see that many of the existing institutional barriers to change had been removed during the occupation. This, however, meant that people defaulted "back" to their real source of security and governance—the tribe and neotribe. Attempts to impose a governance structure totally at odds with that default value were doomed to fail. However, reconstructing the battle space by looking at the reality and by sharing the "authorship," allowed for the coconstruction of a narrative that would be acceptable for both sides. This narrative, in turn, is a symbolic structure that, with time, will embed itself back into Iraqi culture, gaining emotional connotations among the population by lived experience.

The second case is, in some ways, more illustrative of the effects of technology opening up a new battlespace. For al-Qaeda, the battle space has, for the past ten years or so, been much more concentrated in cyberspace; that has been their primary area of operations (AO). Al-Qaeda is engaged in an ontological conflict—a fight for hearts and minds—as much as a physical conflict.

But the rapid spread of blogging and other social network technologies has its own problems, one of which is "content." Content that is not immediately emotionally appealing or is seriously flawed will be rejected. The mutations argued for by the author, a "neutral" voice and thorough research, match the Islamic cultural valuation placed on scholarship and, at the same time, find a ready-made market in parts of Western, non-Muslim, academia. As with governance in Mosul, the goal is to reconstruct the narrative of jihad.

One central difference between a biological theory of evolution and the cultural one presented here lies in the very nature of the coding system. In biological evolution, that coding system is quite resilient, and mutations do not happen that often, which may explain why most biological change is centered around sexual selection (information recombination).

There are certain implications of the cultural coding system being partially communicative (that is, stored outside the individual). In cultural evolution, for example, the coding system is much more subject to "mutation" both initially and on a day-to-day basis. Furthermore, cultural evolution is inherently partially Lamarkian, that is, the inheritance of acquired characteristics. Also, these "inherited" cultural codes may be very strongly embedded in the neurological structures of the brain as a result of early childhood learning; a "learning" that is often stored in narratives.

Can a Darwinian evolutionary theory of culture be predictive without either falling into the determinist or teleological fallacies it has in the past? I believe that it can be, but with only a limited time horizon. In any given work space at particular points in time, there are only a limited number of options available to compete effectively. Which option(s) will be chosen by a group will be constained by their closeness to existing cultural narratives in both form and lived reality. Perhaps this explains why Muslim sympathy for al-Qaeda was so high in the 1980s (opposing an invader), and plummeted after the September 11 attacks (attacks on civilians).[78]

But the danger of falling into the Scylla of determinism or the Charybdis of teleology is always a ready danger when one deals with evolutionary theory and, indeed, with culture. We would be wise to remember that, as with linguistics, we are trying to define and analyze a system of which we, ourselves, are a part.

NOTES

1. I would like to thank the many people who gave me comments on earlier drafts of this chapter: my colleagues in the Carleton Counter-Terrorism discussion group at Carleton Todd MacDonald and Yannick Lepage; my old friend Jerome Barkow at Dalhousie, who continually accuses me of giving him headaches; and my colleagues Tom Odom, John T. Fishel, and Robert L. Thornton at the Small Wars Council. I especially want to thank my friend Maj. Stanley Wiechnik, who took time out of his hectic schedule as XO of the 844th EN BTN in Baghdad to provide me with some excellent ideas. Finally, I want to thank J. S. Bach for initial inspiration and Tomás Luis de Victoria for help during the final push. Any errors and omissions are, obviously, my own.

2. W. H. Calvin, "The Six Essentials? Minimal Requirements for the Darwinian Bootstrapping of Quality." *Journal of Memetics—Evolutionary Models of Information Transmission* 1 (1997); available at http://williamcalvin.com/1990s/1997JMemetics .htm.

3. See Ann T. Jordan, "Organizational Culture: The Anthropological Approach," in Ann T. Jordan, ed., *Practicing Anthropology in Corporate America: Consulting on Organizational Culture*, NAPA Bulletin #14, American Anthropological Association (1994), 3–16.

4. Edward B. Tyler, "On a Method of Investigating the Development of Institutions; Applied to Laws of Marriage and Descent." *The Journal of the Anthropological Institute of Great Britain and Ireland* 18 (1889), 245–272; available at http://galton.org/essays/1880-1889/galton-1888-jaigi-tylor-remarks.pdf.

5. For a much more detailed overview of the complex relationship between the social sciences and evolutionary theory, see Jerome H. Barkow, ed., *Missing the Revolution: Darwinism for Social Scientists* (Oxford, UK: Oxford University Press, 2005). See David Sloan Wilson, *Social Semantics: Toward a Genuine Pluralism in the Study of Social Behaviour, Journal of Evolutionary Biology* 21, 1 (January 2008), 368–373; available at http://evolution.binghamton.edu/dswilson/wp-content/uploads/2010/01/social-semantics.pdf), for an overview of current social scientific use of evolutionary theory.

6. Bronislaw Malinowski, *A Scientific Theory of Culture* (New York: Oxford University Press, 1960 [1944]), 36.

7. Ibid.

8. Ibid.

9. The term *race* is used here as "total membership of a social group" rather than in either the biological sense ("species") or in the ideological sense of differentiation by distinguishing characteristic (such as skin color).

10. Ralph Piddington, *Social Forces: An Introduction to Social Anthropology* (New York: The Macmillan Company, 1957), 34–38. It is important not confuse the concept of "needs" with that of "causes." Such a confusion happened in anthropology in the 1950s, when certain needs were given the status of prime causes or ultimate goals. This created a situation in which the entire concept had to be disposed of due to an obvious lack of relationship to observed reality (cf. Lee, 1959: 70–77). "Needs" should not be viewed as either prime causes or as ultimate goals. Rather, they should be conceived of as an environmental context that creates certain perceived minimal conditions.

11. As such, cultural responses are phenotypic expressions rather than genotypic determinations.

12. He describes this in his chapter "Theory of Organized Behaviour"; cf. Malinowski, 1960, chapter 5. I go into much greater detail on this in section 3, where it forms the basis for my discussion of chartered institutions.

13. See Malinowski, 1960, 120–131.

14. Ibid., 132.

15. Ibid., chapter 11.

16. Ibid., chapter 12; see also Raymond Firth, ed., *Man and Culture* (New York: Routledge and Keegan Paul, 1957).

17. An early version of this was proposed by Richard Dawkins when he coined the term *meme*. The problem with Dawkins's formulation was that he assumed that memes were independant of the biological organisms that they "inhabited." While a useful thought experiment, memetic theory ultimately fails because it cannot point toward any particular observable agents or processes of change.

18. See Alan Page Fiske, *Structures of Social Life: the Four Elementary Forms of Human Relations* (New York: The Free Press, 1991). A short, yet very useful, description is available online at www.sscnet.ucla.edu/anthro/faculty/fiske/relmodov.htm.

19. A more vernacular version would be doing something the same way and always failing.

20. See Alfred Korzybski, *Science and Sanity; An Introduction to Non-Aristotelian Systems and General Semantics*, 5th edition (Lancaster, PA: Institute of General Semantics, April 1, 1995).

21. It is important to note that the "thing" signified does not have to be observable by individuals. It may be a concept, an explanation, a supernatural entity, or anything that can be conceived of by a person.

22. This is the map–territory debate in epistemology. See Gregory Bateson, *A Sacred Unity* (New York: Harper Collins, 1991).

23. In sociobiology, this was referred to as the problem of altruism, or: Why would people take actions that would jeapardize their own survival to help out others with no direct payback?

24. Think about Grimm's tales as a classic example of this genre.

25. As a note, all cultures of which we are aware know of this split and deal with it by "reinterpreting" our experiences within their own symbol systems. See Charles Laughlin, "The Cycle of Meaning," in Stephen Glazier, ed., *Anthropology of Religion: Handbook of Theory and Method*, 471–488 (Westport, CT: Greenwood Press, 1997); available at www.biogeneticstructuralism.com/docs/cycle.rtf.

26. William H. Calvin, *The Cerebral Code: Thinking Thought in the Mosaics of the Mind* (Cambridge, MA: MIT Press, 1996).

27. A "culture area" is a broad geographic area that has similar cultures in multiple states (for example, East Africa, the Caribbean, and so on). Comparative studies at the planetary population level tend to be few over the past fifty years but concentrate on cultural regularities brought about as a result of environment and technology. See, for example, Leslie A. White, *The Evolution of Culture: The Development of Civilization to the Fall of Rome* (Walnut Creek, CA: Left Coast Press, 2007, originally published in 1959).

28. This emphasis on perception is crucial because no pattern of information is capable of accurately representing the sum totality of its environment unless it is the

sum totality of its environment (the classic map–territory problem in epistemology). This is even more problematic than it appears. First, as a species, we abstract and filter our perceptions through culturally created symbol systems such as language. Second, the act of parsing observable reality into discrete components ("naming") tends to create biases in our perceptions ("the map is not the territory"), and we act on those biased perceptions as if they were "reality" ("the map is the territory"). Third, the action of parsing "reality" creates "systems of meaning" that contain predictive and/or explanatory mechanisms. Perhaps most importantly, at least for humans, symbols are capable of being reified (turned in to "things") and symbol systems, once reified, may also metastasize into perceiving "things" that do not exist or, at least, are not perceivable by people using another symbol system. See Roy A. Rappaport, *Ecology, Meaning, & Religion* (Berkeley, CA: North Atlantic Books, 1993).

29. Note that what defines the "environmental level" is, actually, a perception and part of the group's ontology.

30. This "force" does not have to be objectively "real" and may include both non-human actors and conceptual reifications such as the "environment," "God," "Karma," and the like.

31. See Andrew Abbott, *The System of the Professions* (Chicago: University of Chicago Press, 1988).

32. Marshall Sahlins, *Stone Age Economics* (New York: Aldine de Gruyter, 1972).

33. Mihaly Csikszentmihalyi, *Flow: The Psychology of Optimal Experience* (New York: Harper Perennial, 1991).

34. See Marc W. D. Tyrrell, *At the Cusp of the Information Age: Outplacement as a Rite of Passage in Late 20th Century Canada*, PhD dissertation, Department of Sociology and Anthropology, Carleton University, 2000; available at www.nlc-bnc.ca/obj/s4/f2/dsk2/ftp03/NQ52334.pdf section 5.3.

35. See Victor Turner, *The Anthropology of Performance* (New York: PAJ Books, 1988), and *From Ritual to Theatre: The Human Seriousness of Play* (New York: PAJ Books, 1991). In these works, Turner argues that the categories of "work" and "play" have been artificially separated as a result of industrialization, and the immediate linkages between them that are obvious in "traditional" societies are much less so in "modern" societies.

36. Think about phrases like "performance high" or "being in the groove" as examples.

37. People who are able to do this, apparently at will, are usually referred to as "sociopaths." The more common and socially acceptable way is to shift ontological structures (for example, "conversion").

38. This is nalogous to the difference between a base gene code (DNA) and a genetic sequence or "gene."

39. This list is by no means exclusive; there are certainly other possible forms of "copying."

40. A "breach experience" refers to the situation in which an individual comes head-to-head with "reality" and it doesn't match the mental model; cf. Burkart Holzner, *Reality Construction in Society* (Cambridge, MA: Schenkman Publishing, 1968).

41. See Laughlin, 1997, 471–488.

42. It also includes attempts by groups to "sway" general popular interpretations, such as PSYOPS, IO, political agendas, and the like.

43. Broadly speaking, Malinowski's model does suffer from several serious flaws, but at least his model from basic needs through institutions and integrative imperatives is salvageable.

44. See Keith Gomes, "An Intellectual Genealogy of the Just War," *Small Wars Journal*, August 2008; available at http://smallwarsjournal.com/mag/docs-temp/80-gomes.pdf.

45. Even if specific rules are not accepted by one player, components of the overall ontological definition of warfare have been generally accepted. Thus, for example, while the Japanese did not accept many of the specific conventions relating to warfare in World War II, they did accept the principle that war was conducted between "states."

46. I apologize for the brevity of these sections. These examples could be (and in many cases have been) the subject of entire volumes. My treatment of each is necessarily cursory.

47. Jacques Baud, *La Guerre asymétrique ou la Défaite du vainqueur* (Paris: Editions Du Rocher, 2003).

48. Raphaël Baeriswyl, "Use and Perception of Violence: A Girardian Approach to Asymmetric Warfare," *Anthropoetics* 13, 3 (Fall 2007/Winter 2008).

49. Baeriswyl's model of ongoing emergence is, to my mind, limited by two problems. First, "infospace," which he defines as "where opinions are manipulated," is really the work space in which propaganda has been operating for millennia. In a similar manner, "human space," as defined by Baud, is "the space of human life and action, with its cultural, social, economic, moral and political dimensions, where networks are woven, loyalties and hierarchies disputed and opinion and determination forged" that has been around since before writing was invented. The second problem is with the conceptualization of "human space," which has been considered by many people as divisible in terms of battle spaces (vide the concepts of "economic warfare," "political subversion," and so on)

50. Sahlins, 1972.

51. See, for example, O. R. Gurney, *The Hittites* (New York: Penguin, 1991), and Marcel Mauss, *The Gift* (New York: W. W. Norton & Company, 2000).

52. See, for example, Diane Wolkstein and Samuel Noah Kramer, *Inanna, Queen of Heaven and Earth* (New York: Harper Perennial, 1983); n.a., *Enuma Elish: The Seven Tablets of Creation* (San Diego: Book Tree, 1998); *The Illiad*; and Judges 7.

53. See, for example, *The Epic of Gilgamesh*, which chronicles the shift from *ensi* [god-king/incarnate God] to *lugal* ["king"/war leader as ruler] in Babylon.

54. From articles 28, 46, 49. 65 and 123 of "Westphalia," *Law-Ref.org*; retrieved from http://law-ref.org/WESTPHALIA/index.html (no longer active).

55. See Marc W. D. Tyrrell, "The First Culture Turn: Ethnographic Knowledge in the Romano-Byzantine Military Tradition." Paper presented at the 2008 Inter-University Seminar on Armed Forces and Society, Royal Military College, Kingston, November 2008; available at http://marctyrrell.com/uploads/TFCT.pdf.

56. See Ottavia Niccoli, *Prophecy and People in Renaissance Italy* (Princeton, NJ: Princeton University Press, 1990).

57. Sertorius knew all this 2,000 years ago, but who reads Plutarch these days?

58. Rob Thornton, John Fishel, and Marc Tyrrell, "Security Force Assistance Case Study: Mosul, Iraq," *Small Wars Journal*, December, 2008; available at http://small warsjournal.com/blog/2008/12/sfa-case-study-mosul-iraq/. Note that the version published at the *SWJ* was preliminary and missing one chapter; the latest version with the missing chapetr is available at http://marctyrrell.com/wp-content/uploads/2009/02/sfa-case-study-final-with-ch-4-updatedoc.pdf.

In many ways, this case study is unique, not the least reason being that all of the interviews on which it is based are available as open source material to the academic community. A short version, with only the executive summary and the interviews, is available at http://marctyrrell.com/wp-content/uploads/2009/02/sfa-case-study-exec-sum-and-interviews-1.pdf.

59. See ibid., chapter 4, sections 1.4 and 2.

60. Iraq had been governed using a classic "Turkish" model, while the United States developed using a classic "Frankish" model; cf. Macchiavelli's *The Prince*. Each of these models evolved from different initial states (pastoralist versus horticultual) and in wildly diverging forms. While any detailed analysis is clearly beyond the scope of this chapter, suffice it to say that the key survival tactic in Turkish states has always been the development of extended family ("tribal") alliances.

61. Robert Thornton Jr., Joint Center for International Security Force Assistance, "Interview with Dr. James Knight, Provincial Reconstruction Team (PRT) Chief Ninewa, Mosul, Iraq," *The Colloquium*, Fort Leavenworth: USA/USMC Counterinsurgency Center, Volume 1, Issue 1 (August 2008).

62. See Michel Maffesoli, *The Time of the Tribes* (London: Sage, 1996).

63. Such an ideological assumption is really nothing more than a return to the concept of unilinear evolution with "us" on top.

64. This is somewhat of an exaggeration because conceptualizations of "modern" governance structures are part of the mix in the population of Iraq. They are not, however, the dominant form at least as the default.

65. The elections of Allende in Chile and Hamas in the Palestinian Territories come to mind.

66. Mathematician and satirist Tom Lehrer noted this tendency in a song called "Send the Marines."

67. This presumption is one (of many) fatal flaws with Huntington's "Clash of Civilization" argument.

68. The other mechanism is individual learning that then feeds back into a communicative flow.

69. Major Robert Thornton, Joint Center for International Security Force Assistance, "Interview with Colonel Mark Brackney, Deputy Chief Provincial Reconstruction Team," March 11, 2008. Available in Mosul *Case Study: Executive Summary and Interviews*, 65, at http://marctyrrell.com/wp-content/uploads/2009/02/sfa-case-study-exec-sum-and-interviews-1.pdf.

70. In Canada, the primary example is the Royal Commission, while the United States has House and Senate investigations. All modern, liberal democracies have something similar as a way of publicly restoring "trust" in the system.

71. Thornton, "Interview with Colonel Mark Brackney."

72. As a moderately comparable historical analog, consider how the British parliamentary system served to contain the conflict of the great noble houses by providing a venue for nonkinetic competition and producing symbol systems and games that reinforced that competitive system.

73. My thanks to *Milnews.ca* for posting this over at the Small Wars Council. The original post is "The need for proper [jihadi] bloggers," *The Ignored Puzzle Pieces of Knowledge*, March 16, 2009, retrieved from http://revolution.thabaat.net/?p=1046; this link is no longer active, but there is a pdf version available at http://milnewstbay.pbwiki.com/f/ProperJihadBloggers-revolution.thabaat.net-172002Mar09.pdf.

74. By this, I mean that there are stories ("narratives") that valorize such actions.

75. Indeed, a similar strategy has been suggested by Lt. Gen. William B. Caldwell IV; see "Changing the Organizational Culture," *Small Wars Journal* [blog], February 2, 2008; available at http://smallwarsjournal.com/blog/2008/02/changing-the-organizational-cu-1/.

76. See Anthony F. C. Wallace, "Revitalization Movements," *American Anthropologist* (New Series) 58, 2 (April 1956), 264–281.

77. The excuse of U.S. support for the ongoing Israeli "occupation" of Palestinian lands was not enough of a justification for attacking the United States, especially U.S. civilians including women and children.

78. These attitudes are still in place, opposing terrorist (*irhabi*) tactics, while supporting core Islamic values. See WorldPublicOpinion.org, "Public Opinion in the Islamic World on Terrorism, al Qaeda, and US Policies," February 25, 2009; available at www.worldpublicopinion.org/pipa/pdf/feb09/STARTII_Feb09_rpt.pdf

3 EMPLOYING DATA FUSION IN CULTURAL ANALYSIS AND COIN IN TRIBAL SOCIAL SYSTEMS

Steffen Merten

THE IMPORTANCE OF CULTURAL ANALYSIS in counterinsurgency operations is well established. Whether systematically compiled cultural knowledge is employed as a means of building institutions within the indigenous social fabric or for modeling the flow of information through the social system, there can be little doubt that war fighters directly benefit from a deeper understanding of the social context of their operating environment.[1] In the tribal societies of the Middle East and Central Asia the salience of tribe/clan affiliations, and their often strict hierarchical nature, make cultural awareness particularly crucial, especially in light of technological developments in the fields of visual analytics and geospatial/relational data fusion. Data fusion is defined as "the integration of data and knowledge collected from disparate sources by different methods into a consistent, accurate, and useful whole."[2] It is this capability (or previous lack thereof) to "fuse" operationally relevant relational and geospatial data, and its importance in the field of cultural research, that will enhance the way that both analysts and war fighters understand the battlefield. The realization of "multidimensional data fusion" allows the cultural analyst not only to work toward an understanding of the relational structure of the predominant social system (tribal or otherwise) but also to integrate these entities (persons, tribes, and so on) with their spatially fixed anchor points (homes, schools, territories, and the like), allowing for a contextually enriched and actionable understanding of the operating environment.

The main challenge in the complex task of employing data fusion and visual analytics in cultural research stems not from a lack of cultural information, which is abundant in the unclassified literature, but from the challenges posed by the effective cataloging, fusion, and presentation of various data (relational, geospatial, or temporal). This process of properly cataloging and "fusing" data is an important part of visual analytics' focus on creating "automated analysis techniques with interactive visualizations for an effective understanding, reasoning and decision making on the basis of very large and complex data sets," while also "foster[ing] the constructive evaluation, correction, and rapid improvement of our processes and models and—ultimately—the improvement of our knowledge and our decisions."[3] The limiting factor is that data are not being "processed" in a way that is conducive to collaboration and "analytical discourse." It is precisely this lack of collaboration (and implicitly data fusion) that was discussed in the RAND Corporation's 2008 report titled "Analytical Support to Intelligence in Counterinsurgencies" and included a proposal for the creation of COINCOP (Counter-Insurgency Common Operational Picture) that would "provide displays of key information about insurgent networks" including "the insurgents, their assets and their personal relationships (including those with civilians)," and "the location of insurgent cells, their weapons caches, and supply chains for weapons and other war-related equipment." The need is well recognized; it is the means to fuse these data in a "common operational picture" that has been, until now, lacking.[4]

To illustrate the impact of this shortcoming, picture the industrious analyst attempting to unravel the complicated social system for a given province in eastern Afghanistan. Regardless of the possibility for outside collaboration, a talented cultural analyst will use one of several relational analysis platforms to synthesize an exhaustive model of the province's social/tribal hierarchy, including relationships like organization membership, familial ties, and friendships. Until recently, no matter how great the analyst's motivation, the level of data fusion possible between this extensive relational web of key individuals and organizations, and corresponding geospatial data for the province, showing notable places like compounds, schools, or hospitals, was, at best, minimal. In the end, Montague and Capulet would be doomed to remain two distinct ways of understanding the same social system.

This lack of fusion between the geospatial and relational realms has crippled our analytical potential, but by leveraging advances in software development it is possible to fuse these two data sets to produce an analytical product much more meaningful than the sum of its geospatial and relational parts. The fused analytical product allows placement of individuals and organizations within their geospatial and relational context, which, in turn, allows for the inference of individual relational information (tribal affiliation, for example) based on geospatial context and vice versa. For example, after geospatially and relationally mapping the tribal "skeleton" of the aforementioned Afghan province, one may infer an individual's tribal identity based on his or her geospatial location or vice versa. Other examples of contextual analysis using a fused social model will follow.

THE CHALLENGE OF DATA FUSION

While intricate "link charts" showing relational networks like the one shown in Figure 3.1 may prove informative, they remain disparate from the real-time, spatially oriented operating environment, wherein geospatial data generally reside outside their relational context and lose meaning as part of the broader "social skeleton."

To use an example from the Southern Oman, suppose that relational analysis tells us that the Ja`bub and Tabuk tribes are descendents of a common ancestor and that each tribe is composed of eight specific clans. We also have the names of the clans and the names of their respective leaders. In terms of geospatial information, we have a list of coordinates for the homes of the leaders and a map overlay showing which clans are present in each of the area's fifty villages. Even in this relatively simple example, the limits of analysis become apparent as one imagines the analyst attempting to integrate the relational and geospatial data manually. One can picture the dizzying task of plotting these simple data onto a map overlay, with a myriad of colored pieces of yarn and thumbtacks connecting persons to villages, villages to clans, clans to tribes, and so on. Now imagine adding another 10,000 interrelated data points ranging from religious leaders to shipping companies and including attributes like address, sect, friendships, political affiliations, or lineage for each!

The task quickly moves from complicated to impossible. Even if this sort of "manual" integration were possible, the data would likely be useful only as a system overview because effectively parsing the various properties and relationships and examining them would be impossible. Instead we should benefit from the advantages conferred by the analytical science of visual analytics. One of the recommendations of this field is a situation wherein "visualization becomes the medium of a semi-automated analytical process, where humans and machines cooperate using their respective distinct capabilities for the most effective results."[5] As shown in Figure 3.2, the result is an "analytical

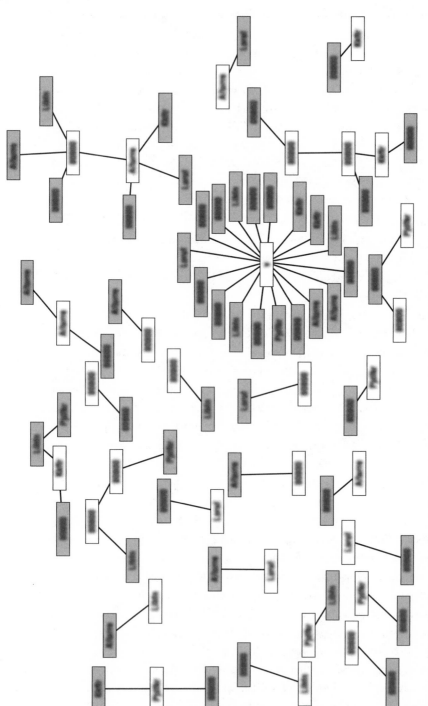

Figure 3.1. "Link chart" showing the relational network or "nexus topography" for the Omani tribal system.

Boxes represent tribes, and the lines connecting them represent relationships like descendency, leadership, or hierarchy. While informative, the data remain apart from their geospatial context.

SOURCE: This figure is based on unpublished research of Omani tribes conducted by the author and generated using Palantir Analytical Platform.

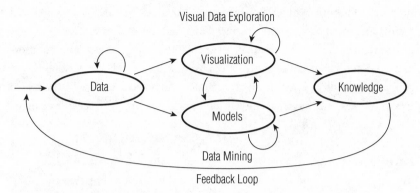

Figure 3.2. Tight integration of visual and automatic data analysis methods with database technology for a scalable interactive decision support.

SOURCE: Daniel Keim, Gennady Andrienko, Jean-Daniel Fekete, Carsten Gorg, Jorn Kohlhammer, and Guy Melancon, "Visual Analytics: Definition, Process, and Challenges," in *Information Visualization: Human-Centered Issues and Perspectives* (Berlin, Heidelberg: Springer, 2008), 154–175.

process" in which the cognitive heavy lifting is assumed by the machine, with data then being presented in a way that allows the analyst to concentrate on more nuanced analysis.

MOVING FROM "ONE-DIMENSIONAL" TO "MULTIDIMENSIONAL" DATA FUSION

Suppose that two commanders decide to fuse their relational data sets outlining the organizational structure of religious leadership for two overlapping areas of Mosul, Iraq. Regardless of the medium of information collaboration (huge whiteboard or otherwise), they would undoubtedly encounter the issue of how to determine whether "Ahmed al Burghouthi" of Sector A is the same person as "Ahmad Bourghuthi" of Sector B and, if so, how to merge or "resolve" these two identities into a single individual. Although names are probably the most often used resolution criterion in relational models, additional information like address, ration card number, or license plate number will often aid in the resolution process. Thus, to properly identify and resolve the thousands or even millions of individual relational nodes, we require an engine capable of conducting the "automated analytical process" mentioned in the previous section. The resolution process employs a series of preprogrammed guidelines for what constitutes a justified resolution, based on combinations of identifying information (name, address, blood type, and so on). If the resolution is found to be justified (they are indeed the same person), the properties for both "Ahmed Bourghuthis," like aliases, skills, friendships, and identifying information, will be knitted together to form a new "Ahmed" integrated within the fused relational network and based on the combined information of both commanders. Even this "one-dimensional" resolution process can get rather dicey when it involves multiple data sets, each with their own terminologies and naming conventions, but software advances have made the process more accessible. Following the development of this automated resolution capability, the next logical step in developing the fusion process is its extension to different types of data, meaning relational and geospatial information. Although recognition of the importance of creating the fused "common operating picture" is widespread, until now efforts to do so have generally taken the form of crude "side-by-side" fusion and data presentation.

For example, during its 2007 deployment to southeast Baghdad, Task Force Dragon of the 3rd Infantry Division clearly demonstrated the benefits of "human terrain mapping" by creating a shared database of relevant cultural and demographic information that proved crucial in its counterinsurgency operations. The effort "created a common human-terrain picture that enabled more proactive initiatives and faster, much more effective responses to events" but still relied almost exclusively on the geospatial framework of analysis, thereby neglecting the cumulative benefits of relational integration. Although relational data like the "location and contact information for each sheik or village mukhtar" were inserted into the geospatial interface showing "the boundaries of each tribal area," "locations of mosques schools and markets," and "nearest locations and checkpoints of Iraqi security forces," these two types of information were not combined in an optimal way. The main medium of analysis remained geospatial, with relational information being simply layered on it in the way that photos or dossiers of leaders in a given neighborhood may be added to the folder containing the neighborhood's tribal map overlay.[6] This distinction between "layered" data and fused data is critical. Whereas data layering can be described as an "additive process," data fusion "goes beyond merely looking at a problem through different lenses; it collects the respective lenses, and looks through them all at the same time for an in-depth view of the problem."[7]

Although the addition of relational information is clearly valuable, these two data media remain distinct, and the actual information fusion (among photos, dossiers, and maps) remains the onerous task of the analyst. Surely efforts have been made to combine these data manually (recall the colored string and thumbtacks mentioned earlier), but this type of crude integration does not leverage the true utility of data fusion. Although crude integration may add value, the analyst requires true fusion of the two data types in a way that allows for fluid analysis of both data sets simultaneously, with each set of entities and nodes, both geospatially and relationally based, being resolved into the same conceptual "space." A solution to this tenuous problem of conflicting data types is an analytical methodology wherein geospatial and relational data are kept in their respectively optimal presentation formats (geospatial as a map overlay and relational as a link chart) but may be analyzed using geographical tools in conjunction with relational tools to move between these two data formats smoothly, thus achieving "multidimensional data fusion." Figure 3.3 shows an example of this type of fluid analysis, where a relational filter isolating a particular set of clans interacts simultaneously with the geospatial display showing where these clans reside. An inverse process could also be performed, with a geospatially bounded search being used to isolate the Beni Ruwahah, with the tribes then being highlighted in their relational context.

An intuitive concern with the fusion of these two data types stems from the fact that our basic unit of relational analysis is generally the mobile (and often highly elusive) individual, while our unit of geospatial analysis is the fixed point in space at a given time (that is, place), and yet this focus on the individual is an integral part of our evolving COIN doctrine. "Man-hunting" expert John Dodson[8] aptly captures both the importance of this level of analysis and the need for further analytical capabilities at the level of individual:

> The fluid, dynamic and surreptitious nature of the HVI [high-value individual] targeting differs significantly from the monolithic nation state threat most analysts were trained for and previously experienced working. The HVI requires intelligence collection and analysis at the lowest level, the individual. This granularity is outside the norm for most current collection systems.[9]

We have come to the crux of the matter: How can we preserve the individual as the root of analysis while marrying it to fixed points in space?

SOLVING THE PROBLEM OF "FIXING" AN INDIVIDUAL IN SPACE

While the concern regarding the incompatability of these two data types is certainly justified (people tend to move around), there are two reasons why it need not derail the analytical windfalls of "multidimensional" data fusion.

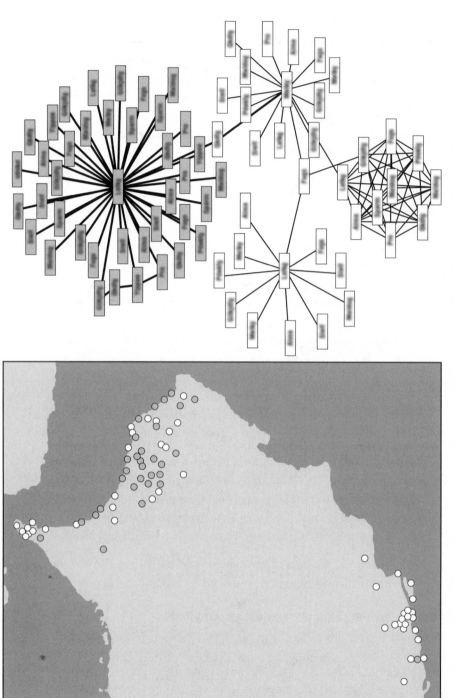

Figure 3.3. A relational filter is applied to a selected set of Omani tribes and clans of the Beni Ruwahah confederation (highlighted in gray on right) and simultaneously highlighted on the geospatial display (highlighted in gray on left).

The first is simply that, although individuals do move, on the aggregate level these swarms of individuals tend toward relatively static spatial distributions, especially in the case of traditional societies. Furthermore, in areas where drastic demographic change is occurring, the model may be updated periodically, and in fact this change may be tracked through time to add a third "dimension" to the analysis. The second is that, while the individual is certainly not "fixed" in space, individuals do tend to orbit certain set "anchor points" that may be used to infer position. In the case of "man-hunting" operations, these "anchor points" limit "the vast majority of the HVI's hiding locations . . . because of an unwillingness to depart from his normative behavior."[10] An example from quantum physics provides a useful metaphor on how this connection may be operationalized.

An electron is an ethereal, intangible thing, difficult to detect directly; not unlike Mao's guerillas, it is "of the people as a fish is of the sea." However, molecular orbital theory provides us with a method for divining "the probability of finding an electron in any specific region [of a molecule]."[11] It is nearly impossible to identify the exact location of an electron orbiting around the perimeter of an atom at any given time, but we can give a probability that the electron will be within specific areas near the atom's positive core. Likewise, persons tend to orbit certain familiar points locked in space, and although we may be unable to geolocate persons with any real meaning (the point would constantly be changing!), we can define the "orbital patterns" for the individual and give an indication of the places that the individual is likely to be near. This is done by linking the individual to points in space that he or she is in turn related to (school, apartment, employer, favoriate night club, and so on), all of which can be plotted in space. Based on this cluster of points we may gain an idea of the "orbital sphere" of the person and take action based on this educated guess as to his or her whereabouts. The result is a fused relational and geospatial method for locating the individual.

Figure 3.4 shows the probable positions, or orbitals, of an electron in orbit around a nucleus. To illustrate the metaphor, imagine that the electron represents an individual named "Bob," with each orbital representing Bob's probability of being near a particular point in space. For example, the 1s orbital might represent Bob's home, where he spends most of his time, the 2s orbital a two-mile radius around his home, the 2p orbitals Bob's six favorite restaurants, and finally the 3s orbital a fifty-mile radius around Bob's home. Although we cannot be certain of where Bob is at any specific time without

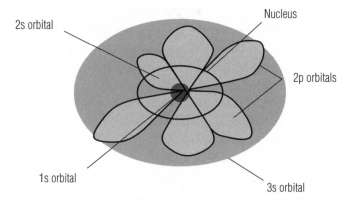

Figure 3.4. Orbital diagram showing the probable locations of particular electrons orbiting the positively charged nucleus of an atom. A useful metaphor for the habits of persons to "orbit" spatially fixed points (home, work, school) in daily life.

watching him constantly (impractical when scaled up), based on Bob's daily routine we can estimate that, at any given time, we are 30 percent likely to find Bob in or around his home (1s orbital); 50 percent likely to find Bob within a two-mile radius of his home; 70 percent likely to find Bob "orbiting" to, from, or around a favorite restaurant (2p orbitals); and 95 percent likely to find Bob somewhere within a fifty-mile radius of his home. The point of this metaphor is not that we need to closely study the routines of the individuals in our social system but rather to show how individuals may theoretically be "anchored" geospatially, based on their relationships to points in space. This concept of relationally "tethering" the individual to points in space provides the critical linkage between our geospatial unit of analysis, the fixed point in space and time, and our basic relational unit of analysis, the person.

THE UTILITY OF "MULTIDIMENSIONAL" DATA FUSION

Suppose that the analyst is interested in whether IED attacks occurring in an Afghan valley are related to a blood feud declared against coalition forces. Because the valley does not have a particular address and corresponding boundary, the attacks occurring in that valley must be separated from others in the sector using a geographic filter, that is, by drawing a circle around the perimeter of the valley using a mapping tool. Now that the attacks have been isolated geospatially, we could apply a data layering technique by simply overlaying a map of tribal boundaries onto the map of IED attacks and use any one of several methods to sleuth a significant relationship between the two layers. Although this tried-and-true method of data layering may offer valuable insights into the relationship between attacks and tribes in the valley, its use is limited by its lack of truly integrated relational information, as shown in a second example.

Now consider the same question of relationship between IEDs and tribes using a fused data set. Although several paths are available to detect a relationship, we would probably begin with the isolation of the IED "events" using a geospatially bounded search, but at this point we might slip into the relational realm and display the "IED events" as a series of nodes on a link chart. Perhaps then we would link each "IED event" to the persons involved in the attack by things like arrests, license plate numbers, fingerprints, and so on, then identify the tribal affiliations of these persons using their surnames, and finally determine the tribal leaders that likely authorized the attacks. We may then return to the geospatial interface, to plot the known addresses for each of the tribal leaders likely to have authorized the attacks.

Although the first example yielded the relationship between the tribal system and a particular set of IED attacks using geospatial analysis, the layering method does not harness the elegance of the relational data, limits the analyst to systemwide trends and leads to an analytical dead end. In contrast, consider the use of the fused data set. In the second example, the analyst is free to sift through relationships between the attacks and their environment geospatially (using a tribal area overlay, for example), then to examine the filtered data relationally (perhaps through arrests) to leverage linking data like vehicle identifiers or fingerprints to determine the persons or organizations involved in the attacks and how they may be located and affected. The true value-added aspect of data fusion is this ability to present entities (events, persons, organizations, places, and the like) within their spatial, relational, or even temporal contexts and to move among these data domains seamlessly. This analytical flexibility creates the type of virtuous circle of knowledge refinement that is one of the key concepts of visual analytics (see Figure 3.5).

Consider the example of the infamous Jemaah Islamiyah bomb maker and Malaysian terrorist leader Noordin Mohammed Top. Suppose that the analyst is tasked with determining possible locations where Top may be hiding on the island of Java, based on Dodson's man-hunting principles of familiarity, survivability, safety, and vulnerability, which effectively limit the target's

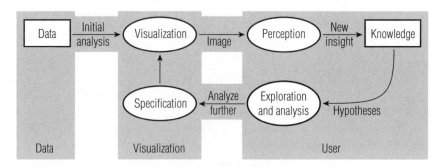

Figure 3.5. The sense-making loop for visual analytics.

SOURCE: J. J. van Wijk, "The Value of Visualization," from *IEEE Visualization* (2005), p. 11; available at www.win.tue.nl/~vanwijk/vov.pdf.

location based on past experience and practical constraints.[12] The analyst will likely begin by plotting Noordin's past and present relationships to persons or organizations onto the link-chart. Relationships may then be presented geospatially by showing the locations of related individuals on a map based on address information, thus making the relational information actionable. Should the analyst opt to continue the investigation further, perhaps by delving deeper into Noordin's friendship ties in the Jaipur area, these ties may be isolated using a geofilter and reexamined more closely relationally. The important element of these examples is that data fusion empowers the analyst with the freedom to move among data dimensions and refine knowledge freely.

In addition to the geospatial and relational data dimensions, mention should also be given to the fusion of temporal data. By fusing this third data dimension, the researcher may not only leverage the previously discussed power of "bidimensional" data fusion (geospatial and relational) but also observe trends in the social system over time. To give another example, recall the case of Noordin Top and suppose that, in addition to isolating his relationships and plotting them geospatially, we are also able to display changes in these relationships and other events (like movements) over time. Perhaps we will notice that Noordin's past movements tend to follow a seasonal pattern or that police crackdowns on his followers tend to precipitate Top's relocation. These types of observations and complex analyses are only possible through the integration of temporal attributes within the already fused georelational system and are likely to present the next frontier in data fusion.

THE SUITABILITY OF TRIBES FOR FUSION ANALYSIS

Now that the value and need of multidimensional data fusion has been established, I will discuss why this method of social modeling is especially appropriate for use in understanding tribal social systems. An important element of this suitability lies in what French sociologist Emile Durkheim refers to as "mechanical solidarity." Grahame Thompson (2003) explains:

> Mechanical solidarity typifies a segmentary community, often small in scale, in which there are clearly separated roles between its members and clear standards by which their behavior can be assessed. This produces collective conscience in a "mechanical" way as the members of the community interact along these strictly demarcated lines. People "know their place" and then act accordingly.

Now contrast this idea with the "organic solidarity" prevalent in "advanced industrial economies," which refers to a functionally differentiated society of a more complex character. In this case, solidarity is more difficult to generate. The complexity of the functions in a differentiated society implies a greater variability of social relations, where the social roles members are called upon to play are less clear-cut (and often multiple) and the behavioral norms associated with those roles equally complex.[13]

The mechanical solidarity prevalent in tribal social systems in turn reinforces the effects of social "structure" (those factors such as social class, religion, gender, ethnicity, and customs that seem to limit or influence the opportunities that individuals have) while detracting from "agency" (the capacity of individual humans to act independently and to make their own free choices).[14] From the point of view of the cultural analyst, this situation effectively simplifies the relational system by increasing the importance of social hierarchy and often disaggregating segmentary (tribal) communities in a system (province) socially as well as spatially (that is, tribesmen tend to associate with other tribe members and live within tribal territories). The same reasons that author and historian Steven Pressfield gives for tribes being a "natural-born warfighting unit," including "obedience, respect for elders, hostility to all outsiders, loyalty, fidelity, the obligation for revenge and blood payback," also effectively simplify the social system through increased mechanical solidarity.[15]

REPRESENTING TRIBAL SYSTEMS: POINTS NOT LINES

To exploit the theoretical suitability of tribal systems for fused analysis we must first identify effective ways of representing tribal territories. There are several ways to determine tribal authority within a given territory, but among the simplest is to represent the presence of tribal elements by plotting individual data points geospatially and then relating these points to one another. Through the use of source language ethnographic or historical documents, survey/census data, or personal interviews, the researcher may assemble a compilation of data points corresponding to tribally linked persons, villages, companies, neighborhoods, and the like. When displayed collectively geospatially, these points effectively show the distribution of the tribal group as the sum of its individual "parts."

The advantage of this method is that it allows a more realistic and meaningful geospatial representation based on the most granular unit of analysis available. Ideally, this unit would be the residences and other geospatial "anchor points" of individual tribesmen, but where these data are unavailable, tribal identification to the village level is still much more meaningful than the traditional boundary-line method. Instead of presenting a tribe geospatially as a polygon, the tribe would be shown as clusters of points among populated areas throughout the map, with points corresponding to villages, valleys, or neighborhoods inhabited or controlled by members of the tribe. This form of presentation allows for the realistic blending of tribal boundaries, as several tribes may be present in a particular urban center or grazing area, and drift within these boundaries may be tracked incrementally over time, as demographics change.

CONCLUSION

The point of this chapter has been to outline ways that data fusion may be achieved and how it can dramatically enhance the analytical capabilities of cultural analysts, especially in tribal social systems. By using visual analytics theory and technology to conduct the labor-intensive aspects of data fusion and accepting the theoretical justification of fusion among the geospatial, relational, and temporal data dimensions, the field of cultural analysis seems poised to make a major contribution to COIN doctrine. The software developers racing to fill this technological need include I2, Access Pro, and a company called Palantir Technologies, which has proven especially well suited for data fusion during the author's ongoing analysis of the Omani tribal system and is discussed in detail by Hartunian and Germann.[16]

However, these software advances must also be accompanied by two caveats. The first is that, no matter how powerful or versatile the technology, a deep understanding of the social system will always depend on "expert opinion familiar with the culture, indoctrination procedures, and institutional foundations" that lend significance to relationships, as well as the skill, intuition, and innovation of the analyst/collector.[17] This is especially true in the case of tribal social systems, where linguistic skill, cultural knowledge, and analytical experience are not a luxury but a requirement. Without the skills required to accomplish tasks like imbedding source language information in the analysis, proper transliteration to English, or understanding the nuance of complex tribal systems, the analysis is best left undone. With this in mind, we must also refrain from attempting to reinvent the wheel by tapping existing sources of social data ranging from deployed company intelligence officers to civil affairs teams operating outside the combat zone. While the need for effective human terrain analysis is especially acute in the combat zone, as a colleague put it, "Building these models in the war zone is like trying to build a bike while running beside it." Just as we have accumulated a wealth of geospatial data for use in any future deployment throughout the globe, we must have the strategic foresight to match and fuse this information with its relational context. In the end, by harnessing technology to fuse geospatial, relational, and temporal data in a meaningful way, we may drastically enhance the field of cultural analysis and further empower the war fighter in the mission of defeating contemporary and future insurgency.

NOTES

This chapter originally appeared in the November 1, 2009, edition of *The Culture and Conflict Review* and is reprinted here with permission.

1. Montgomery McFate, "The Military Utility of Understanding Adversary Culture," *Joint Force Quarterly* 38 (third quarter 2005): 42–48.

2. *Encarta World English Dictionary,* North American edition (Redmond, WA: Microsoft Corporation, 2009); available at http://encarta.msn.com.

3. Daniel Keim, Gennady Andrienko, Jean-Daniel Fekete, Carsten Gorg, Jorn Kohlhammer, and Guy Melancon, "Visual Analytics: Definition, Process, and Challenges," in *Information Visualization: Human-Centered Issues and Perspectives,* 154–175 (Berlin and Heidelburg: Springer, 2008).

4. Walter L. Perry and John Gordon IV, *Analytic Support to Intelligence in Counterinsurgencies* (Santa Monica, CA: RAND National Defense Research Institute, 2008).

5. Keim et al., 2008, 154–175.

6. J. Marr, B. G. Johncushing, and R. Thompson, "Human Terrain Mapping: A Critical First Step to Winning the COIN Fight," *Military Review* 88 (March/April 2008), 37–51.

7. Hartunian and Germann, 2008.

8. John Dodson, "Man-Hunting, Nexus Topography, Dark Networks and Small Worlds," Joint Information Operations Center, *IOSphere*, Winter 2006; retrieved on July 9, 2013, from www.au.af.mil/info-ops/iosphere/iosphere_win06_dodson.pdf.

9. McFate, 2005b, 42–48.

10. Ibid.

11. John Daintith, ed., *Oxford Dictionary of Chemistry* (New York: Oxford University Press, 2004).

12. Dodson, 2006.

13. Grahame F. Thompson, *Between Hierarchies and Markets: The Logic and Limits of Network Forms of Organization* (Oxford, UK: Oxford University Press, 2003).

14. Peter L. Berger and Thomas Luckmann, *The Social Construction of Reality: A Treatise in the Sociology of Knowledge* (Garden City, NY: Anchor Books, 1966).

15. Steven Pressfield, "How to Win in Afghanistan," blog.stevenpressfield.com, 2009.

16. Hartunian and Germann, 2008.

17. Todd J. Hamill, Richard F. Drecko, James W. Chrissis, and Robert F. Mills, "Analysis of Layered Social Networks," *IO Sphere* (Winter 2008).

Part II

CULTURE AND CONFLICT

From Methodology to Practice, Lessons from Afghanistan

4 WEAPONS OF THE NOT SO WEAK IN AFGHANISTAN
Pashtun Agrarian Structure and Tribal Organization

Thomas J. Barfield

AFGHANISTAN IS A COUNTRY WITH A REPUTATION. It bested two short British attempts at occupation in the nineteenth century and one long Soviet attempt in the twentieth. The international community wonders if it will go for four in a row to mark the twenty-first. While resistance to political domination is now attributed in some form to practically everyone, resistance in Afghanistan is still of the old-fashioned type—they shoot at people. But scratch beneath the surface of this history, and one finds that resistance of this type does not originate in the country's urban centers or in its most productive agricultural areas, but that it is at the margins where people still find open resistance a useful political option. One reason for this is that governing powers found it easier to pay such people off than to fight them continuously. Example: I saw a sign at the beginning of the Khyber Pass that declared it was "closed after sunset" (and another that prohibited taking pictures of tribal women). Given that the overloaded painted trucks that sped through the pass often drive without lights at night, this seemed a sensible safety regulation. But it was nothing of the sort. The British, like their Mughal predecessors, had had a problem with the tribes of the Khyber who supported themselves by raiding caravans. The Mughals paid them not to, and the British followed this tradition. But, in the spirit of bargaining, the tribes had insisted that the treaty apply only to daylight hours. The sign should have read, "Khyber Pass: No government after dark." Pakistan, as the world is now learning, inherited and has continued this policy more quietly.

The people causing this trouble were the Pashtuns, now straddling the border between Afghanistan and Pakistan, long experienced at holding their more sophisticated neighbors to ransom, as Rudyard Kipling observed in an oft-quoted line from "Arithmetic of the Frontier":

> A scrimmage in a Border station—A canter down a dark defile—Two thousand pounds of education Drops to a ten-rupee *jezail*.[1]

The Pashtuns (also called Pathans or Pakhtuns) are the largest tribally organized group in the world, numbering between 20 and 24 million divided more or less equally between Afghanistan and Pakistan. In Afghanistan they constitute a plurality but not a majority of the country's population and have provided its national leaders for the past 250 years. In Afghanistan they are divided politically and linguistically into two large descent groups: the Durranis, who inhabit the southwest in the regions bordering Baluchistan and who have Kandahar as their center; and the Ghilzais of eastern Afghanistan, who border and often overlap Pakistan's Northwest Frontier Province (NWFP). The Pashtuns in the NWFP are mostly comprised of a third large descent group, the Karlanri. While the Pashtuns in Pakistan constitute a relatively small percentage of the country's total population, they are the overwhelming majority in the NWFP. Here they are divided among the autonomous groups who live in the Federally Administered Tribal Areas (FATA) of the NWFP that border Afghanistan and those who inhabit the settled regions of the NWFP that are ruled by the Pakistani state from the provincial capital in Peshawar.

The Pashtuns have dominated national politics in Afghanistan since the foundation of the Afghan state by Ahmad Shah Durrani in 1747. But while other ethnic groups may view such Pashtun domination as monolithic, there has always been a rivalry between the more numerous Ghilzai Pashtuns in the east and the Durrani Pashtuns in the south. Indeed, in the 1970s a Ghilzai Pashtun friend of mine in Afghanistan complained that it was the majority Ghilzais who won the country's wars but the minority Durranis who always seemed to end up ruling the country and excluding them from power. He noted that in the first Anglo–Afghan War it was the Ghilzai tribes who had taken on the British, most notably by destroying their retreating army in 1842. It was they who had forced the abdication of the Afghan Amir and started the second Anglo–Afghan war in 1878. It was their revolts in 1929 that had overthrown the reform-minded King Amanullah. What they got in return each time was a restoration of Durrani Mohammadzai monarchy, followed by punitive military campaigns directed by the Kabul government to put them in their place. While my friend's relatives had held high positions in the police and military, they complained of a glass ceiling that kept them well below the power and privilege held by the ruling Durrani Mohammadzais (sardars) under King Zahir Shah and later his cousin President Daud. These Persian-speaking poseurs hardly deserved to be called Pashtuns, he claimed, and yet here they had ruled the country for more than 200 years.

I took these complaints to be a bit of sour grapes mixed with some tribal chauvinism because my friend had easily overlooked the contribution of the Tajik Kohistanis, the Sunni Persian-speaking population north of Kabul, to Afghanistan's long history of resistance to foreign invasions and rebellion against its own rulers. They tended to be as involved as the eastern Pashtuns in these matters but stood even lower on the political food chain than the Ghilzais. Yet when conflict broke out in Afghanistan in 1978 with the coup that toppled Daud and brought the Soviet-backed Peoples Democratic Party of Afghanistan (PDPA) to power, I was struck by an undercurrent of revenge long in the making. The dominant Khalq (Masses) faction that came out of the military was not only mostly Pashtun, in contrast to the more Persian-speaking Parcham (Banner) faction, it was Ghilzai Pashtun. So, in the guise of communists, the Ghilzais had finally taken the top slots.

But, unlike with the old dynastic line, faction fighting among these Ghilzai communists was so intense that within a year they were murdering one another. This internal struggle so weakened the power of the PDPA government that the Soviets invaded the country in December 1979, hoping to stabilize the situation there. As war enveloped all of Afghanistan, another of my friend's observations seemed to be repeating itself. Most of the significant Pashtun military commanders, whether on the PDPA side or the mujahideen side, were overwhelmingly Ghilzais. Where were the Durrani generals, and why was the most severe fighting in eastern rather than southern Afghanistan? Following the Russian withdrawal in 1989 and a subsequent unresolved civil war among ethnically based factions, the Taliban emerged on the national stage in 1975. Because they were based in Kandahar, the center of the Durrani Pashtuns, I thought that this would prove my biases wrong and that here was the Durrani reply to Ghilzai mismanagement. But no; although based in Qandahar, the Taliban's leader, Mulla Omar, was a Hotak Ghilzai, and most of his ministers were also Hotaks. The Hotaks had been the princely lineage before the rise of the Durranis and were the closest Ghilzai group to Kandahar. In addition, that movement gave precedence to clerics rather than tribal leaders, so its organizational base was more religious than tribal. It also recruited foreign fighters more readily than Afghan ones.

But with the American invasion and the toppling of the Taliban in 2001, the words of my friend came back to me again. After twenty-five years of war it was a relatively low-profile Durrani from the south—Hamid Karzai—who suddenly got the new top spot in the new government in the Bonn Accord and went on to be elected president. He was a member of the Popalzai clan, the direct descendants of Ahmad Shah Durrani who had founded the Durrani Empire in 1747. At the same time, the most powerful Ghilzai commanders were coming to blows arguing over who would be governor of Jalalabad, the provincial center where the Ghilzais were the majority. The election of Karzai as president in 2004 appeared to put the Ghilzais back in their secondary position at the national level, as not a single one of the most powerful ministries went to them.

So why was it that the Ghilzai seemed to thrive politically in time of war and anarchy and so often produced the major military figures who were self-made men? Why did the Durranis end up winning the peace from a position of weakness and gain the ability to restore leadership to families that had dominated Afghan politics for generations with leaders who lacked a strong military base? And what light does this throw on the renewed Taliban insurgency, one of the first in Afghan history to have its base in the Durrani south rather than the Ghilzai east?

It is these questions that I would like to address in this chapter. I do not believe that the answer lies in ideology but in the dynamics of social organization that itself is rooted in the long-term structure of their respective agrarian economies. The more the agrarian structure was subsistence based and patterns of land ownership were fragmented, the less scope there was for the emergence of powerful hereditary leaders, let alone dynastic families. This can be seen today most graphically among the Karlanri in Federally Administered Tribal Areas of the NWFP in Pakistan, where the land barely supports the population. The Ghilzai in Afghanistan have a more productive agriculture base than that, but it was a production system that provided little scope for class distinctions. They maintained an egalitarian political order that was as opposed to the power of its own leaders as it was to attempts by governments to centralize power in Kabul. Successful leaders in this system were aggressive risk takers whose positions were based on their personal achievements, which were hard to institutionalize. By contrast, the Durrani Pashtuns in southern Afghanistan had come into possession of large tracts of lightly taxed agricultural land during the founding of the Durrani Empire. These rich irrigated lands located around Kandahar and Peshawar supported a hierarchical political system that required large agricultural surpluses to sustain them. It supported an elite of landowners whose tribal followers had in many cases been reduced to their economic clients. In this system, power was relatively easy to maintain and pass on to descendants who rarely faced the personal power struggles required of Ghilzai leaders. Perhaps more important, they could count on the support of their home regions if they entered national government. Ghilzai leaders could not—if they left their territories to enter the national stage, rivals at home resented their success and undermined them at every turn.

Such dynamics still have an impact on Afghan politics today. To understand them we should look first at the classic model of the interaction between a subsistence-based agrarian (and pastoral) system and one based on irrigated agriculture and cities as propounded by the medieval Arab social theorist and historian, ibn Khaldun. Afghanistan fits his model well, but, as we will see, some modification is needed to explain the rise of the more hierarchical tribal organization that was characteristic of ruling dynasties there.

IBN KHALDUN: MODELS OF AGRARIAN ECONOMIES AND SOCIAL ORGANIZATION

Ibn Khaldun was born in Tunisia in 1332 and died in 1406 in Egypt.[2] In 1375 he took four years of sabbatical from his usual work as a court official to write a multivolume history of the world in the quiet of a village on the edge of the desert. It was in the "Introduction," or *Muqaddimah*, to this work that ibn Khaldun laid out his model of history and society, a new "science of culture" (*'ilm al-'umran*).[3] This introduction was designed to provide the background to his larger history of events, to explain his methodology, and to lay out a number of models that explained a series of historical cycles that underlay the rise and fall of dynasties and the relationship between "desert civilization" and "sedentary civilization."

Desert civilizations were those human communities based on subsistence agriculture or pastoralism that organized themselves along kinship lines under conditions of low population density. They were located in geographically marginal areas that proved difficult for outsiders to dominate effectively or that did not repay the cost of doing so. The specific examples he cited included desert nomads (camel-raising Bedouin), steppe nomads (Turks), and mountain villagers (Kurds and Berbers). Sedentary civilizations were those human communities based on surplus agricultural production that sustained dense populations and created complex economies. They were located in broad river valleys and irrigated plains that allowed for the emergence of nucleated villages and cities. Such communities were organized on the basis of residency but divided by class and occupational structures with considerable division of labor. They were centers of learning and high culture as well as markets for regional trade and international commerce. In filling a blank map, the communities at the margins overspread the greatest geographic space, but the people concentrated in the limited areas of irrigated agriculture or in urban centers equaled or exceeded them in numbers. More significantly, the sedentary areas controlled the region's productive capital and produced the bulk of its wealth.

The two systems were not sealed off from each other. On the contrary, they had intense interactions and close connections, particularly because of population movements. Ibn Khaldun contended that desert civilizations must have predated sedentary ones because they were less complex socially and simpler economically, a supposition confirmed by modern archeology. Once cities arose, however, there was a constant population flow from the marginal subsistence areas in the mountains, deserts, and steppes toward the cities and irrigated valleys. By contrast, city residents showed no desire to take up the harder and more austere life of the desert nomad or mountain villager. The push factor in this equation was demographic: The healthier periphery produced more people than its limited subsistence base could support. The pull factor was cultural and economic: City life has always been more appealing than that found in mountain villages or nomad camps. Cities and productive agricultural lands provided opportunities to indulge in rare luxuries for the rich and powerful, while the poor were attracted by the constant demand for new workers. In fact, this population flow was essential to the survival of premodern cities because their death rates exceeded their birth rates. Urban centers could not maintain a stable population (let alone grow) without a constant influx of migrants. Over time, this could lead to what amounted to a wholesale population replacement. The disappearance of the Sumerian as a living language in ancient Mesopotamia was a product of the constant influx of Akkadian speakers from the countryside, whose language displaced it. But the reverse also was true because the cultural power of city life was so strong. Immigrants drawn from many disparate groups of people adopted the lingua franca of the cities that they moved to and lost their own native tongues over the course of a few generations.

DESERT CIVILIZATION

Economic Structure

In a subsistence economy nearly everyone produces the same things, so there are no great differences in standards of living or much internal trade. In desert civilization, therefore, the chief might eat and drink more than an ordinary person, but he eats and drinks the same things. Wealth is measured in terms of property (land and livestock particularly) rather than money. This was brought home to me in Afghanistan by a nomad trader who showed me the goods he had brought into the mountains to trade with Tajik villagers. I commented that it could not be much of a business because these villagers had no money. He rebuked me, saying, "Just because people have no money does not mean they are poor. Here they have livestock." He explained that villagers had goats with so little local value that they were eager to barter them for his imported goods. As an example, the trader showed me a box containing a half dozen unbreakable tea glasses he had purchased for 100 afghanis in a city bazaar that he would barter for a goat valued in the village at 500 afghanis. I apologized and told the trader that this was indeed a good return, but he only laughed and remarked that I had missed the real profit in his trade. When his own flocks returned to the lowlands, each Tajik goat would then be worth 1,500 afghanis in the local bazaar, meaning that his initial 100 afghani investment would yield a 1,400 afghani profit per animal.

In the absence of a money economy, people support themselves at a basic level. When surplus comes their way, they invest in relationships. Hospitality, communal feasts, gift giving, and other forms of redistribution raise the status of the givers, and it is this social esteem or fame that is more cherished than money. Indeed, a leader gains and retains power through his ability to give to the group in some fashion. Bedouin poetry in particular praises the sheikh who is so lavish with his hospitality that he keeps nothing for himself. But such a subsistence economic base provides little basis for class differentiation, economic specialization, or capital accumulation. If societies rooted in subsistence economies often seem timeless and unchanging, it is because their replication remains trapped within such narrow limits.

Social and Political Structure

Desert civilizations had specific social attributes. The most important of these was their strong group solidarity based on kinship and descent. This generated *'asabiya*, or group feeling, which bound all member of a social group together when facing the outside world. In such a system, the group interest trumps individual interest to such an extent that loyalty to the group supersedes everything else. Positive acts by any member of the group redound to the group's benefit; any shame likewise tarnishes the reputation of the group as a whole. More significantly, attacks or slights against an individual are met with a collective response. Take crime as an example. One does not seek justice through government institutions (which often do not exist) but by mobilizing the kin group to seek retribution or compensation. If one man murders another, the murdered man's kin are collectively obligated to seek blood revenge. Similarly, the murderer's kin are collectively responsible for his act (and may even be targets in revenge killings), although they had no direct role in it. If compensation is agreed on to end the threat of revenge, the whole group is liable for its payment. Not only do overt acts such as assault, murder, or theft demand a collective response, so did threats to a group's honor and reputation.

In Afghanistan, it is the Pashtuns who are the best examples of this system through the *Pashtunwali*, a code of principles thoroughly rooted in the primacy of maintaining honor and reputation. The military advantage of this solidarity was particularly evident in times of conflict. When such groups entered into battle, they were renowned as fierce fighters because individuals would rather die than shame themselves in front of their kin by running away. Life would not be worth living afterwards if they did. Of course, the group itself could decide to run away (and usually did) if the odds turned against them, but they retreated together. That was only good tactics, and there was no honor to be lost in deciding to fight another day when victory was more certain.

This strong group solidarity was undermined by a number of structural political weaknesses, however. The first was that these descent or locality groups were necessarily of small size. Second, because such groups were relatively equal in numbers and had a strong cultural predisposition toward equality, it was difficult for a leader to consolidate power. In such a system, every man and every group could at least imagine the possibility of becoming dominant and resented being placed in a subordinate position. Anyone in a leadership position was therefore plagued by jealous rivals who would be happy to replace him or at least throw obstacles in his way if they could not. This pattern was so ubiquitous among close relatives in Afghanistan that it acquired a specific term in Pashto, *tarburwali* (the rivalry of cousins). Third, even if a man succeeded in surmounting this rivalry, the position of leader itself was structurally weak. It lacked the right of command and so depended on the ability to persuade others to follow. It was therefore tough being a chief of a people whom you had to cajole into action and where criticism by rivals was constant. For this reason, ibn Khaldun noted, religious leaders were often more successful than tribal ones in uniting large groups. Coming from outside the system and calling on God's authority, they could better circumvent tribal rivalries.

SEDENTARY CIVILIZATION

Economy

Sedentary civilization has luxury as its defining characteristic. This luxury is the product of a complex division of labor, where money trumps kinship. In cities, everything one needs or wants is obtained with money, and so kinship ties atrophy. Five hundred years later and a half a world away from ibn Khaldun's medieval Islamic cities, Adam Smith made the same point more broadly, noting

> . . . that without the assistance and co-operation of many thousands, the very meanest person in a civilized country could not be provided, even according to what we very falsely imagine, the easy and simple manner in which he is commonly accommodated. Compared, indeed, with the more extravagant luxury of the great, his accommodation must no doubt appear extremely simple and easy; and yet it may be true, perhaps, that the accommodation of an European prince does not always so much exceed that of an industrious and frugal peasant, as the accommodation of the latter exceeds that of many an African king, the absolute master of the lives and liberties of ten thousand naked savages.[4]

Cities also supported a wide range of locally produced and imported foods, as well as goods and services that ranged from the utilitarian to the extravagant. Many of these products were vital to the survival of even distant rural communities. Their need for goods they could not produce for themselves forced subsistence mountain villagers and nomads into dependency relations with urban markets:

> While (the Bedouins) need the cities for their necessities of life, the urban population needs (the Bedouins) for conveniences and luxuries . . . They must be active on the behalf of their interests and obey them whenever (the cities) ask and demand obedience from them.[5]

I experienced an example of this at first hand with the salt trade in the mountainous province of Badakhshan in the 1970s. Although I had thought the summer nomad encampments were self-sufficient, in fact they continually sent donkey and horse caravans to the distant provincial capital of Faizabad to buy salt because it was a necessary dietary supplement for their grazing sheep. Because the local mountain villagers had cows and goats, they also made the same buying trip for salt as did the nomads but purchased cloth, metal tools, sugar, and tea as well. Villagers were therefore keen to sell surplus wheat to the visiting nomads for the cash they would need for these purchases. It was clear that geographic isolation did not imply economic isolation.

The division of labor and surplus production also supported centers of learning and artistic production. Although one might find Sufi mystics in remote regions, centers of Islamic teachings were always urban based. They were financed through government patronage but also by private donations of money, irrigated land, and urban property to pious foundations, the revenue from which supported shrines, schools, and the members of the clergy that ran them. These institutions served as bastions of power for orthodox religious sects. Heterodox sects, by contrast, tended to thrive in the marginal areas beyond the control of status quo institutions. It is no accident that the core Shia and Ismaili populations in Sunni-dominated Afghanistan are found in its most remote mountain regions or that older pagan groups survived here until a century ago. Indeed, one scholar has suggested that this is a reoccurring pattern: Whatever tradition the center holds as orthodox, the mountainous margins will set themselves off against it.[6]

Social and Political Structure

Two defining social characteristics of sedentary civilization are identification by residence (not kinship) and hierarchical divisions based on class. It is a world of strangers who are economically dependent on one another in all aspects of daily life but have no reason to interact socially. People may boast of having a particularly prestigious bloodline, but such descent groups cannot survive intact in a world where the individual interests supersede group interests. More important, social rank had less to do with ancestors than control of wealth. Signs of class inequality are ever present in dress, food, and housing. Indeed, in this setting we are no longer dealing with undifferentiated commonalities ranked on a scale of more versus less. Here we experience differences in kind so large that no single generality can encompass them. We stop talking about food and explore the realm of cuisine in which members of different classes have different diets. Similarly social status can be distinguished immediately by dress, some types of which may be legally mandated or prohibited to make their distinctions binding. It is where women are much more commonly veiled and secluded than their sisters in the countryside because they do no work outside of the household.

The political strengths of sedentary civilization lay in its centralization, higher degree of wealth, and larger size. Political leaders had "royal authority," the ability to issue commands with the expectation that they would be obeyed. Unlike the desert chieftain, a ruler here was not a consensus builder or redistributor of wealth but an acquisitive autocrat. He secured his power by accumulating wealth for himself and the state on a grand scale through various forms of taxation, control of trade or markets, and large-scale ownership of productive land. Such wealth was necessary because it undergirded centralized authority. It paid for a government bureaucracy composed of appointed subordinates who carried out the ruler's commands with a police force behind them. Punishment awaited those who refused to pay taxes or who had the temerity to ignore a decree. Perhaps most important, the revenue paid for an army that protected the state from invasion from without and against rebellion from within. Such military forces in the medieval Islamic world consisted of paid mercenaries or slave soldiers. While ibn Khaldun takes this as a given, it is a significant departure from Western history. Although mercenary forces were never absent, the ancient Greek polis (city state), Alexander the Great, or the Roman Republic and early Empire all recruited soldiers from their own people and often made military service an obligation of citizenship (or a way to obtain it). Even in feudal Europe, the nobility justified its dominance of society based on their obligation to provide military service as mounted knights and were expected to fight in battle themselves. In the Islamic world, such mass participation in warfare was characteristic only of desert civilization. Warfare by states was in the hands of military professionals who were the often unruly but paid servants of the state, not the ordinary inhabitants of any class.

This very complexity, hierarchy, and wealth created political weaknesses as well as strengths. Urban and peasant populations were not as tough as the people from the margins, physically or mentally. A structure of centralized political authority where officials could easily abuse their authority and accumulate personal wealth tended to spawn corruption. This weakened the state by siphoning off its revenue and alienating the population. But perhaps most significantly, these populations were uninvolved with government. As its passive inhabitants it mattered little to them who the ruler was, hence concepts of patriotism, citizenship, or indeed any sense of political obligation to the state were almost entirely absent. This often proved a fatal weakness because the wealth of cities served as magnets for attacks by poor but militarily powerful desert civilization peoples, particularly the camel-riding Bedouin and the horse-riding Turkish nomads. Ibn Khaldun noted that most of the ruling dynasties in the medieval Islamic world had their origins within such groups who formerly lived at the margins of powerful regional states and empires. Taking advantage of periodic military weakness and economic decline within sedentary states, they made themselves masters of societies far more complex than those in which they were born. In the process, peoples from the margins regularly established themselves as ruling elites in regions in which they conquered and then settled.

The division of marginal areas in Afghanistan into mountain, steppe, and desert zones creates a pattern very similar to that seen in North Africa or the Arab Near East, but the order of their importance is very different. In this region it was the Turko-Mongolian horse-riding nomads from the north who played the dominating political role historically, one they did not lose until the rise of the Pashtuns in the mid-eighteenth century. Mountain peoples also played a larger role than elsewhere in the Islamic world. These include the Aimaqs in the Paropamisus, the Hazaras in the center of the Hindu Kush, the Tajiks in the northeastern mountains, the Pashtun in the mountainous regions straddling the border between Pakistan and Afghanistan, and the small but culturally distinctive linguistic groups in Nuristan and the Pamirs. By contrast, desert nomads play an insignificant significant role, and, unlike in Arabia, nomads do not form exclusive tribal or ethnic groups. In particular, the Pashtun nomads in the south and east share common descent groups with other Pashtuns who are sedentary, as do the much smaller number of Baluch in the deserts further south.

Even now, at the beginning of the twenty-first century, ibn Khaldun's model can be applied directly and very fruitfully to Afghanistan. Although not untouched by the economic and social changes that have fundamentally transformed or even eliminated "desert civilization" communities in other parts of the Near East, North Africa, or Central Asia, Afghanistan remains a place that ibn Khaldun would easily recognize. Its rural economy remains largely subsistence based, and its road and communication infrastructure is only minimally developed. Once leaving the few main highways, particularly in mountainous areas, one quickly encounters a world in which people move only on horseback, on foot, or by riding donkeys. They measure travel time in days, not hours. Wherever the destination, they will cheerfully tell a traveller that the place is "*dur nist*" (not far) so as not to disappoint, even though it will still take all day or more to get there. These are people whose goal in agriculture is to feed themselves and their families, not to produce crops for the market. Although hospitable, they draw the boundaries of community tightly and distrust strangers. Differences in wealth, rank, and status are minimal when compared to those on the plains on in the cities. Most important, these communities are still beyond the direct control of a weak Afghan central government in Kabul. What power that state had gained in the century prior to the communist coup of 1978 was then lost in the quarter century of war that followed it.

Ibn Khaldun would also be familiar with the cultural tensions in Afghanistan between the people of the plains and cities and those who inhabited the country's mountains, deserts, and steppes. To city people those in the hinterlands are more barbarian than civilized. Who (except perhaps an anthropologist like myself) would live with such people voluntarily? As a foreigner, I was often more comfortable dealing with nomads and villagers than some of my urban Afghan acquaintances. I at least respected their culture, which most city people (particularly educated ones) either held in contempt or feared. Of course people in the hinterland viewed city dwellers as weak willed and corrupt. And people in the countryside had little good to say of the political elites in the capital, regardless of their ethnic origin. Yet one of the most interesting things about this divide, unlike so many others in Afghanistan, was that it could be crossed by individuals. People migrating to the cities who may have been steeped in rural values found them impossible to maintain in an urban setting (or perhaps it would be safer to say that their children did). This tension was particularly marked under Taliban rule. On first sight, the harsh restrictions the Taliban imposed on daily life in Kabul (no music, no games or kite flying, required beards and prayers) appears rooted solely in their severe vision of Islam. But beneath the surface lay an older and deeper conflict that ibn Khaldun would have well understood. The Taliban's hatred of the residents of Kabul, and the Kabul people's contempt and fear of the Taliban, had less to do with Islam than it did with the long-standing clash of values between luxury-loving urbanites and puritanical rural villagers who had come to wield power over them. But, as ibn Khaldun also observed, if these mountain puritans were closer to being good in a moral sense than were city people, it was only because their rural life offered far fewer opportunities for corruption. And having power and wealth in an urban setting could always be counted on to change that equation over time.

With this larger context in mind, let us now leave ibn Khaldun's model and return directly to the Pashtuns.

THE PASHTUNS

Who Is a Pashtun?

The three ideal criteria for Pashtun identity are Pashtun descent, speaking Pashto, and conducting life in accord with Pashtun cultural code of values.

Descent plays a key role because it gives rise to the Pashtun model of tribal organization based on nested sets of egalitarian clans and lineages defined by patrilineal genealogies stemming from a common ancestor. In the absence of government institutions, such descent groups act to organize economic production, preserve internal political order, and defend the group against outsiders. The relationships among each of these lineages, and even extended families, rests on segmentary opposition; that is, lineages are supported by, or opposed to, one another based on their degrees of relatedness and the problem confronting them. This ideal, though often honored in the breach, gives rise to the ethnographic cliché often cited by anthropologists and tribesmen alike: "Me against my brothers; my brothers and me against our cousins; my brothers, cousins, and me against the world." The tribe marks the outer limits of both ordinary ethnic identification and political leadership.

In addition to descent, Pashtun identity has strong cultural boundaries, the first being command of the Pashto language. (This can be a bone of contention in Afghanistan where Pashtun elites such as the Mohammadzai royal lineage became Persian speakers over time.) But Pashtuns also insist that being a "real Pashtun" demands that one not just speak Pashto but "do Pashto," that is follow the precepts of the *Pashtunwali*. This is a code of conduct that stresses personal autonomy and equality of political rights in a world of equals. Thus it is more than a system of customary laws; it is a way of life that stresses honor above all else, including the acquisition of money or property. It is a code that is practically impossible to fulfill in a class-structured society or in areas where governments prohibit such institutions as blood feuds and demand tax payments.

It is therefore the people who inhabit the most marginal lands and who are poor and beyond government control who see themselves as the only true Pashtuns. These include the Ghilzai border regions of eastern Afghanistan and the Karlanri FATA regions of the NWFP because only they can maintain the strict standards of autonomy demanded by the *Pashtunwali*. In richer rural areas, such as the irrigated plains around Peshawar or Kandahar where governments have been long established, this is less possible. Here there are two patterns: (1) relatively poor egalitarian lineage groups that are no match for the power of states authorities and (2) local lineages that are dominated by hereditary landlords who have reduced their fellow tribesmen to the status of clients. In the first case, it is not possible for the community to meet the standards of autonomy required by the *Pashtunwali*, while in the second is the land-owning elite who overtly display these values because only they have enough political autonomy to meet its standards of behavior and enough resources to meet demands of required hospitality. In Swat, Pakistan, for example, Pashtun landlords created political factions composed of clients to compete with other powerful landlords, but it was clear that the khans were politically and economically superior to these clients.[7] Pashtuns, even wealthy ones, who moved to large cities were even farther removed from the values of the *Pashtunwali* because there they were enmeshed in state systems of government that restricted autonomy and cash economies that valued money more than honor. The higher Pashtun elites rose in stratified urban societies, the weaker their ties with the rural hinterland became.

These distinctions were formally recognized by the British raj when it divided the NWFP into two zones: the FATA (which was not under direct state rule and had almost complete internal autonomy) and the more prosperous settled zones and cities (which were ruled by colonial administrators directly and subject to all state laws and regulations). Pakistan inherited and has maintained this same system since its independence. Afghanistan never formally recognized politically autonomous tribal zones but did grant many distinct privileges in regards to taxation and conscription to the tribes that straddled the Durand Line. The Afghan Ministry of Tribal Affairs also provided subsidies to the tribes in this region and dealt with their problems outside of the usual government administration.

POLITICAL LEADERSHIP AS A PRODUCT OF PASHTUN TRIBAL DYNAMICS

Egalitarian Pashtun Tribes

The Pashtun ethos among the Ghilzai and the FATA is rabidly egalitarian. Each individual is in theory no better by birth than any other. Leaders in such egalitarian tribal organizations gain their positions by displaying special skills in mediating problems within the tribe or successfully organizing raids and wars against its enemies. It is an achieved status not automatically inherited by a man's sons, for there are always potential agnatic rivals (particularly patrilineal cousins, *tarbur*) ready to seize any opportunity to replace an incumbent or his heir if the opportunity presents itself. For this reason, leadership has rarely remained for long in a single lineage. Indeed, as ibn Khaldun was first to point out, such leaders lacked "royal authority," the ability to command. Such a role had little inherent power, and without the ability to command it was hamstrung by time-consuming consensus building to carry out any major action.

The necessity of proving leadership by building a social consensus is seen most clearly in the Pashtun *jirga* (an assembly called to settle disputes or approve plans for collective action), in which effective leaders must build a consensus in support of their decisions. In settling a blood feud, for example, the community lacks the authority either to impose a punishment on the murderers or to force the murder victim's kin to accept blood money. Instead, mediators must convince the aggrieved parties to accept a settlement even though this may take an extended period of time. If they are successful, such mediators gain prestige and more followers. This dynamic also crops up when Pashtun leaders have to deal with states. Pashtun khans or maliks may appear to be leaders of their tribes, but their ability to negotiate is limited by the knowledge they can impose nothing on their followers. As Akbar Ahmed noted, "The prejudice against ranks and titles and the hierarchy they imply is strong in tribal society and is summed up by the choice the Mahsud mahshar [headman] speaking on behalf of the clan elders, gave the British, 'Blow us all up with cannons or make all eighteen thousand of us Nawabs.'"[8]

The tendency toward political fragmentation among the Ghilzais had been noticed by the first British envoy to the Kingdom of Kabul, Mountstuart Elphinstone, in the early nineteenth century. Comparing them to the ruling Durranis, he wrote,

> The internal government of the Ghiljies is entirely different from that of the Dooraunees. The chiefs of the former have now lost all the authority which they possessed under their own royal government. There is reason to doubt whether that authority ever was so extensive, as that introduced among the Dooraunees on the Persian model. It is more probable that the power of even the King of the Ghiljies, was small in his own country, and that the tulmultuary consent of the people to support his measures abroad, was dictated more by a sense of the interest and glory of the tribe than by any deference to the King's commands. Some appearances however warrant a supposition that his power was sufficient to check murders and other great disorders. Whatever the power of the King may have had formerly, it is now at an end, and that the aristocracy has fallen with it; and although it has left sentiments of respect in the minds of the people, yet that respect is so entirely unmixed with fear, that it has no effect whatever in controlling their actions. No Khaun of a tribe, or Mullik of a village, ever interferes as a magistrate to settle a dispute, or at least a serious one; they keep their own families and immediate dependants in order, but leave the rest of the people to accommodate their differences as they can. This may be presumed not to have always been the case, because it has not generally produced the compulsory trial by a Jeerga, (or assembly of elders) which subsists among the Berdouranee [i.e. the Karlanri], so long habituated to strife; neither has it exasperated the tempers, nor embittered the enmities of the Ghiljies, as it has with the people just mentioned.[9]

The maintenance and persistence of this egalitarian ethos over time has a strong ecological base. The FATA area of the NWFP and the neighboring Ghilzai areas of eastern Afghanistan are resource poor and marginal to urban centers. Arable land is scarce and not very productive in any event. Resources such as timber or pasture are under community, not private, ownership. The economy is subsistence based. In such an environment those who rise to political prominence find it hard to secure their positions over time. What surplus wealth they have is consumed by obligations of hospitality and other expressions of generosity that maintain their political support. Seeking outside revenue is therefore a strong priority for leaders who have so little at home, but this is a two-edged sword. Subsidies from governments or political movements to resident leaders build their followings but can provoke jealousy, generosity's evil twin.[10] Leaders in eastern Afghanistan or FATA are thus never able to soar far enough above their rivals to permanently subordinate them. And public acceptance of such permanent subordination would violate the basic principle of political autonomy that undergirds the Pashtunwali.

Hierarchical Pashtun Tribes

The Pashtuns (and the Bedouin Arabs) are classic examples of egalitarian segmentary tribes. But not all tribes based on descent follow this pattern, nor do they all have such egalitarian ideologies. Invading Turco-Mongolian tribes from Central Asia whose dynasties dominated Iran and Turkey for almost a thousand years, for example, were explicitly hierarchical. This difference was reflected in both their social structure and their political organization. Kinship terms made distinctions between elder and younger brothers, junior and senior generations, and noble and common clans. These created a structure of nested descent groups, similar to those of the Pashtuns, but where clans and lineages were ranked hierarchically along genealogical lines. Only the leaders of noble clans had the ability to compete for high political office, and the cultural tradition among the Central Asian tribes of drawing leadership from a single ruling lineage was strong and produced dynasties of unparalleled duration. The direct descendants of the Mongolian Xiongnu leader, Modun (who founded his empire in 200 BC) ruled over the Mongolian steppe for 600 years in greater and lesser capacities, as did the direct descendants of Chinggis Khan for 700 years. The unbroken line of Ottoman sultans ruled in Turkey for more than 600 years. Babur, the founder of the Mughal Empire in north India who was buried in Kabul, was a product of such a tradition.[11]

The tribal leaders in such hierarchical systems have true royal authority: They command followers who recognize their subordinate status. The hierarchical ideology of such social structures made the cultural acceptance of status differences more natural, for no honor was lost in assuming a junior role in a larger group, nor did vesting leadership in a ruling clan or paying tribute to it create discontent. The most notable example of this structure in the Afghan–Pakistan border region is the Baluch, who have permanent khans from long-lived dynasties to whom taxes and political fealty are obligatory. Such is the ideological divide between the two systems that Fredrik Barth found that Pashto speakers who accepted the political protection of Baluch khans were no longer considered to be Pashtuns.[12] Because they had publicly surrendered their autonomy they had become, in the eyes of their neighbors, "Pashto-speaking Baluch."

If the Pashtuns have refused to accept the cultural legitimacy of a hierarchy, they have been forced to adapt to its consequences. The majority of the Pashtuns in the NWFP do not live in the autonomous tribal regions but in the state-administered regions where they are subject to the laws of Pakistan. In contrast to the border regions, these are lands that are more highly productively agriculturally, depend on irrigated agriculture, have strong market economies, and support the major urban center of Peshawar. Indeed, the densely populated Peshawar Valley and surrounding areas have been under direct state rule since pre-Islamic times. Before Pakistan became a state, the region was directly administered by the British, by the Sikhs, by the Afghan amirs, and by the Mughals before them. Similarly, in southern Afghanistan the rich irrigated land in Kandahar and Helmand has produced a more complex economy than in eastern Afghanistan and the emergence of powerful local lineages that have been able to secure their power by dominating the agricultural economy. Before the rise of the Afghan state, Kandahar was a bone of contention between the Safavid Empire in Iran and the Mughal Empire in India and came under the rule of each at various periods of time.

In terms of styles of leadership, Pashtuns from the irrigated plains rely more on wealth and inherited political authority to maintain their positions. The Durrani clans of southern Afghanistan, for example, more often consist of a landlord and his clients, all Pashtuns but now no longer equals. Such leaders faced only limited internal lineage challengers to their rule and focused more on competition with similar leaders from other such clans who competed for resources in the same region. In Kandahar, the historic and continuing rivalry among the major Durrani clans is centuries old. The Popalzai, Karzai's clan, provided the Sadozai lineage of Afghan amirs who ruled from the founding of the Afghan state in 1747 until 1818. Their rivals, the Barakzais, produced the Mohammadzai royal lineage that ruled Afghanistan from 1826 to 1978. Locally these clans faced two other rivals, the Alikozai and the Achakzai, who have been powerful regional elites in southern Afghanistan for the same period.

There is a similar dichotomy in Pakistan's NWFP as well. When Akbar Ahmed compared tribal area Mohmands with settled area Mohmands, he found that the latter were so encapsulated by the state that they had little effective leadership and were well on their way to becoming a subjected peasant class.[13] In Swat, Barth observed the historical development of powerful land-owning khans who dominated their clients.[14] Swat was therefore more structurally similar to Kandahar in political organization: The egalitarian ethos of the FATA tribes was missing, but the land-owning khans provided the backbone of resistance to state penetration. The price for FATA's autonomy has been lack of economic development, education, and services.

The leaders of southern Durrani groups have great time depth when compared to the Ghilzais and more wealth at their disposal because they own so much land. They have also played an important political role in representing the region's interests in dealings with the central government. As a result, they have been generally more educated and sophisticated than their rural Ghilzai counterparts and more comfortable in national politics. However, although they have more security of command and property, they are also more subject to more coercion. The river valleys and flat surrounding deserts are much more vulnerable to military attack than are isolated mountain villages. Landed estates are subject to confiscation, and the irrigation network itself is exquisitely vulnerable to disruption. The once densely populated region of Seistan of western Afghanistan became a depopulated desert when its irrigation system failed (historians still debate whether the cause was geological or disruption by war).

IMPLICATIONS FOR LEADERSHIP WAR AND PEACE

These differences may explain the first question introduced at the beginning of this chapter. The Ghilzais do best in times of anarchy because their poor subsistence-based regions cope better with economic or political disruption and are harder to coerce because of their isolation. The high level of competition and relative ease of entry into the political sphere means that ambitious and talented men have had a better chance to rise in times of war and political anarchy when military leadership is most highly valued and poor social or economic background is not a barrier. In terms of filling military commands, Ghilzais were more prone to enter the army or interior police in the twentieth century because the Durranis already commanded the more prestigious positions. During the Soviet occupation, personal charisma and ability accelerated their advancement in both the PDPA and the mujahideen. By contrast, the Durrani leaders were disadvantaged by the outbreak of war. Their regions were more vulnerable to retaliation, their populations more concentrated, and the topography less favorable to guerilla war than was eastern Afghanistan. The power of Durrani leaders had also always been more political than military. In the communist ranks the Durrani were more often to be found with the urbanized Tajiks who formed the Parcham faction than allied with their more rural coethnics in the military ranks of the Khalq faction. The Durrani elite who opposed the PDPA used its established wealth and connections to seek asylum in Europe or North America. Their Ghilzai counterparts sought refuge in Pakistan from where they could still engage in resistance against the regime if they chose.

In time of peace, or at least emerging stability, the situation was reversed. Here the defects that hindered them were either irrelevant or positive advantages. The Durranis had a long-established elite who could negotiate for them. Their leaders were able to make deals that would be accepted by their followers, while Ghilzai leaders could never be sure their followers would back them. Their Durrani elite by its very nature had higher levels of education and sophistication than their Ghilzai counterparts. This gave them an advantage in the world of diplomacy, where dealing with non-Afghans was key to success. Indeed, the bulk of the cabinet officials in the new government were educated Afghans who had been in exile in Western countries, a fact that riled the existing mujahideen commanders who saw them as carpetbaggers. Still, money talks: The Durrani were past masters of winning subsidies from world powers, while the Ghilzai mujahideen leadership had dealt only with Pakistan.[15] In a continuing civil war conflict situation, Karzai would have never emerged at the top. But in a contest where dealing with the outside world took precedence, he had signal advantage over Ghilzai rivals. The latter were not secure enough in their own regions to make a play for national power. Karzai had that security because the Durrani elite stood to back him regionally as a way back to national prominence for the Pashtuns as a whole and the Kandaharis in particular. In this political ecology, assets in time of war became liabilities in times of peace.

SOME THOUGHTS ON THE RESURGENT TALIBAN
AND THEIR WAR OF RELIGION

The current revival of the Taliban represents an usual situation in Afghan history. Resistance against Kabul or foreign occupation has usually had its epicenter in eastern Afghanistan (Ghilzai country) and Kohistan (the plains north of Kabul, including the Panjshir valley). Throughout Afghan history, Kandahar and the south have either come to an accommodation with the powers that be or been a secondary area of resistance. The Afghans expelled the British from Kabul in both Anglo–Afghan Wars, but the British never lost control of Kandahar.

The Taliban were organized as a religious movement, but their followers and leaders are predominantly Pashtun. By 1999 they controlled all of Afghanistan except the Tajik northeast until they were expelled from Afghanistan by the American invasion of 2001. While their emergence was a surprise, their movement's dynamic followed a well-worn path. Scholars have long noted that religious leaders could transcend tribal boundaries and unite people in the name of religion who would not otherwise cooperate. Commenting on the structurally similar Bedouin tribes, ibn Khaldun argued that religion was uniquely suited to bringing rival tribes together because:

> The Bedouins are the least willing of nations to subordinate themselves to each other, as they are rude, proud, ambitious and eager to be leaders. Their individual aspirations rarely coincide. But when there is religion (among them) through prophethood or sainthood, then they have some restraining influence on themselves. The qualities of haughtiness and jealousy leave them. It is then easy for them to subordinate themselves and unite (as a social organization).[16]

The Taliban used the failures of the mujahideen warlords during the Afghan civil war to attract a wide following in the south. Eliminating robber bands around Kandahar beginning in 1994, they went on to incorporate an increasing number of Pashtun groups, mostly by convincing them to join the movement. An advantage of a religious movement for rival Pashtun leaders was that there was no honor or prestige lost in subordinating oneself to the will of God or God's agents. The movement also served to give the Pashtuns the dominant role they expected to play in Afghan politics without having to cede any ground to specific rival clans. The Taliban expansion into Pashtun areas was largely peaceful, with tribal leaders and local mujahideen commanders defecting to their cause in return for retaining their local power under a Taliban administration. When they moved out of Pashtun regions, they relied more on force and came to depend on outside support from Pakistan and international jihadi groups like al-Qaeda. Their restoration of order was welcome, but their severe religious policies and their inability to provide any governmental services alienated them from the population. The tribal

Pashtun elite in the south refused to ally themselves with the Taliban when the Americans moved on Kandahar and Mullah Omar decamped to Pakistan by motorcycle.

After four years of quiet in the south, the Taliban made a concerted effort to show they are still a powerful military force. While this proved that they remained players in Afghan politics who need to be reckoned with, the more likely reason for initiating large-scale conflict was that the Taliban (and their Pakistani backers) saw the changeover to NATO troops in the south as a sign of weakness they could and should exploit. Certainly the types of attacks they made, the size of the groups involved, and the numbers of casualties they took were significantly larger than in the past. It was also apparent that the trouble they caused remained confined to the Pakistan border region. The Taliban and its leaders have always represented an alternative to the traditional Durrani tribal leadership structure and a threat to it. As the jihadi factions in the NWFP have done, they would like to use their access to vast sums of outside money, arms, and their fervent Islamic ideology to displace much of the established tribal leadership.

But in southern Afghanistan this is less easy to do, in part because their tribal opponents now also have access to outside funds and can depend on a powerful international military force to take on the Taliban. Thus, although the Taliban were able to replace the traditional tribal structure in the late 1990s, weakened as it was by the period of civil war anarchy, in the present context they may find it more difficult. Durrani leaders have a much greater capacity to cut deals with the Kabul government and mobilize larger numbers of people than do the eastern Ghilzais if they decide that this is in their interest. Having lost out once to Mullah Omar and company, they are not likely to accommodate the Taliban again if they think they can be defeated. As a Ghilzai, he is at a disadvantage, centering his resistance in Durrani tribal territory, although by stressing its religious basis this conflict is muted. Areas under current Taliban domination have come into existence where the absence of significant Kabul government or international forces to oppose them have given them an almost free ride. And it has been the failure of the Kabul government to provide economic benefits and security that have made the Taliban look like an attractive alternative again, not sympathy for their ideology.

But perhaps a greater problem is that the south has never served a good center for rebellions of any type because it provides a relatively poor base for an insurgency, and its population has historically been inclined to sit on the fence rather than take the lead. Its leadership has always seen politics rather than military prowess as the best long-term strategy. In geographical terms it offers little to sustain an insurgency. The terrain is flat, with little ground cover, and the population is concentrated in villages dependent on irrigated agriculture. Despite former Pakistani President Musharraf's comments that the Taliban is a danger because it has solid Afghan roots, in fact its ideology is more Pakistani than Afghan. Its leadership bases itself in Pakistan and could not wage an insurgency without with the recruits, bases, and safe refuge it finds there. The Taliban succeeded in the past in an environment of anarchy; to the degree that anarchy returns, so do the Taliban.

NOTES

1. A *jezail* was a locally produced Afghan musket. Rudyard Kipling, *The Works of Rudyard Kipling* (Roslyn, NY: Black Readers Service, n.d.).

2. For a biography, see Muhsin Madhi, *Ibn Khaldun's Philosophy of History: A Study in the Philosophic Foundation of the Science of Culture* (Chicago: University of Chicago Press, 1971).

3. For a full translation, see *Ibn Khaldun: The Muqaddimah: An Introduction to History* (3 vol.), trans. Franz Rosenthal (Princeton, NJ: Princeton University Press, 1958). Translations cited here are from the one-volume abridged 1967 edition: Ibn Khaldun, *The Muqaddimah: An Introduction to History* (abridged edition), trans. Franz Rosenthal (Princeton, NJ: Princeton University Press, 1967).

4. Adam Smith, B.I, Ch.1, "Of the Division of Labor," in paragraph I.1.11, *An Inquiry into the Nature and Causes of the Wealth of Nations* (London: W. Strahan and T. Cadell, 1776).

5. Ibn Khaldun, *The Muqaddimah: An Introduction to History* (abridged edition), trans. Franz Rosenthal (Princeton, NJ: Princeton University Press, 1967), 122.

6. Robert Canfield, *Faction and Conversion in a Plural Society* (Ann Arbor: University of Michigan Press, 1973).

7. Fredrik Barth, *Political Leadership among the Swat Pathans* (London: Athlone, 1959).

8. Akbar Ahmed, *Pukhtun Economy and Society* (London: Kegan Paul, 1980), 141–142.

9. Monsturat Elphinstone, *An Account of the Kingdom of Caubul* (Delhi: Manoharlal, 1998 [1815]), 439–440.

10. Charles Lindholm, *Generosity and Jealousy* (New York: Columbia University Press, 1980).

11. Thomas Barfield, "Tribe and State Relations: The Inner Asian perspective," in Philip Khoury and Joseph Kostiner, eds., *Tribes and State Formation in the Middle East* (Berkeley: University of California Press, 1991), 153–185.

12. Fredrik Barth (ed.), "Pathan identity and its maintenance," in *Ethnic Groups and Boundaries* (Boston: Little Brown, 1969), 119–134.

13. Ahmed, 1980.

14. Barth, 1969, 119–134.

15. As one of Kipling's famous poems, "Ballad of the King's Mercy," went, "Abdur Rahman the Durani Chief, of him is the story told, He has opened his mouth to the North and the South, they have stuffed his mouth with gold." See Rudyard Kipling, "The Ballad of the King's Mercy," 1889; retrieved on July 9, 2013, from www.kipling.org.uk/rg_kingsmercy1.htm.

16. Ibn Khaldun, *The Muqaddimah: An Introduction to History*, trans. Franz Rosenthal. (Princeton, NJ: Princeton University Press, 1967), 121–122.

5 RELIGIOUS FIGURES, INSURGENCY, AND JIHAD IN SOUTHERN AFGHANISTAN

Thomas H. Johnson

> *The more we stress Islam as a unit of analysis, the more we face the dangers of abstraction and unwarranted generalization. Islam keeps us mired in debates about normativity, where an emphasis on Muslims allows us to appreciate the dynamic nature of Islam as a lived experience.*[1]
>
> **—Peter Mandaville, *Global Political Islam***

RELIGIOUS AUTHORITIES PLAY A CRITICAL ROLE in the present conflict in Afghanistan.[2] Consider, for example, the fact that virtually all Taliban leaders, from the senior regional leadership down to subcommanders at the district level, are mullahs (religious leaders).[3] Indeed it is reasonable to argue that the present conflict in Afghanistan represents a classic insurgency wrapped in the religious narratives of jihad.[4] Although a broad majority of the foot soldiers in this insurgency might be "accidental guerrillas,"[5] the leaders are for the most part committed Afghan religious figures.[6] Hence, to understand this conflict and its nuances, it is important to attempt to understand the religious figures and phenomena in Afghanistan as well as their societal roles.[7]

The role of religious figures in insurgencies and jihads has been a mainstay of Afghanistan's history. David Edwards argues that Afghan religious personalities are central to the moral authority as well as to the "contradictions" of Afghan society. These contradictions, together with the "artificiality of the Afghan nation-state," reflect critical historical components of the "deep structure" of Afghan conflict.[8] Regimes ranging from Hamid Karzai's to the era of Amanullah Khan (1919–1929) have been existentially threatened by, and have had difficulties in subduing, rural religious conservative insurgencies. This has especially been the case when Afghan state authority has been perceived to challenge or offend traditional Islamic values. The national political dominance in Afghan politics of organized religious groups compared to dynastic monarchical groups, however, is a rather new phenomenon.[9] Historically, the degree of regime success in subduing an Afghan insurgency has largely been a function of the extent to which the regime is viewed as legitimate in the eyes of the population. Critical here is the fact that, since the time of the Achaemenids and the Parthians, history has demonstrated that the legitimacy of Afghan governance is derived from two immutable sources: dynastic sources, usually in the form of monarchies and tribal patriarchies; and religious sources.[10] This problem of legitimacy is especially acute at the local and village level of rural Pashtun society, where dynastic and religious authority has been paramount for over a thousand years.[11]

The objective of this chapter is to briefly address issues of Islam, politics, and the dynamics of religious authority in southern Afghanistan—the traditional spiritual center of the country and a significant focus of Taliban insurgent activity.[12] In doing so, this chapter will examine the following topics: the cultural and religious mores and tropes of Loy Kandahar, the *ulema shura*[13] of southern Afghanistan; the role that the Afghan media plays in legitimizing figures of religious authority and how certain religious figures manipulate this media attention; the Taliban's strategic use of symbols and the media to gain legitimacy; and the Tablighi Jamaat and Sufis in southern Afghanistan. These extremely complex topics will be addressed using anecdotal experience and evidence, interviews conducted in the region over the last few years, and other data gathered, in part, in greater southern Afghanistan.

The fundamental question that this chapter seeks to address is that of Islam's public persona: Who speaks for Islam in Afghanistan? The extent of the historical and cultural tradition of these religious figures' political involvement is then examined, for where there is religious influence there is also bound to be some element of power play. Subsidiary questions look into what the sources of these religious figures' influence are, how these sources are changing, and what the fundamental factors of this influence are—that is, the base societal conditions in southern Afghanistan and how they shape the way religious figures can operate.

Southern Afghanistan is an interesting case study in part because so little has been written on the exact dynamics of the interaction between religion and politics, even for a group as prominent as the Taliban. The area of "greater Kandahar" remains the spiritual and strategic heart of the present conflict, and as such an increased understanding of the religious dimension can help prevent mistakes borne of ignorance and impoverished assumptions. There is no doubt that religious figures have played, are playing, and will continue to play a central role in militant mobilizations in Afghanistan. Understanding such mobilizations from a cultural perspective is ultimately the goal of this chapter.

CULTURAL AND RELIGIOUS INFLUENCES IN SOUTHERN AFGHANISTAN

Nearly all Afghans are Muslim, with Islam serving as a common frame of reference and key cognitive driver for the vast majority of the population. Undoubtedly, Islam is the only characteristic that nearly all Afghans have in common. Yet popular Islamic ideas and beliefs are rooted in a mix of culture, self-interpreted religious views, tribal values, money, influence, and personal connections. Although religion has clearly helped to shape Afghan values systems and codes of behavior for generations, it would nevertheless be wrong to infer that this fact results in unanimity of opinion concerning all things Muslim. Islam is not a monolithic entity in Afghanistan, just as Christianity is not a monolithic entity in the United States or Europe. Afghan Islam encompasses a wide range of opinions—including reformists, foreign-educated progressives, ascetics, radicals, Salafists, Deobandis, Talibs, and conservative judicial scholars, among others. All of these can be progovernment or antigovernment (and sometimes both), West-loving or West-hating; there is no uniformity of opinion. Moreover, it would be a mistake to assume that all southern political, economic, and social behavior is driven merely by religious dynamics. A variety of intervening variables such as the urban–rural divide, geography, culture, *quams* (a communal group, whose sociological basis may vary; it may be a clan—in tribal zones—a village, an ethnic group, an extended family, or a professional group), and affinity groups are also important influences that must be recognized.[14] These intervening variables of influence will be the next topic of assessment and discussion.

Rural Population Distribution

The most important and relevant division within southern Afghan society, the divide between urban and rural populations, is often glossed over by Western analysts. Cleavages between the urban and rural populations of Loy (Greater) Kandahar[15] have long been a driving force of southern politics, social interactions, and conflicts as well as aspects of Islamic practice.

Population statistics dating back to 2004 (the best and most recent data available) demonstrate that only 12 percent of southern Afghans belong to urban communities in Loy Kandahar; rural society makes up 88 percent of

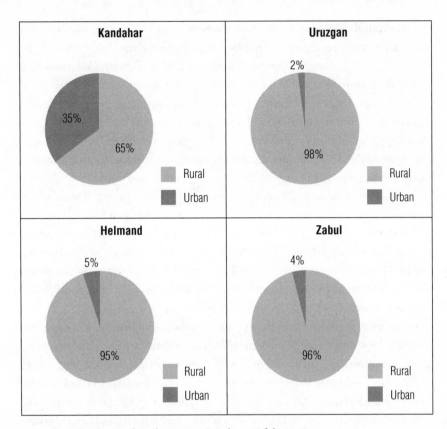

Figure 5.1. Population distribution in Southern Afghanistan.
SOURCE: Afghanistan's Central Statistics Office, 2004.

the population (see Figure 5.1). When you look outside Kandahar Province, the figures become even starker, with only 5 percent, 2 percent, and 4 percent for the residents of Helmand, Uruzgan, and Zabul provinces, respectively, living in urban environments. The south is primarily a rural environ, and this fact is important when we consider the role religious figures play in southern Afghanistan. There is no question that urban and rural Afghanistan have distinct cultures.[16] These cultures in turn play a significant role in determining how a particular person or group of people will behave and respond to certain types of authority figures—be they religious or political or conservative, moderate, or radical.

Attempts to modernize the south (and the never-ending conflict between the traditional and the modern) are central concerns of the area's ideological battleground. Attempts to institute modern political or social agendas have not necessarily been meet with enthusiasm in Loy Kandahar. Consider, for example, how the south responded to the recent "democratic" elections held in Afghanistan. While the vast majority of Afghan provinces had registered voter turnout rates for the 2005 provincial elections of 60 to 70 percent, the provinces of Kandahar, Helmand, Uruzgan, and Zabul had rates of 25.3 percent, 36.8 percent, 23.4 percent, and 20 percent, respectively.[17] Interviews conducted this past summer among village elders and leaders in Kandahari districts suggest that there was little interest in the 2009 presidential election or local provincial and district elections in the south.[18] In fact, it was further posited during these interviews that the Taliban were not overly interested in attempting to disrupt these elections because of the apparent apathy of the Kandaharis toward them.[19] Though the day of what would ultimately turn out to be a blatantly corrupt election did see a spike in insurgent activities, it was not as intense as the Americans or International Security Assistance Force (ISAF) expected.

The village continues to be a pivotal and defining institution of life and culture in southern Afghanistan, and many villagers view Kandahar City with suspicion and disdain. For a society that—at least on one level—is as traditional as Afghanistan, the concern of much of the southern rural population is that Kandahar City is a source of corruption and iniquity. Indeed, the Taliban regularly play on this belief and consider the city as the area where infidels live. Further, the Taliban use this justification to legitimize their attacks in the city.[20]

Geography

The effect of Afghanistan's geography is often underestimated as a factor that influences social behavior. In southern Afghanistan, the distances involved, the high levels of insecurity, and the sometimes difficult terrain between villages have helped give rise to the "one-family-one-mosque" phenomenon, which is discussed in the following pages. In addition, isolated and fairly inaccessible locations are prevalent in the south, helping to create a culture of "traveling mullahs" who satisfy the need for figures of authority—sometimes simply to mediate local disputes. Many of these mullahs also help to solidify the Taliban narrative through preaching and, indeed, encouraging and prompting individuals to join the insurgency against Kabul and the "infidels."

The geography of irrigated lands of southern Afghanistan, especially around Kandahar City, has also played a role in defining certain social norms and influences. As Thomas Barfield has suggested "these rich irrigated lands ... [supported] a hierarchical political system that required large agricultural surpluses to sustain them. It supported an elite of landowners whose tribal followers had in many cases been reduced to their economic clients."[21] This factor has significantly influenced the agrarian economy of southern Afghanistan as well as the development of important land-owner families in the politics and social structure of the region, such as the Durrani Mohammadzais and Popalzais.

Kandahar's typography also influences the security situation in the province. The southern half of Kandahar is dominated by sparsely inhabited deserts and a porous border with Pakistan, accented by the large border crossing at Spin Boldak, where both licit and illicit goods transit through every day. The northern portion of Kandahar consists of wadis (dry riverbeds) and hilly terrain and lacks reliable roadways, making the region ideal for guerilla activity and the use of improvised explosive devices. Furthermore, the rocky, inhospitable terrain of western Uruzgan Province, which borders northern Kandahar, has provided a necessary refuge for the training, resting, and cycling of Taliban foot soldiers into the southern Afghanistan provinces.

PASHTUN SOCIETY AND CULTURE

Pashtun society and culture is the dominant influence in southern Afghanistan, not least because Pashtuns make up the vast majority of the population and because the south has been historically the heartland of Pashtun influence in Afghanistan as a whole. Exact demographic statistics are impossible to come by, and the last accurate census was conducted decades ago, but it is safe to assume that at least 85 percent of the population in southern Afghanistan is ethnically Pashtun.

At the expense of overgeneralizing, Pashtuns tend to be pragmatic individuals who usually come to recognize early in their lives the core importance of their religion and relations with religious authorities.[22] Village mullahs, whose role in rural communities has evolved over the centuries, are complemented by religious figures such as sayyids. The family lineage of sayyeds is traced to the lineage of the Prophet, *qazis*, or religious law experts/shari'at judges—either *mawlawi*, who teach at a higher level in religious schools (madaris) or *pirs*, who teach at Sufi madaris or at collective prayer sites where Sufis congregate.

Depending on a particular situation, people will be more or less tempered by their interactions with and the roles of local religious figures, resulting in one of the reasons that the religious make-up and identity of many southern Pashtuns are so difficult to define. For a traditional religious elder—a mullah or *mawlawi*, for instance—mediation and conflict resolution are essential parts of his mandate and identity, but this role also forms part of the basis of that same identity and authority. Both in Pakistan and in Afghanistan as well as in the border areas, religious elders have played this role since the early nineteenth century. Sana Haroon, for example, explores the little-understood traditional role of the rural mullah as the Pashtun equivalent of the circuit-riding judge in nineteenth century America, serving as an impartial arbiter of disputes between clans (*khels*).[23] Even in a *jirga* (a village council that has legislative and judicial authority for the tribal community), the authority of the elder mullah in convoking religious legitimacy over the proceedings is greater than many appreciate, especially in the form of mediation. The implications of this authority for the present insurgency in Afghanistan are significant, and the Taliban are well aware of this and use it to their advantage.[24] Nevertheless, in deference to the implicit implications of the role of the rural mullah, religious authority extends only as far as the people let it. The idea of near-total subservience to figures of religious authority has little basis in fact in Afghanistan. A good example of this that is little understood in the West is the obscure phenomenon of "one-family-one-mosque" that is especially prominent in southern rural areas.

Loy Kandahari villages will often consist entirely of members of a single extended family (*kahol*) or clan (*khel*). Where different families or groups co-exist in one area, there will often be one mosque for each of the individual families. Though particularly prominent in the south, this has been observed in communities from Khost Province in eastern Afghanistan to Farah Province in the southwest.[25]

Although this phenomenon is also witnessed in the Afghan environs of rich or wealthy landowners who are known to construct mosques to help improve their public standing, one would expect it to be rarer in poverty-stricken rural areas. The one-mosque-one-family concept promotes religious dynamics that are highly personal and relatively immune to rhetoric and manipulation by outside forces, and it is often difficult for mass movements and popular uprisings to significantly penetrate these mosques. For example, a prominent family will be responsible not only for physically building the mosque but also for the selection of the mosque's mullah. During a recent research trip in southern Afghanistan, the author asked a prominent land owner, who had built a new mosque for his family in the village of Deh-e Bagh in the Dand District of Kandahar Province, what would happen if the mullah of the mosque started preaching in a way inconsistent with his family's beliefs or political orientations. The elder responded that "this would never happen because I hired the mullah and I would fire him if such preaching occurred. He works for me and will follow my instructions concerning such matters."

While the one-family-one-mosque concept has a tendency to insulate people from certain aspects of political Islam, the concept of jihad has the opposite effect.[26] Historically, the connection between Islam and jihad has been extremely important for Kandahar, with disenfranchised Afghans responding to the unifying call of jihad as a reaction to perceived corruption, government failure, and outside interference.[27] In fact, jihad has traditionally represented a kind of public sphere of Kandahari Islam, where religious authority figures can command more immediate support and obedience of the public. The call of "Islam under threat" is an extremely powerful incentive for public and communal action and historically has been a consistent motivator and force for Kandaharis to stand behind.

EVERYDAY ISLAMIC TRADITIONS

Islam, of course, is not just about following rules. The core of Islam—as with most religions—is the cultural provision of principles for living a moral life, and the regular daily cycle of prayers can remind the faithful of these values. It is for this reason that Kandaharis will often make reference to the idea of living a more moral life, even if they do not necessarily always follow this policy to its conclusion. A sampling of the key dimensions of southern Afghanistan's Islamic traditions is presented in the following paragraphs.

Namaz

Islam affects the everyday life of a southern Afghan in a variety of ways. The five daily prayers, *namaz*,[28] for the most part, are integrated into the rhythm of the Afghan day. It is not seen as an interruption to stop what one is doing to pray. A corollary example of this is the use of a *patu* (*patkai*) on which to pray. A woolen blanket used during the day (especially during the winter) as a wraparound cloak is taken off and put on the floor, and prayers are made there. The *patu* is a good indication and reflective of the effortless ubiquity of Islam in the daily life of Afghans.

Zakat

Another Islamic concept that demands mention is *zakat* (alms for the poor). Zakat is followed and often employed by the Taliban as a motivating force to encourage villagers to contribute funds or assets to their cause.

Sharia Courts

Yet another extremely important dynamic are sharia (Islamic law) courts that represent a popular alternative to government legal institutions, which have been marred by years of corruption and inefficient legal processes. In numerous areas, especially in the rural southern Pashtun hinterlands, the Taliban are perceived as not only doing a better job of governance—via "shadow" provincial and district governments—and providing justice than Kabul; the Taliban are also seen as more legitimate than the distant and unpopular leadership in Kabul.[29] Throughout southern Afghanistan, the Taliban have established parallel government systems, including provincial and district level administrators, police chiefs, and judges; just how effective or widespread these informal power structures are is difficult to assess.[30] But one element of the Taliban's shadow government that has been particularly popular throughout Loy Kandahar is the alternative judicial system. Today, faced with a choice between a protracted case before an inscrutable system of state justice, in which the individual who can pay the highest bribes to the most people over the longest period of time invariably wins, the Pashtuns are instead turning in droves to the rapid, transparent justice of the mullahs of the Taliban. Justice and, particularly, mediation are indeed a traditional part of the mullahs' role in the community, and the Taliban have masterfully played on this reality.[31]

Madrasah

The institution of the madrasah, too, is an important feature of the day-to-day landscape of southern Afghanistan. The role that madaris have played in the political life of southern Afghanistan has fluctuated over the years and, since the 1980s, permanently changed in character—endowing the religious clergy with political power and influence. This culminated in the "clerical revolution" (with popular backing) of the Taliban in 1994. According to Olivier Roy, the Afghan Taliban is the only contemporary Islamic movement whose basis is a network of rural madaris, effectively tapping the well of rural southern Afghan conservatism and puritanism.[32] The full history of this change is beyond the scope of this chapter, but the profound effect this has had on communities should not be underestimated.

RELIGION AND AUTHORITY IN SOUTHERN AFGHANISTAN

> [We should regard] as political all actors and activities involved
> in the establishment, maintenance or contestation of particular
> visions of public morality ("the good") and of social order.[33]

Both mullahs and formally trained Islamic legal scholars, *alim* (singular of
ulema), are significant and influential religious figures in southern Afghanistan. Although village mullahs have ideally studied Islamic traditions (*hadith*)
and Islamic law (*fiqh*), their actual formal education will vary from basically
none to significant madrasah training. All mullahs, however, will lead mosque
prayer sessions and conduct religious rituals such as birth rites, marriage, and
funeral services at the village level. They are basically "ritual practitioners," in
the words of Olivier Roy.[34]

Mullahs have traditionally served as spiritual advisors to village elders,
jirgas, and *shuras* and, for the most part, have been inconsequential to village
politics. It has also been suggested that mullahs serve as the custodians of the
principals of *Pashtunwali* and "use their religious authority to pass binding
judgments rooted in [*Pashtunwali*] in the area of the tribal jirga."[35] This is an
important social dynamic in southern Pashtun Afghanistan.

Historically the vast majority of mullahs have rarely been militant. A mullah's basic legitimacy customarily has come from his application of sharia and
defense of the Islamic community.[36] The role of the mullah has changed drastically with the rise of the Taliban, however. Though they were once primarily
apolitical, serving the role of a glorified notary public, mullahs are now the
leading political and ideological figures and voices of the Afghan insurgency.
The present role of many mullahs in providing narratives and information to
the village population has become a critical source of their influence and the
subject of the next section of this chapter.

Who controls the flow of information is vitally important in southern Afghanistan, and the control of religious information is intimately influenced by
language and the relative lack of education realized in the southern Pashtun
areas. Most of the population does not understand Arabic. This results in the
Muslim faithful being almost entirely dependent on the local mullah to teach
and interpret the words and lessons of the Koran. In many instances, especially in the rural southern hinterland, the mullah himself has no in-depth
knowledge of Arabic and thus will rely on local traditions and oral narratives
in his religious teachings and lessons. This interpretive duty results in considerable power for the mullahs.

The control of information also has an impact on the role of religious figures as mediators; they are seen as both being impartial and possessing a broader perspective as well as having pertinent legal expertise that allows them to pass judgment on certain issues. For example, consider the institution of the "Friday sermon," a speech to the gathered faithful, which often touches on political issues (remember that there is considerably less distinction between politics and religion when compared with much Western religious thought). In many respects this sermon is an extension of their authority. Mullahs now regularly pass judgment on local political or governmental personalities as well as critique political and social situations.

Mullahs gain some of this authority through the receipt of foreign aid, much in the form of *zakat* (giving of wealth), particularly from Middle Eastern and South Asian sources. Some of this aid, distributed through mosques, is most certainly aimed at strengthening the authority of the religious figures. Mullahs have become a focal point of resource distribution, and as such their authority has been strengthened:

> This religious interpretation of the rebellion was promoted by the *ulema* and the *mullah*s, a group strongly united in their struggle against the communist authorities, who had proclaimed a *jihad* against the regime. Represented everywhere in the country, they constituted an informal but efficient network for the transmission of information, as the rebellion of 1929 had already shown. In instances where the uprising was coordinated, for example in Logar [sic] or in Ghazni, the *ulema* played the leading role. In most insurrections the sermons of the mullahs were crucial: the people often assembled at the mosque before marching on the government command post. In the mosques, the habitual scene for discussion among the villagers, the mullah would use his influence to put forward a religious exegesis of resistance to authority, and his intervention often served to convince the hesitant by removing their doubts as to the illegitimacy of the authorities. . . . With the proclamation of *jihad* by the *ulema* the rebellion took on a universal nature.[37]

The social and political role of mullahs and ulema has been crucial throughout the past forty years of Afghan history. Looking back even further to the past two centuries, and including the Pakistani border areas, a trend of increased influence is evident, legitimized by a wide variety of dynamics. In Kandahar, mullah networks and the ulema council[38] operate side by side as of 2009, but broadly speaking they are ideologically opposed to each other. The legitimacy of both these groups is drawn from a variety of sources, but three factors are worth considering here: tribes, age, and wealth.

Regardless of what members of ulema may say in interviews, the tribe that someone comes from is an important factor in the level of respect for that person—even before graduating from a madrasah.[39] Similarly, age is important only in that it takes time for an *alim* to mature as a figure and gain respect in society. *Shia ulema* tend to be younger, and a younger, more active member of the Shia clergy can advance and make a name for himself—within reason. It is doubtful, however, that Afghanistan, outside of the Hazarajat, will ever be fertile ground for the Shia.[40] Thus, ulema in Afghanistan tend to be older members of society.

Wealth—of paramount importance to the nonreligious or tribal oligarchy—is relatively unimportant for the ulema and mullah network. Popular opinion, as well as a whole host of folklore and proverbs, considers mullahs as de facto poor. The image of the mullah asking for money from the rich man is a common stereotype in Kandahari society. In many respects, however, this is a self-created narrative. In fact, grants of land and financial contributions to the mosques, and the establishment of madaris connected to the mosques, have served to make the mullahs among the wealthiest men in some rural areas in terms of total assets.[41]

In Kandahar, aside from the significant role that the religious clergy took post-1994, there was no ulema council in the form that currently exists. The traditional role of the religious clergy was to assist in religious administrative duties (all the traditional aspects that we commonly associate with the clergy), to serve as part of the Haj and Awqaf ministry, and to serve in the Ministry of Justice. The ulema council in the south (with Kandahar as the focal point) represents a sector of the religious clergy that has remained relatively unradicalized by war. For example, consider Haji Mahmoud (originally from the Khakrez District of Kandahar Province).[42] He is a writer, poet, and member of the ulema council and views his role as being quite simple: encouraging those who wish for a continuation of the conflict to start interacting with society in a more peaceful manner.[43]

Members of the ulema council claim a salary of around $200 each month. Aside from their general duties, one of their main activities seems to be producing a government-funded magazine—*Islami Diwa*—each month. The current head of Kandahar's ulema council is Mawlawi Sayyed Mohammad Hanafi (Alizai by tribe and originally from Helmand Province). He was selected and appointed to that position by Asadullah Khaled, the former governor of Kandahar—a fact that helps illustrate one aspect of the relatively unclear relationship between the Afghan government and the ulema in Kandahar.

The council consists of approximately sixty or seventy clerics from within the city and five or six from every district in the province, leading to a total of 140 or 150 mullahs and *mawlawis* who participate in the council. Some of the clergy in the city occasionally offer advice or counsel to the Afghan government (to the governor, for example), and there is even the possibility of outreach to Kabul via the central ulema council there and its head, Shinwari Saheb (Borhanullah Shinwari, former Afghan attorney general). The council's political "face" also extends as far as appearances in the local media: Members write articles for newspapers and magazines, speak regularly on radio programs, and are quite frequently invited as guests onto local television stations.

Interactions of the Afghan domestic security apparatus—for example, Afghanistan National Development Strategy (ANDS)—with the ulema in Kandahar are clouded in secrecy, and it is difficult to determine the nature of explicit relationships with any degree of certainty. It is relatively clear, though, that government agencies are at the very least attempting to use the ulema as their eyes and ears in the districts. With tens of thousands of agents around the country, the ulema and mullah networks around the province would be a ripe resource for domestic security services, but it is highly likely that there are a significant number of paid informants among the ulema.

Some members of the religious clergy—certain prominent families within the city, for example—use religious legitimacy as a way to enhance their personal status and business interests. This can be purely an issue of status (for example, being called in to advise the governor on a regular basis) or can be financial (that is, receiving more contracts from foreign militaries for construction projects or private and convoy security duties). There is, however, very little contact between NATO/ISAF and the ulema of southern Afghanistan. In some ways, this is regrettable:

> Lack of familiarity, not knowing how to engage, and political sensitivities in donor home countries can partly explain the lack of engagement from the side of the international community. Further, stereotyping of religious leaders and institutions as militant fundamentalists—often equated with the Taliban and radical madrasas—makes it difficult politically to include religious actors and institutions as partners in civil society. Within the Afghan government and the international community, many seem to be have concerns about mak-

ing religious actors more powerful by granting them formal authority and recognition.[44]

Afghan ulema in southern Afghanistan have been targeted by members of the insurgency on a regular basis since 2001. Approximately twenty-four members of the official ulema council have been killed since 2001, along with dozens of mullahs and other religious figures, including Mawlawi Mohammad Rasoul (killed outside the Qadiri Mosque in Kandahar City), Qari Ahmadullah (killed in his home on March 1, 2009), Mawlawi Abdul Qayyum (shot outside the Red Mosque in Kandahar City), and, most well-known, Mawlawi Fayyaz, the first president of the ulema council and son of Mawlawi Darab Akhundzada.[45] Mawlawi Fayyaz famously stripped Mullah Omar of his legendary *Amir ul-Mumineen* (commander of the believers or faithful) status during a public sermon (although it is debatable whether Fayyaz actually had the religious authority to do so) and survived numerous attempts against his life before insurgent gunmen eventually succeeded in murdering him.

Afghan ulema are probably targeted because they offer a legitimate opposition to the radical mobilizations and motivations offered by the Taliban to young madrasah students and the unemployed. This is not to suggest that the insurgency is primarily motivated only by ideology or religion. Many ulema council members are actively and deliberately provocative. They write articles, make pronouncements, and issue statements arguing, for example, that suicide bombing is an illegitimate form of jihad.

It is important to recognize that Afghanistan, and especially southern Afghanistan, is a region where conflict and war have been staples of daily life for over thirty years. This changes a society. Money (and the resultant status it brings) becomes one of the most important assets—people have less opportunity to exercise the luxury of having principles. It is clear that Islam throughout Afghanistan is radicalized and further politicized by conflict.[46] This has resulted in less room for nuance in argumentation or for an intellectually formulated opinion, and this ultimately works against the members of the ulema council. At the same time, conflict also has a tendency to reinforce the need for figures of authority like the mullahs within society.

PROMINENT ISLAMIC GROUPS AND INFLUENCES IN SOUTHERN AFGHANISTAN

Just as the distinctions between the religious and the political[47] are blurred in Pashtun and Afghan culture, so do the spheres and figures of authority frequently shift from the religious to the political (and back again). These dynamics are influenced by the respective experiences and historical roles that these figures played during the 1980s anti-Soviet jihad and the ensuing civil war. Yet it is important to recognize that certain sectors of the population and influence groups prominent in other parts of the country were entirely absent in the major southern Afghan politico-religious debates of the past thirty years. For example, the Afghan Islamists of the 1970s and their ideological discussions at Kabul University[48] (and later in Peshawar during the 1980s)— Burhanuddin Rabbani, Abdul Rasul Sayyaf, Gulbuddin Hekmatyar, and Ahmad Shah Massoud—were not very important or influential for the Talibs of the south.[49] Ultimately, many of these key players and parties of the anti-Soviet jihad had little influence in critical events of the region. It was the polarization of the parties along ethnic, tribal, and geographic lines that would eventually help shape the politics and narratives of the rest of the country.[50]

Deobandism

Deobandism is one of the principal Islamic philosophical influences in southern Afghanistan and a prominent force in Afghan political Islam. In theory, the Deobandi school of Islam shares many of the same beliefs as Sufism;[51] however, the two schools are not in concert on the means of achieving their similar objectives to remove corruption and materialism from Islam. Whereas Sufism was a reaction to conditions under the Umayyad Caliphate—the second of the four Islamic caliphates after the death of Mohammad—Deobandism arose as a reaction to the British colonialism in India. The two key founders of Deobandism were Hazrat Maulana Mohammad Qasim Nanautavi and Hazrat Maulana Rasheed Ahmed Gangohi, who founded the Dar ul-Ulum madrasah in Deoband, India, in the mid-nineteenth century that has shaped resistance tropes in the subcontinent ever since. There are thousands of Deoband madaris in Pakistan and Afghanistan. A paradox between Deobandism and Sufism is that many Deobandis are also members of Sufi brotherhoods.

The teachings of Deobandism focus on strict adherence to Islamic ethical codes and the independence of Muslim lands. Attacks on Muslim lands are considered attacks on Islam and worthy of jihad.[52] According to Deobandism, a Muslim man's first obligation is to his faith and then to his country. Yet Deobandism does not recognize national boundaries per se but rather holds the boundaries of the greater Islamic community (or *ummah*) paramount.

Muslims have an obligation and duty to wage jihad in defense of Muslims anywhere they are threatened.

Deobandism falls under the Hanafi school of Sunni Islam and shares much in common with the teachings of many great Islamic reformers, such as Mawdudi in Pakistan, Sayyed Qutb in Egypt, and Ibn Taymiyyah, who all advocated Islamic statehood following the principles of sharia, though they differed on the means acceptable to bring this about.[53] Deobandism does not focus on mysticism and asceticism in the way that Sufism does but does encourage pious practice and is a major faith throughout South Asia. Rather than representing discrete and opposing religious worldviews, however, it is perhaps more accurate to say that these schools represent different modalities for gaining and engaging religious knowledge: one more scriptural, the other more emotive. Deobandis are comfortable with Sufism as expressed through pious and devotional practices but take issue with the social structure of Sufism as manifested by the *tariqat* (brotherhoods).

The Afghan constitution of 1931 guaranteed the right of the ulema to attend private religious schools, most of which were Deobandi, and until the Soviet invasion in 1979 the majority of the Afghan ulema were educated in these madaris.[54]

Tablighi Jamaat

Faizani probably enjoyed his greatest support among military officers. He used the traditional *zikr* circle as an avenue not just for spiritual enlightenment but also for political organizing. In tapping into the officer corps in this way, Faizani was following a long-standing tradition of Sufi association with the military, a tradition that went back at least to the turn of the last century and that had periodically generated considerable paranoia within the government.[55]

The involvement of religious groups in political activities is probably one of the most misunderstood and yet crucial elements in recent Afghan history. In light of this, it is instructive to briefly examine the activities of groups like the Tablighi Jamaat and Sufis. Secretive by nature, these groups represent large numbers of Afghans, yet they remain less understood (and almost completely undocumented), and their role in Afghan society underappreciated. Part of the explanation for this relates to the urban–rural divide in Afghan society. Most of the members of Sufi societies as well as the Tablighi Jamaat are rural and poor and not members of the urban elite.[56] This is an important reason why these groups are misunderstood by both outsiders and fellow Afghans.

Tablighi Jamaat was founded in the late 1920s by Mawlana Muhammad Ilyas Kandhalawi, himself a prominent member and advocate of the revivalist conservative Deoband tradition. Present members are committed to *dawa* or "the call." Many of their activities are dedicated to persuading and proselytizing others to join them in either conversion or simply just reforming and becoming a "proper Muslim." To pursue this goal, the Tablighi Jamaat has established missionaries throughout the world.[57]

The organization holds meetings throughout Pakistan and Afghanistan and has a proclivity for meeting in large regional centers. Their annual Lahore meeting seems to be the biggest in the two countries, with hundreds of thousands of attendees. At these events, the discussion revolves around religious subjects, with members of the Tablighi Jamaat projecting an avowedly apolitical stance, refusing even to talk about the situation in either Afghanistan or Pakistan. At a meeting in Kabul, however, a colleague witnessed a full lineup of almost every single significant midlevel mujahedeen commander from Nangarhar Province sitting in a circle together and discussing different interpretations of a certain *hadith*.[58] So although politics is apparently absent from the surface of such meetings, there is—in Afghanistan at least—some amount of networking happening at Tablighi Jamaat meetings and events.

The Tablighi Jamaat's explicit relationship with members of the insurgency is distant and seemingly detached, and, despite certain ideological similarities by virtue of their shared idolization of the culture of the village, there are no strong ties with the Taliban. A number of Kandaharis have suggested to the author that they do not like the Tablighi because "many come from Pakistan" or because they are not Kandahari and they project themselves as knowing Islam better than Kandaharis do. In fact, it was suggested that Tablighi were not welcomed in local mosques and had been even asked to leave.[59] Some Western scholars have argued that the Tablighi Jamaat networks are used by al-Qaeda to radicalize vulnerable sectors of society,[60] and U.S., British, Pakistani, and Afghan governments have monitored these networks closely.[61]

Sufis

The role of Sufism (Islamic mysticism, *tasawwuf*) in Afghanistan is similarly misunderstood.[62] The so-called mystical side of Islam, Sufism, focuses on the personal relationship between the believer and God, with the believer seeking to individualize that connection through prayer, training, and discipline (*marifa*). The modalities of the transmission of religious knowledge and the nature of the *piri–muridi* (master–student relationship) tradition in Sufism are little understood but seemingly have important implications for the Afghan insurgency. Mullah-led militant mobilizations connected closely to Pashtun cultural mores and fraternity have a long history on the Afghan–Pakistan frontier. The piri–murdi system represents a basic reformist ideology and a mode of knowledge transmission where a teacher is inherent in the knowledge. Thus, mullahs who learn from the same teacher, or from teachers who had a common master, share the same ideology. This system has served as a kind of social institution and network that past jihadist movements in South Asia, such as the Hindustani fanatics Akhund Ghaffur, Mullah Najmuddin of Hadda, and the Faqir of Ipi, have exploited.[63]

The Sufi mullahs and their *murids* (committed) and Talibs operate a complex and mutually supportive network of insurgent religious authority. Their information operations—carried out through mosque, madrasah, and *langarkhana* (a place where food is prepared and distributed to the poor) via pedagogy[64]—have, as previously suggested, underpinned past insurgencies and jihads and presumably have helped to frame the discourse of the present Taliban jihad and insurgency. An understanding of this process is a vital starting point for any campaign to combat it.

Sufism and the majority of Afghan ulema look at Islam from two different perspectives. The ulema focus primarily on the orderly interpretation of Islamic law and doctrine, whereas the Sufis focus on the love of God through asceticism and ritual practice.[65] This division in the interpretation of Islam through the eyes of the ulema and the Sufis became increasingly important again during the twentieth century, particularly during the formation of the Afghan state and during the anti-Soviet jihad. John Esposito describes the rise of Sufism in this way:

> Reacting with disdain and dismay to the worldly seductions of imperial Islam, they were motivated by a desire to return to what they regarded as the purity and simplicity of the Prophet's time and driven by a deep devotional love of God that culminated in a quest for a direct, personal experience of the presence of God in this life.[66]

Sufism affects rural Muslims in southern Afghanistan in a variety of ways. For example, the prevalence of *ziarat*s (shrines) built over the graves of alleged holy men and women can be found throughout the south, and many venerate them. In the absence of real medicine or doctors, villagers place their faith in a culture of miracles and signs instead—here Sufi mysticism plays a role. A nuanced understanding of the interplay between the religious and the political phenomena in southern Afghanistan should include an appreciation of the importance of these beliefs to the vast majority of people.[67] This also has implications for understanding aspects of the Taliban. A recent article published on the BBC's news with the headline "Can Sufi Islam Counter the Taliban?" described the experiences of visiting a Sufi shrine in Pakistan and talking to various experts and locals about the alleged relationship between the Taliban and Sufism.[68] After the explosion at the tomb of Rahman Baba, the much-loved Pashtu Sufi poet, there were many more articles to this effect.[69] Is Sufism a force, these articles asked, that can stand up against radicalism and so-called Talibanism? In the West, this has been a seductive idea for scholars and think tanks, many of whom are familiar only with the tamer variants of Sufism. The increasing number of attacks targeting Sufi shrines throughout South Asia is of particular concern. Groups operating in the Khyber Agency of the FATA, as well as in the Swat Valley, have repeatedly attacked Sufi shrines and targeted Sufi *pirs* for assassination over the last few years. The shrine of Bahadur Baba, located in hills near Nowshera, east of Peshawar, was rocketed by militants in March 2009—almost exactly one year after militants destroyed the 400-year-old shrine of Abu Saeed Baba, also near Peshawar.[70] The attacks have been attributed to Lashkar-i-Islam, a militant group based in Khyber and led by their charismatic and vehemently anti-Sufi commander, Mangal Bagh. Demonstrations protesting the destruction of Sufi shrines have created widespread distaste for local militant factions such as Lashkar-i-Islam, prompting some Sufi elders such as Pir Samiullah to form tribal militias. Samiullah's militia attacked Pakistani Taliban forces in the Swat Valley last year, killing approximately 100 militants. Samiullah was killed by militants linked to the Taliban in December 2008, who later exhumed and hanged his corpse in Mingora, the provincial capital. The bloody clashes between Samiullah's forces and Mullah Fazlullah's Taliban fighters in the Matta area of Swat have left hundreds dead since December.[71]

The RAND Corporation published a study in 2003 that advocated encouraging "the elements within the Islamic mix that are most compatible with global peace and the international community and that are friendly to democracy and modernity."[72] This study was widely rumored to be the public face of a U.S. intelligence community plan to "engage with Sufis" around the world as a strategy against Islamic radicalism. Such discussions fail to properly assess the realities of Sufism as experienced on the ground in southern Afghanistan and approach the matter as if religious practices in Afghanistan are similar to those in Pakistan. The two most important Sufi orders in Afghanistan— the Qadiri and Naqshbandi—are organized into brotherhoods. Pir Sayyid Ahmad Gailani heads the Qadiri order, which consists primarily of Pashtuns of southern and eastern Afghanistan.[73] The Naqshbandi order of southern and northern Afghanistan is lead by the Mujaddidi family (Sebghatullah Mujaddidi).[74] Additionally, the analysis of Sufism's main ideas and practices in these discussions is derived from a reading of classical texts (mainly poetry), which, while important, fails to give a proper picture of the way Sufism interacts and has created religious networks.

Recognizing the importance of Sufism in Afghanistan, the Taliban have attempted to manipulate certain Sufi customs and traditions. Some Taliban have even sought to identify themselves as part of the Sufi tradition.[75] This is similar to the dynamic that Bernt Glatzer describes of the "southern Pashtun tribesman seeking political leadership beyond his village" through the manipulation of "networks based on locality, economy, sectarianism, Sufi orders, religious schools, political and religious parties and so on."[76]

Pir Sayyid Ahmad Gailani has stated that "a majority of Taliban are Sufis, mostly followers of the Qadiri and Naqshbandi movements."[77] Some analysts have even alleged that Mullah Mohammad Omar, the nominal leader of the movement, is a member and local leader of the Naqshbandi order. Although many experts intensely dispute this contentious claim, Gailani states "Mullah Omar was raised as a Sufi before later embracing the more severe Wahhabi-inspired Islam."[78] Even a brief examination of the Taliban's current propaganda output on its website, *Al-Emarah*, emphasizes that Taliban poetry and songs published in Pashtu rely strongly on the imagery, style, and forms used by the well-known classical Pashtun Sufi poets. Further, the biographies of jihadi "martyrs" posted on the website and in Taliban magazines call to mind the Sufi hagiographic traditions. Similarly, the authority of Mullah Omar's leadership rests in part on his risky but brilliant propaganda move in 1996 of taking the *khirqa* (a garment that Afghans believe to be the Prophet Mohammed's cloak) out of Kandahar's royal mausoleum for the first time in sixty years and displaying it in a public rally as a way to identify himself with the Prophet.[79] Mysticism similar to that practiced by Sufis has long surrounded Mullah Omar. Omar reportedly started the Taliban after a dream in which Allah came to him in the shape of a man, asking him to lead the faithful. The *khirqa*, for example, is believed by many Pashtuns to contain supernatural and mystical powers. This action in part represented Omar's absolute faith in his perceived divine right to rule and gave him legitimacy in his role as leader of the Afghan people ordained by Allah. After Omar showed the cloak of the Prophet Mohammad to those present and received general acceptance by public, he invited the people to accept him as their leader by raising hands.[80] Whereas Omar had been a relative nonentity before this piece of religious theater, the audacious stunt catapulted him to a level of mystical power. Soon afterward, Omar was named Amir ul-Mumineen, or "commander of the faithful"—not just of the Afghans but of all Muslims. He was given this title by almost 1,500 mullahs and religious scholars who were present in Kandahar.

As in Iraq, Sufi groups in Kandahar have allied themselves with the insurgency since 2003. A significant proportion of the rank-and-file members of the Taliban in southern Afghanistan (and increasingly in Pakistan) believe in the local traditions and customs that are identified as Sufi.[81] Analyses of who the Taliban are and what they stand for have yet to convincingly offer an account of the movement's popular appeal and fail to account for apparent Sufi aspects of the movement. It seems clear that the tradition of Sufism, rather than the practice (as associated with dervishes, for example), has been important in shaping the structure of rural resistance to secular authority. The full extent of Sufi contributions, however, to the networks that make up the insurgency in Afghanistan and Pakistan has not been properly explored, and there is not place here for a full discussion. It should be noted, though, that this is an important cultural feature that should not be underestimated.

CONCLUSION

The lack of strategic innovation on the side of the international coalition is striking, and the difficulties in Afghanistan are in large part due to an intellectual failure to understand the country's social and political dynamics.[82]

The international community and, in particular, the U.S. and NATO forces have failed to thoroughly or systematically understand the religious foundations of the Taliban insurgency and jihad. Indeed, a rigorous and methodical examination of the Islamic realities of southern Afghanistan is potentially the most important arrow missing in the foreign forces' quiver. Although this lack of understanding has direct implications for U.S. and NATO kinetic military operations, it is even more important to the information operations. A counterinsurgency is first and foremost an information war. One critical reason why the U.S. and NATO forces are not winning in Afghanistan is because they misunderstand certain components of the information battle space—most importantly those that involve religious dynamics. How can the United States and NATO protect the people of Afghanistan—the central tenet of successful counterinsurgency—if they do not understand the fundamental religious and societal drivers of the Afghan people?

Although this chapter has merely scratched the surface of these extremely complex issues, it leaves no question that Islam and Islamic religious figures continue to play a critical role in the everyday life and politics of southern Afghanistan. Today, Sufism and Deobandism work together with traditional tribal mores in shaping the cognitive structures of southern Afghans. These beliefs, for the most part, influence the populations' social, political, and economic interactions. Both government and Taliban insurgent leadership have attempted to both shape and act in accordance with these normative structures, as well as to develop narratives to achieve the support and acquiescence of the southern, mostly rural Pashtun population. Ultimately, however, the ongoing conditions of the conflict environment that grips Afghanistan will most certainly influence and mix with these beliefs and narratives to alter the fabric of Afghan society and thus will be the final determinant as to the future path of Afghanistan.

NOTES

This essay originally appeared as Thomas H. Johnson, "Religious Figures, Insurgency, and Jihad in Southern Afghanistan," 41–65, in "Who Speaks for Islam? Muslim Grassroots Leaders and Popular Preachers in South Asia," *NBR Special Report*, no. 22, February 2010, Copyright (c) The National Bureau of Asian Research (NBR).

1. Peter Mandaville, *Global Political Islam* (London: Routledge, 2007), 20.

2. Unless otherwise specified, the term *religious figures of authority* extends to include the Taliban as well as other figures who would not necessarily identify themselves as such or who work together with the government.

3. Author's interview with senior State Department and Department of Defense analysts and officials, Washington, DC, March 2009. Traditionally, mullahs have served as village spiritual advisors as well as elementary teachers and are paid by donations from the community, often supplementing their income through farming or a trade. Mullahs vary considerably by educational background from being illiterate to having some madrasah (Islamic school) education. It should be noted, however, that there are many cases where a Taliban commander will adopt (or be given) the title "mullah"—still implicitly suggesting the importance of religious figures in this insurgency/jihad.

4. For a discussion of Taliban narratives, see Thomas H. Johnson, "The Taliban Insurgency and an Analysis of *Shabnamah* (Night Letters)," *Small Wars and Insurgencies* 18, no. 3 (September 2007): 317–344.

5. On "accidental guerrillas," see David Kilcullen, *The Accidental Guerrilla: Fighting Small Wars in the Midst of a Big One* (New York: Oxford University Press, 2009). Kilcullen argues that an accidental guerrilla is an individual motivated to fight due to an encroachment on the local social network or way of life.

6. Some observers argue that the social changes made during the 1980s Soviet–Afghan War are what gave power to religious leaders and village mullahs. See, for example, Thomas H. Johnson and M. Chris Mason, "No Sign until the Burst of Fire: Understanding the Pakistan–Afghanistan Frontier," *International Security* 32, no. 4 (Spring 2008): 70. It is also important to note that millions of Afghan refugees settled in Pakistan during the anti-Soviet jihad and were indoctrinated by Islamist mullahs in these camps. Many of these refugees eventually returned to Afghanistan as committed Islamists.

7. See generally, Olivier Roy, *Islam and Resistance in Afghanistan* (Cambridge, UK: Cambridge University Press, 1990).

8. David Edwards, *Heroes of the Age: Moral Fault Lines on the Afghan Frontier* (Berkeley: University of California Press, 1996), 1–32.

9. William Maley, "Introduction: Interpreting the Taliban," in William Maley, ed., *Fundamentalism Reborn? Afghanistan and the Taliban* (New York: New York University Press, 1998), 8. Until the rise of the Taliban mullahs, overt religious figures never held political power nationally in Afghanistan.

10. On Afghan governance during this period, see Louis Dupree, *Afghanistan*, 2nd ed. (Oxford, UK: Oxford University Press, 1980).

11. See Johnson and Mason, 2009, 4–5, and Dupree, 1980. For an excellent review of political legitimacy in Afghanistan, see Thomas Barfield, "Problems of Establishing Legitimacy in Afghanistan," *Iranian Studies* 37 (2004): 263–269; and Thomas Barfield, *Afghanistan: A Cultural and Political History (Princeton Studies in Muslim Politics)* (Princeton, NJ: Princeton University Press, 2012).

12. It is important to note that the terms *Taliban* and *Talib* are not used here as a blanket term for anyone opposed to the Afghan government but rather as terms referring to religious students educated in madaris (Islamic schools, plural of madrasah).

13. *Ulema* is a collective term for doctors of Islamic sciences and graduates of Islamic studies or private studies with an *alim* (one who possess the quality of *lim* or knowledge of Islamic law, theology, and traditions). A *shura* is a council or consultative body.

14. Roy, 1990, 242.

15. "Loy Kandahar" refers to the geographical area encompassing Uruzgan, Helmand, Kandahar, and Zabul provinces.

16. Roy, 1990, 10–29.

17. Sean M. Maloney, "A Violent Impediment: The Evolution of Insurgent Operations in Kandahar Province 2003–07," *Small Wars & Insurgencies* 19, no. 2 (June 2008): 205.

18. Personal interviews of district and village elders, Kandahar City, May–June 2009.

19. Ibid.

20. Personal interview with a Kandahari citizen, Kandahar City, September 2008. This same interviewee told the story of a friend who was apprehended by Taliban. This friend told his abductors that he was a nurse—not a government employee or official—and served all people. The Taliban replied that they had "permission" and a duty to kill all "Muslim infidels" (but not their women and children) who live in Kandahar City.

21. Thomas J. Barfield, "Weapons of the Not So Weak in Afghanistan: Pashtun Agrarian Structure and Tribal Organizations for Times of War and Peace" (paper presented as part of the Agrarian Studies Colloquium Series entitled "Hinterlands, Frontiers, Cities and States: Transactions and Identities," Yale University, New Haven, CT, February 2007), 3.

22. Ralph H. Magnus and Eden Naby, *Afghanistan: Mullah, Marx, and Mujahid* (Boulder: Westview Press, 2000), 70–97.

23. Sana Haroon, *Frontier of Faith: Islam in the Indo-Afghan Borderland* (London: C. Hurst and Company, 2007).

24. The author is indebted to M. Chris Mason for bringing this interesting point to his attention.

25. Based on the author's discussions with and empirical observations of Conrad Jennings. The author also observed this phenomenon firsthand in villages in Kandahar's Dand District in June 2009.

26. It seems reasonable to assume that "privatizing" mosques significantly dampens the collective Islam, where the mosque serves as the meeting place for social events or for the rallying of its members to combat an injustice or perceived threat. See Roy, 1990, 31.

27. See Barbara D. Metcalf, "'Traditionalist' Islamic Activism: Deoband, Tablighis, and Talibs," Social Science Research Council, 2001, 1–8; available at http://essays.ssrc.org/sept11/essays/metcalf.htm.

28. The prayers take place at dawn (*fajr*), at noon (*dhuhr*), in the afternoon (*asr*), at sunset (*maghrib*), and at nightfall (*ishaa*).

29. This was a common theme among the sixty or so village elders, tribal leaders, and even some Afghan government leaders interviewed by the author in various locations in Afghanistan, in August and September, 2008, and May and June, 2009. It is important to note, however, that the desire of locals for Taliban court systems is due to the corruption and inefficiency of the government's system. In rural communities,

most of the legal matters relating to land and crime would never have been legislated by the government (even in the 1970s), and, as such, that people go to the Taliban courts is not so surprising. For a discussion of the Taliban court systems, see NPR (National Public Radio) Special Series, "Afghanistan: In Search of Justice," National Public Radio website, December 12–17, 2008; available at www.npr.org/series/98121740/afghanistan-in-search-of-justice.

30. CBS News, "Taliban Shadow Gov't Pervades Afghanistan," December 27, 2008; available at www.cbsnews.com/stories/2008/12/27/world/main4687823_page2.shtml.

31. For an important scholarly statement and analysis of the impact of culture on Afghan law, see Thomas Barfield, "Culture and Custom in Nation-Building: Law in Afghanistan," *Maine Law Review* 60, no. 2 (2008): 358–373.

32. Olivier Roy, "Has Islamism a Future in Afghanistan?" in William Maley, ed., *Fundamentalism Reborn? Afghanistan and the Taliban.* (New York: New York University Press, 1998), 204.

33. Mandaville, 2007, 6.

34. Olivier Roy, *The Failure of Political Islam* (Cambridge, MA: Harvard University Press, 1994), 28.

35. Haroon, 2007, 68.

36. Roy, 1994, 3, 29.

37. Gilles Dorronsoro, *Revolution Unending: Afghanistan, 1979 to the Present* (New York: Columbia University Press, 2005), 106–107.

38. See the text of the Ulema Shura Declaration, Kabul, March 19, 2009 in Thomas H. Johnson, "Religious Figures, Insurgency, and Jihad in Southern Afghanistan," 65, in "Who Speaks for Islam? Muslim Grassroots Leaders and Popular Preachers in South Asia," *NBR Special Report*, no. 22, February 2010. One of the author's interviewees suggested that a number of the members in the ulema council were only elders. Author's interview, Kandahar City, September 2008.

39. Based on numerous personal interviews, Kandahar City, August and September 2008.

40. This is not to suggest that Shia do not exist in the south. There are pockets of Shia Pashtuns in the Loy Kandahar, but their societal and political importance is slight.

41. I am indebted to M. Chris Mason for this point.

42. Haji Mahmoud served as an MP in Kabul during the reign of Zahir Shah.

43. Interview of Haji Mahmoud from a series of interviews of Kandahris by Conrad Jennings, 2006–2009.

44. Mirwais Wardak, Idrees Zaman, and Kanishka Nawabi, "The Role and Functions of Religious Civil Society in Afghanistan: Case Studies from Sayedabad and Kun-

duz," *Cooperation for Peace and Unity*, July 2007; available at www.cmi.no/pdf/?file=/afghanistan/doc/Kunduz%20and%20Sayedabad%20Report%20-%20Final.pdf, 8.

45. Bashir Ahmad Nadem, "Religious Scholar Shot Dead in Kandahar," *Pajhwok Afghan News*, January 6, 2009, available at www.pajhwok.com/viewstory.asp?lng=eng&id=67799; Bashir Ahmad Nazim, "Religious Scholar, Four Guards Killed in Kandahar," *Pajhwok Afghan News*, March 1, 2009, available at www.pajhwok.com/viewstory.asp?lng=eng&id=70485; and A. Jamali, "Taliban Forces Are Now Attacking Sunni Leaders in Afghanistan," Jamestown Foundation, *Eurasia Daily Monitor*, June 2, 2005; available at www.jamestown.org/single/?no_cache=1&tx_ttnews%5Btt_news%5D=30481.

46. For general information about the influence of conflict on Islam in Afghanistan, see Roy, 1990.

47. For more on this distinction, see Dale F. Eickelman and James Piscatori, *Muslim Politics* (Princeton, NJ: Princeton University Press, 1996).

48. Much of this movement owed its organization and ideology to the influence of Egypt's Muslim Brotherhood (Al-Ikhwan Al-Muslimin) and had as its chief ideologues Ghulam Muhammad Niazi, Rabbani, Sayyid Musa Tawana, and others who studied at al-Azhar University in Cairo and later taught on the faculty of theology at Kabul University.

49. Other anti-Soviet jihadi Peshawar party political leaders such as Yunus Khalis and Mohammad Nabi Mohammdi had considerable influence over the Taliban in the south, particularly in Kandahar, during this time period. Many of the Taliban core from Kandahar fought under the command of Nabi Mohammdi's local factions, including Mullah Omar. Khalis even helped radical elements in the eastern Afghanistan rise to power, including Jalaluddin Haqqani, who single-handedly destroyed the Zadran's *malik* system after he ran Mohammad Omar Babrakzai out of Paktia, the most powerful Zadran *malik* during the 1980s. Mohammadi's faction helped spread the rise of madaris in southern Afghanistan and attracted many Talibs from Kandahar such as Mullah Omar.

50. For more on the polarization, see Roy, 1998, 206.

51. "The Deoband School drew heavily on the Sufi tradition of Afghanistan and was highly orthodox in its interpretation of Islam." Peter Marsden, *Taliban: War, Religion, and the New Order in Afghanistan* (London: Zed Books, 1998), 79.

52. Dorronsoro, 2005, 50–51.

53. Ibid., 51.

54. Ibid., 50.

55. David B. Edwards, *Before Taliban: Genealogies of the Afghan Jihad* (Berkeley: University of California Press, 2002), 230.

56. Much of the Afghan urban elite identify with the more ideologically purist Hizb-e Islami.

57. For an introduction to the Tablighi Jamaat and some of the suspicion this group has generated in the West, see Susan Sachs, "A Muslim Missionary Group Draws New Scrutiny in U.S.," *The New York Times*, July 14, 2003; available at www .nytimes.com/2003/07/14/national/14ISLA.html?pagewanted=1.

58. Observation of Conrad Jennings, summer 2007.

59. Personal interviews, Kandahar City, August 2008.

60. John Walker Lindh of "American Taliban" fame was allegedly indoctrinated by Tablighi Jammat before joining the Afghan Taliban. The UK cricket team coach murdered by assassins is thought to have been killed by Tablighi Jamaat operatives.

61. Paul Lewis, "Inside the Islamic Group Accused by MI5 and FBI," *Guardian*, August 19, 2006; available at www.guardian.co.uk/uk/2006/aug/19/religion.terrorism.

62. For overviews of Sufi history and philosophy, see Julian Baldick, *Mystical Islam: An Introduction to Sufism* (New York: New York University Press, 1989); Annnemarie Schimmel, *Mystical Dimensions of Islam* (Chapel Hill: University of North Carolina Press, 1975); and J. Spencer Trimingham, *The Sufi Orders of Islam* (Oxford, UK: Clarendon Press, 1971).

63. For more history on this topic, see Haroon, 2007, 33–64.

64. *Tariaq* is the Sufi method of instruction.

65. For general information on this distinction, see Haroon, 2007.

66. William L. Cleveland, *A History of the Modern Middle East*, 3rd ed. (Boulder, CO: Westview Press, 2004), 101.

67. Many rural Pashtuns, particularly in the Katawaz, are very superstitious. The Islam of swaths of rural Afghanistan has more in common with mysticism than is commonly supposed. The role of djinns, for example, is akin to that of evil spirits. This aspect of Sufism—the fear of rural peasants of the frightening mystical powers of the Sufis—is much more powerful than the adherence to Sufi beliefs, which is negligible.

68. Barbara Plett, "Can Sufi Islam Counter the Taleban?" BBC News, February 24, 2009; available at http://news.bbc.co.uk/2/hi/south_asia/7896943.stm.

69. Ghulam Dastageer, "Militants Blow Up Rehman Baba's Shrine," *International News*, March 26, 2009; available at http://thenews.jang.com.pk/top_story_detail.asp? Id=20760.

70. Tom Hussain, "Pakistani Taliban Target Sufi Shrines," *National*, March 10, 2009; available at www.thenational.ae/apps/pbcs.dll/article?AID=/20090310/ FOREIGN/157439541/1002.

71. The author would like to thank Matthew Dupee for contributing to this analysis.

72. Cheryl Benard, *Civil Democratic Islam: Partners, Resources, and Strategies* (Santa Monica, CA: RAND Corporation, 2003).

73. Gailani ancestor Abd al-Qadir al-Jilani founded the Qadiri order.

74. The Naqshbandi order formed the base of the Jebhe-yi Nejat party at the time of the Soviet invasion. The Qadiri brotherhood formed the base of the Mahaz-i Melli party. The Naqasbandi order originated in Bukhara during the fourteenth century.

75. Interviews by Conrad Jennings in Kandahar City in 2007–2008, however, suggested that the Taliban banned some Sufi activities in Kandahar during their rule (1996–2001). These interviewees suggested that the Taliban opposed Sufi groups. They argued that there was a huge contradiction between Taliban and the Sufis and that they did not like each other. These interviewees also mentioned that the Taliban did not respect the Sufi shrines and mistrusted the *pirs* as well.

76. Bernt Glatzer, "Is Afghanistan on the Brink of Ethnic and Tribal Disintegration?" in William Maley, ed., *Fundamentalism Reborn? Afghanistan and the Taliban* (New York: New York University Press, 1998), 177–178.

77. Farangis Najibullah, "Can Sufis Bring Peace to Afghanistan?" Radio Free Europe/Radio Liberty, March 5, 2009; available at www.rferl.org/content/Can_Sufis_Bring_Peace_to_Afghanistan/1503303.html. This article goes on to state that "one prominent Taliban figure, Abdul Hakim Mujahed . . . says that the Taliban 'consist of people from various backgrounds,' and that while some 'oppose' Sufis, others have 'great respect' for them and are even followers."

78. Ibid.

79. The cloak had been folded and padlocked in a series of chests in a crypt in the royal mausoleum at Kandahar; "Myth had it that the padlocks to the crypt could be opened only when touched by a true *Amir ul-Mumineen*, a king of the Muslims." Joseph A. Raelin, "The Myth of Charismatic Leaders," BNET, March 2003; available at www.findarticles.com/p/articles/mi_moMNT/is_3_57/ai_98901483. For a discussion of this incident, see Ahmed Rashid, *Taliban: Militant Islam, Oil, and Fundamentalism in Central Asia* (New Haven, CT: Yale University Press, 2001), 20.

80. Author's interview of an eyewitness to Mullah Omar's donning of the *khirqa*, Kandahar City, September 2008.

81. Based on numerous interviews of Kandahris by Conrad Jennings, 2006–2009.

82. Giles Dorronsoro, "Running Out of Time: Arguments for a New Strategy in Afghanistan," Centre for International Policy Studies (CIPS), University of Ottawa, CIPS Working Paper, no. 3, July 2009.

6 THE DURAND LINE

Tribal Politics and Pakistan–Afghanistan Relations

Feroz Hassan Khan

> *There is no desire on our part to interfere with their (tribesmen)*
> *freedom. We shall be happy to meet them and enter into such*
> *arrangements with them, as would be in the mutual interests of*
> *both, and Muslims generally.*[1]
>
> **—Muhammad Ali Jinnah, founder of Pakistan**

"FRONTIERS," SAYS LORD CURZON, "are indeed the razor's edge on which hang suspended the modern issues of war and peace, of life and death to nations."[2] Nowhere else is Lord Curzon's prediction truer than in the case of the borderlands dispute between Pakistan and Afghanistan. The historical and cultural dimensions that bind Pakistani relations with Afghanistan are critical to the stability of the South Asian region. As seen many times before in history, Afghanistan and its frontiers are central to conflicting spheres of interests, with a major impact on the geostrategic environment of the region and beyond.

Afghanistan is important to Pakistan for several reasons, and among them are geographical contiguity; social, cultural, religious, and ethnic links; and mutual strategic interests. But commonalties and shared interests have never translated into a harmonious relationship. For the greater part of Pakistan's history, relations with Afghanistan have been tricky, characterized by mutual suspicions, accusations of policies of interference, and even attempts to destabilize one another.

The tribal areas of Pakistan have a unique cultural heritage. Among a people known to be brave, hardy, and deeply religious, tribal culture and customs have proven to be strongly resistant to change as its peoples are often wary of outside influence. Sociopolitical, religious, and cultural cleavages in a geographically sensitive area have made the tribes pay a heavy price, particularly compounded by the fallout of anarchy, wars, and instability in Afghanistan. Located at the confluence of great mountains and having a turbulent history, the broader region was once referred to as the "cockpit of Asia," standing at the "crossroads of global and regional politics."[3] Tribal politics and the involvement of various players—a hostile India and an often unfriendly Afghanistan and Iran—have impinged on Pakistan's internal security environment. Pakistan's participation in the Global War against Terrorism (GWOT) has also provided a favorable ground for foreign agencies and domestic sympathizers to make ingress in these turbulent areas bringing it into sharp international focus.

Afghanistan is undergoing substantial violent conflicts and insurgencies and thus facing immense security challenges. Even the militarily strong international community has been unable to extend its security umbrella beyond Kabul, which in turn has perpetuated and deepened the political and economic power of regional commanders. NATO lacks adequate troops to defeat the resurgent Taliban and to deploy additional provincial reconstruction teams (PRTs); the new Afghan National Army (ANA) does not have the ability to extend the writ of the central government across the whole of Afghanistan. This weak security structure has led to an increase in cross Pakistan–Afghan border movement, nonrepatriation of Afghan refugees from Pakistan, and resurgent drug trafficking, cumulatively creating a negative impact on internal dynamics of Pakistan.

This chapter is divided in six sections. The first section will explain the significance of the issue of Durand Line within the context of Pakistan's national security. The second will explain the sensitivity of the tribes manifested in the Pashtunistan issue; the third section will explain the complexities of cross-border movements in tribes; the fourth section will analyze the role of major regional players in the milieu; the fifth section explains Pakistani strategy to deal with the issue, especially in the past five years. Finally, the conclusion gives some recommendations for the future of the region.

THE BORDER ISSUE AND THE TREATY QUESTION

The Durand Line marks the western border between Pakistan and Afghanistan. The border was delineated in 1893 in an agreement between British India and the amir of Afghanistan as a consequence of a series of crises, two major wars, and geopolitical great-power politics in the nineteenth century between czarist Russia and Great Britain. Named after Sir Mortimer Durand, it "is a 2,450 kilometer (1,519 mile) border between Afghanistan and Pakistan; from the spur of the Sarikol range in the north to the Iranian border to the southwest."[4] The border remains contentious, especially for the divided Pashtuns, who consider this simply a line drawn on water. After the British left the Indian subcontinent in 1947, dividing it into India and Pakistan, the new state of Pakistan inherited the problem. Afghanistan refused to accept Pakistan as legitimate, cast the sole vote against Pakistan's membership in the United Nations, and laid claim to the Pashtun territory in Pakistan—thus marking an unhealthy beginning between the two countries. The legitimacy of the Durand Line and Pashtun nationalism are two major issues of controversy in Pakistani–Afghan relations.[5]

Both countries have accused each other of wrongdoings: "Modern inquiries into this vexing controversy are often mystified by the differing nature of Afghan claims."[6] Kabul's complaints against Pakistan range from supporting the right of self-determination for the Pashtuns to claiming Pashtun (and Baluch) territory under control of Pakistan; challenging the validity of the boundary agreement or conversely questioning the legitimacy of Pakistan as successor state; accusing Pakistan of enforcing an economic blockade and conducting forward policy and using Afghanistan as strategic depth; and continued cross-border support of the Taliban to destabilize Afghanistan. Pakistan's position in the dispute is a good deal clearer. Pakistan had accused Afghanistan of being heady and obstinate in making irredentist claims over a long-settled border and insists that the international boundary with Afghanistan is historically and legally settled. It exercises exclusive jurisdiction over the Pashtuns residing on its side, who are politically and economically integrated into the country. Pakistan also alleges that Afghanistan connives with hostile powers (India and the Soviet Union), allows the Afghan territory to be used for covert activities in Pakistan (including sabotage, terrorism, and violent mob attacks on the Pakistani Embassy), and in inciting Pashtun and Baluch subnationalism in Pakistan, leading to periodic crises such as in 1948, 1949, 1955, 1961, and 1973.[7] Pakistan denies using trade blocs to cause harm, doing so only when Afghanistan acted with hostility. After the Soviet occupation and events since then, the border issue was revived only around the summer of 2003. The Pakistanis were quick to note that this happened no sooner than a semblance of stability and governance returned to Afghanistan. History is turning full circle.

Afghanistan has made four major arguments regarding the border issue at various times. First, the Afghans argue that they never truly accepted the border treaty with the British, and, if they did, it was under duress. Afghanistan believes that it has a right to repudiate the treaty. Second, Afghanistan never believed that the 1893 agreement was an international border but was a line demarcating British and Afghanistan "zones of influence." Third, Afghanistan did not accept Pakistan as a successor state to British India. Lastly, the Anglo–Afghan Boundary Treaty of 1893 was stipulated for 100 years and has lost its validity and shelf life after November 1993. Each of the preceding arguments has been debated and analyzed several times over the past century and examined from all legal, political, and security perspectives.

The argument that the treaty was signed under duress—as Afghanistan and Britain were unequal—hence stands invalid and is highly debatable from historical records. A treaty is analogous to a contract between two parties and, if proved to have been made under coercion or duress, stands invalidated. To prove this, it is important to establish that the conditions of negotiations were such that there was no free will on the part of the amir of Afghanistan. A judgment to this effect must also distinguish among compulsions, pressure, and duress.[8] It is true that, in the geopolitical great game of the nineteenth century, the Afghans were used as pawns, and the nation suffered under British forward policy and trade embargoes. If these broader conditions are taken into account, it lends credence to the Afghan claim of existence of coercive environment. But closer examination of history reveals that Amir Abdul Rahman had an interest in the agreement. His objective of consolidating the Afghan nation required peace and a "defined line beyond which the British would not push was therefore of great advantage to Afghanistan at this particular period."[9] Also, the treaty was arranged at the request of Amir Abdul Rahman and negotiated for one month. The Afghan negotiating team comprised of elites from the government, including tribal chiefs, army generals, experts, and eminent religious leaders. Further, British India had already suffered defeat of sorts in the two Afghan wars. The agreement of 1893 was not between a conquering or occupying force and a defeated power. International law does not allow a state to denounce a treaty merely because one of the parties to the given treaty happened to be a colonial or more powerful state. Should that argument be accepted, nearly all boundaries of contemporary nation-states would be put to question.

The second argument was about the interpretation of whether it was truly a boundary treaty or instead one creating zones of influence. This brings into question the interpretation of the treaty and language issues. Several sessions of the treaty were held in the Persian language between the amir and Durand in private, as the amir did not know English, although Durand was a Persian scholar. Afghans claim that the amir in his mind had signed off, demarcating a "frontier" as opposed to a border. They also claim that the British had subsequently allowed Afghanistan to exercise influence over Pashtun tribes on both sides of the divide. The British government at Whitehall, London, was conditioned to European boundaries in a strict sense. The nuance of interpretation between "frontier" and "border" was complicated due to the existence of the tribes, which "the British government did not want to incorporate into their administrative system. [However] in the international aspect this was of no account, for the Amir had renounced sovereignty beyond this line."[10] The treaty has been reaffirmed several times with the British: ratifications in the Anglo-Afghan treaty of 1905 with Amir Habibullah, the Rawalpindi Treaty of 1919, and the Anglo-Afghan Treaty of 1921 (King Amanullah). All three documents contain language that appears that Afghanistan agreed "to ratify or at least accept the 1893 Durand Line Agreement."[11] After the British left, the Afghan government unilaterally denounced the treaty in the Afghan Parliament in 1949 on the basis of *rebus sic stantibus* or change of circumstances. International law, however, does not allow denunciation or withdrawal from a treaty that establishes a border.[12]

The third argument proffered by the Afghanistan is to challenge the succession of state. First, a legal basis of succession of the state was made to renounce the treaty. Afghanistan did not vote for Pakistan's membership in the United Nations, a move that caused Pakistan to suspect India's involvement. In the first place, India had not wanted a partition, and anything that undermines the idea of Pakistan strengthens India opposition of the two-nation theory. India abets the Afghanistan government's claim of Pashtun territory and has stoked Pashtun nationalism (covered later in this chapter) not for the love of the Pashtuns but for the animosity of the idea of Pakistan. Afghanistan "in consultation with India, argued the successor state to British India, can terminate it (Durand Line Agreement)."[13] This matter was settled when Noel Baker, Secretary of State for the Commonwealth, stated in his speech to the British House of Commons on June 30, 1950, that

> His Majesty's Government in the United Kingdom have seen with regret the disagreements between the Governments of Pakistan and Afghanistan about the status of the territories on the North West Frontier. It is His Majesty's Government view that Pakistan is in international law the inheritor of the rights and duties of the old Government of India and of his Majesty's Government

in the United Kingdom in these territories and that the Durand Line is the international frontier.[14]

A few years later a communiqué issued on March 8, 1956, at the conclusion of the SEATO Ministerial Council Meeting held at Karachi, reaffirmed the recognition of the Durand Line as the internationally recognized boundary.[15] Finally, the United States accepted the Durand Line as international boundary and declared Pashtunistan campaign as a "farcical stunt on the part of the Royal Family of Afghanistan to promote its own interests."[16]

The fourth argument is that the 1893 Agreement was no longer in force after a lapse of 100 years. Again, Indian and Afghan media have been in the forefront on propagating this argument. But there exists no such clause in the text of the treaty (Annex A), and in any subsequent revalidation by successive Afghan rulers this fact has never been mentioned. And if the validity were to expire in 1993, what was the logic behind Kabul government's rejection of the treaty in June 1947?[17] In general, Afghanistan has tried to challenge the *locus standi* of Pakistan. According to international law, a treaty between two countries does not require any revision unless both parties desire change. International agreement can be revoked only bilaterally and not unilaterally. Unless provided in the treaty, its duration becomes permanent for all times to come. Moreover, the same Afghan Amir Abdul Rahman signed similar boundary agreements with the imperialist Russia and Iran in the same period. Though the amir objected to them on the basis that neither the Afghans nor the Persians were consulted, yet those agreements hold good today with successor states Tajikistan, Uzbekistan, and Turkmenistan, and so on.[18]

THE PASHTUNISTAN ISSUE

> You want to know whether I am first a Pashtun, a Muslim, or a Pakistani. I am a six thousand year old Pashtun, a thousand year old Muslim and 27 year old Pakistani. Therefore, I will always be a Pashtun first.[19]
>
> **Khan Abdul Wali Khan (1975)**

On August 31, 2003, a section of people in Afghanistan celebrated Pashtunistan Day. The Pashtuns scraped old wounds, recalled the historic injustices, and distributed maps showing Pashtunistan boundaries up to the Indus River in Pakistan. This issue had been nearly trashed into dustbin of history since the departure of Sardar Dawood, who was obsessed with this issue. Pakistani intelligence analysts soon found the clues leading to the central governments of Kabul and to some recently opened consulates in Afghanistan.

By this time the Pakistani military operations in support of Operation Enduring Freedom were well underway. It had been nearly two years then that inroads into hitherto no-go areas in the rowdy tribal areas had been made by the Pakistan military. It was apparent that Pakistan was taking advantage of the environment and attempting to integrate the tribal areas into the settled area of Pakistan. Now, a decade later, Pakistan has apparently shifted strategy from military coercion as a means to enforce integration to a policy of restoring tribal autonomy to the tribal leaders and revamping the political agent system, while keeping the military in the background.

Pashtun nationalism has long historical evidence of its depth and width. Long before the British had arrived, the Pashtuns defended their identity against the oppression of the Mughals. Later, like the Baluchis, the Pashtuns felt cheated by the British of their birthright; the British had annexed their territories between Indus and Khyber and added insult to injury by dividing them across the Durand Line. The divide resulted into dilution of Pashtun majority in Afghanistan and made them a minority under the Punjabi-dominated Pakistan. Of all tribal groups in Iran or Afghanistan, the Pashtuns have had perhaps the most pervasive and explicit segmentary lineage ideology on classic pattern, expressed not only in written genealogies but in territorial distribution.[20]

The Pashtun nationalist movement began as anti-British sentiment in the 1920s and 1930s, originating under Khan Abdul Ghaffar Khan's "Red Shirts." The idea of "Pashtunistan" emerged as it became clear that the British were to leave India and divide it into India and Pakistan. The partition plan gave only two choices, to join either India or Pakistan. Ghaffar Khan, allied to the Indian National Congress, opposed Jinnah's Muslim League. On June 3, 1947, the British plan was announced, calling for a referendum in the Northwest Frontier Province. To counter this, Ghaffar Khan gave a declaration known as the Bannu Declaration on June 22, 1947, in which he demanded that the Pashtuns be given the choice to have an "independent Pashtunistan." The British referendum in the province was boycotted by the Red Shirts and rejected by the Afghans; instead, the question of the right of self-determination of the Pashtuns was raised. The cry for autonomy, from a close ally to the Indian National Congress, juxtaposed with the Afghanistan's renunciation of the

Durand Treaty in 1949, made early fissures in Pakistan–Afghanistan relations and raised doubts in Pakistan about machinations by India.

The vexing issues with the tribes in the borderlands made the British devise a two-pronged strategy: a forward policy of pushing the forces into areas, building forward cantonments, and using force with a policy of "masterly inactivity," which involved moving forces to settled areas in the plains and avoiding mountains, a haven for guerilla warfare, which the Pashtuns had mastered over the centuries. British gave autonomy, and, as Pashtun tribal law held sway, it used subsidies and administrative levers to punish erring tribes under the Frontier Crimes Regulations (FCR). The underlying motivations of the nationalism movement were fueled further when Pakistan decided to convert West Pakistan into one unit to be at par with the majority Bengalis in East Pakistan, where they were always the majority. The Pashtuns and Afghanistan resisted this merging of their brethren east of Durand Line with the utmost nationalistic fervor.

Pakistani Pashtuns, however, were gradually integrated into the national system in all spheres of life, rising to become presidents, military leaders, and top bureaucrats; they developed political and economic stakes in the system. Yet the Pashtun tribes have preserved their norms and customs jealously. Afghanistan's position over the question of Pashtun nationalism has often been contradictory. For Afghan to become a strong state, incorporation of tribal cleavages has made integration even more difficult. But Afghanistan's position has been contradictory and ambiguous. Officially the Afghan government consistently says that they do not seek to incorporate or absorb the transborder tribes; all they seek is recognition that Pashtuns in Pakistan are entitled to be a separate entity, with a right to self-determination and autonomy if they choose, and that Afghans cannot repudiate their own brothers, leading to ambiguity about official policy and chauvinistic claims of Pashtuns zealots.[21] So what makes Afghanistan insist on keeping the Pashtunistan and Durand line issue alive? Three reasons can be discerned. First is the belief, like many in India, that Pakistan is not a viable state and that internal forces or wars with India will lead it to collapse. Second is the grandiose memory of past Afghan glory that had ruled Peshawar, Punjab, and Kashmir. This was especially true during the leadership of Sardar Dawood (as prime minister from 1953 to 1963 and later as president from 1973 to 1978), who was a descendent of Amir Dost Muhammad (Peshawar Sardars). Thirdly, major support of Pashtun segments sustains power in Kabul. Even if the demands are not pragmatic and have made Afghans pay a heavy price, this has remained a domestic compulsion. For all of these three reasons, Afghanistan wants to retain its historical claims across the Durand Line.[22]

Pakistan is of course concerned and will not countenance any notion of self-identity beyond what is acceptable to all ethnic groups in the nation, underplaying the notion of separateness, preserving the delicate ethnic balance in its body politic, and preventing centrifugal tendencies. Pakistan's insistence on keeping Afghanistan out of its affairs has in turn reinforced Pashtun nationalists in Afghanistan who appease Pakistani tribes and Pashtuns even more. Such complexities have made it impossible for Pakistan to concede to a simple Pashtun demand of renaming the North West Frontier Province (NWFP) into "Pashtunistan."

THE COMPLEXITIES OF CROSS-BORDER MOVEMENTS

This section will discuss the complications arising out of the cross-border movements of tribes astride the Durand Line; the impact of refugees and drugs; and finally the role of external actors in the milieu. Each of them has compounded Pakistan national security and imposed constraints on Pakistan.

A year after the agreement, Sir Mortimer Durand was transferred to another assignment, breaking the momentum, and the border remained undemarcated, ill defined, and highly porous. The "Durand Line" was spread over a difficult mountainous stretch (2,430 kilometers) and was never fully staffed, neither by the British nor by Pakistan and Afghanistan. Border tribes have traditionally enjoyed rights of free movement. In the past three decades this became a source of trouble on several counts. Infiltration from tribal areas to fight wars in Afghanistan became part of life for jihad against the Soviets; the influx of refugees and transit trade into Afghanistan got intertwined with smuggling and Afghan jihad. Since then it had become difficult to tell genuine refugees apart from militants and smuggling from genuine trade and drug traffickers.

There never existed any proper uniform system of checking the cross-border movement. Officially there were two designated exit/entry points, that is, at Torkham (NWFP) and Chaman (Baluchistan). Over time, smaller checkpoints have developed. Today there are fourteen custom check posts (at the border) and 334 crossing points (categorized as frequent and unfrequented routes). Though no formal survey exists of those frequented/unfrequented routes, an estimated 6,000 and 15,000 people cross daily from Torkham and Chaman, respectively. The broad categories of these crossers include businesspeople, tribesmembers, carriers involved in smuggling, NGOs and international agencies personnel, and illegal immigrants. The overwhelming majority of Afghan travelers crossing the border do not possess any identity documents.

This system has worked well, and the border has remained soft for the tribal people who moved back and forth without issues and bureaucratic hassles. There are three categories of tribes in the context of movement across the border. The first category is the "divided tribes," which include those tribes whose lands have been divided by the Durand Line. They live along the border on both sides. These include Mashwani, Mohmands, Shinwaris, Afridis, Mangals, Wazirs, and Gulbaz. The second category is the "separated tribes," those tribes who essentially do not have land ownership across the border but are a major or minor part of it and reside in FATA or across the border. These are smaller subtribes or sections of the major tribes mentioned under divided tribes. The third category is the "assured tribes." The Wakhi and Kalash tribes of Chitral are assured tribes who enjoy traditional and conventional rights to cross the border without possession and production of legal travel documents. This historically acquired right has been in vogue for centuries and is assumed to have the sanctity of acceptance of the governments of Pakistan and Afghanistan.

The Durand Line Treaty of 1893 and its subsequent treaties—in 1905, 1919, 1921, and 1930—do not address the question of providing "easement rights" for the divided, separated, or assured tribes to move back and forth across the border. There are no documents or policy with the NWFP/Baluchistan Government or any political agent that state a clear policy on the subject. To facilitate legal moves across the border and check illegal crossings, a policy of permits (*rahdari*) has been in vogue, and the entire mechanism is staffed by Custom Check Posts, Federal Immigration Agency (FIA) Posts, Frontier Corps (FC) Posts, Mobile Check Posts (*Nakas*), *Khasadars* (local police), and *levis* (revenue collectors). This system is ineffective, corrupt, and biased.

Large numbers of Afghan and Pakistani tribesmembers (living within ten miles) move across on a daily basis without any *rahdari*, or permit. Intermarriages, free trade, and purchase of property are also allowed. Pakistani passport holders and foreign nationals traveling in vehicles or those carrying "transit trade" and other goods are checked by the FIA at the Torkham and Chaman border posts. Afghan diplomatic missions in Pakistan issue "red passes" for entry into Afghanistan, whereas Pakistani diplomatic missions in Afghanistan issue "route passes." Shipment of U.S. and coalition forces is exempted from red passes.

In 2003 the Baluchistan government issued passes (*rahdari*) for crossing over into Afghanistan. The system was generally accepted by the law enforcement agencies (LEAs) on both sides. However, it was apparently misused and hence suspended in 2004. The old passes, though invalidated, are still being used and are accepted by LEAs staffing the exit and entry points. It is not possible for these agencies to routinely check such large number of crossers and vehicles. Further, a dichotomy also exists with regard to movement of local vehicles without valid documents or permits.[23]

The procedures of controlling, checking, and maintaining records involves three major issues. First, the FC, assisted by police, *levis*, or *khassadars*, is the primary agency to check cross-border movement at frequented routes or crossing points. Border tribesmembers are not subjected to any scrutiny and are allowed on personal visual recognition or identification by *khassadars*, *levis*, or border police. Second, proper records are not maintained except for a few handwritten registers at crossing points. The total number of crossers, compiled from these registers, is reported on a daily or monthly basis to the respective FC headquarters. Third, Afghan refugees are generally allowed to proceed after checking their Afghan identity cards and letters of recommendation from respective governors or area commanders. For this reason, those Afghans who are not in possession of any valid documents prefer to cross using unfrequented routes.[24]

From Pakistan's standpoint, cross-border movement control is extremely challenging because it must take into account the cultural, traditional, historical, and legal aspects, especially the easement rights, a task that is compounded by the presence of over 2.6 million Afghan refugees. The government of Pakistan (GOP) claims it has never denied that hostile elements are not crossing the border but insists that it is impossible to give ironclad guarantees of border control, given the circumstances. The GOP dismisses allegations that the government or Inter Service Intelligence (ISI) is either involved or abets or even sponsors such movement. In other words, the GOP is insisting that its limitations must be understood with objectivity and sympathy. Elaborating the difficulties, one official told the author that India has deployed five times more forces along the line of control in Kashmir, which is one-third of the length of the Pakistan–Afghan border, yet has been unable to control in-filtration for seventeen years.[25]

The Pakistan government feels it is not possible to enforce a stricter policy than is already in place, as it would bring the way of life to a standstill, given the fact that these areas are remote with no basic infrastructure, a lack of fa-cilities, and the perpetuation of a tribal and nomadic culture. Tightening of screws on security and bureaucratic procedures and tampering with the exist-ing arrangement will deteriorate law and order, create local issues, and lead to possible revolt. Given the volatile nature of the two western provinces of Pakistan and the precarious domestic political situation, the GOP will not push the envelope harder on its side alone, unless a concerted joint strategy is formulated, which, given the trust deficit between the United States and Pakistan, seems even more distant. Well before the 2011 incidents, the GOP had proffered six point steps to be undertaken jointly between Afghanistan/ Coalition Forces and Pakistan. The measures suggested by Pakistan were in-stitutionalization of a system of proper documentation at the crossing points; installation of a computerized database system to record each crossing and sharing of data on required basis; timely sharing of actionable information; the opening of more authorized routes, having adequate security and immi-gration staff at both ends; the sealing of the Pakistan–Afghan border in con-cert with the Afghan Army and Border Militia; the fencing of the border at selected points; and the laying of mines on suspected illegal crossing places.

Two combined factors—refugees and drugs—have compounded the pre-dicament of security in the tribal borderlands. In 1979, after the Soviet inva-sion of Afghanistan, over 6 million Afghans were displaced and sought refuge in Pakistan and Iran. The influx of refugees into Pakistan reached at its peak in 1990 when over 3.7 million (including 0.5 million unregistered) Afghan refugees were present in the country. Later, another influx of 0.4 million refu-gees entered Pakistan between 1990 and 2001 due to factional fighting, the Taliban takeover, and drought. Another 0.3 million came after 9/11, from 2002 to 2005. Thus, the total figure reached 4.4 million. The year 2004 was the dead-line for the closure of all refugees camps in Pakistan, but that deadline was ex-tended to May 2006. However, even after the expiration of the given deadline, the problem persists.[26]

The Pakistani government has issued the following provincewise break-down to the author: Khyber–Pakhtun Khwa, 1,589,515; Baluchistan, 686,011; Punjab, 175,871; Sind, 112,950; Islamabad, 29, 531; and Azad Jammu and

Kashmir, 13,079. This brings the registered total of Afghan refugees to 2,606,957 (2.6 million). The issue is further compounded for Pakistan when approximately 68 percent of the total refugees are living outside the camps and 61 percent of Afghans belong to areas bordering Pakistan.[27] There is, however, a disparity between international agency reporting and Pakistani figures.[28] The U.N. High Commission for Refugees (UNHCR) is urging Pakistan to accept Afghan refugees as economic migrants and ensure local integration, which Pakistan is refusing, asking instead for "compulsory registration" of all refugees, failing which all "unregistered refugees will be treated as illegal immigrants and deported," though Pakistan has never followed up with this threat. Pakistan is also curbing the "recycling process" and blocking the return of refugees from Afghanistan, which then pits the Pakistan government against human rights NGOs (nongovernmental organizations). The fragile security situation in the areas bordering Pakistan, lack of any socioeconomic development, and substantial cuts in the UNHCR budget are the main reasons inhibiting refugees' return. The Pakistan government also complains that the Afghan government is reluctant to accept their people due to lack of capacity to absorb them.

The refugee/repatriation issue and cross-border movement issues are further compounded by drug production in Afghanistan and trafficking. Recent increases in poppy cultivation and narcotics production in Afghanistan are reported to have reached their historic peak. CNN reported on September 17, 2006, that 92 percent of world narco-trade emanates from Afghanistan. Pakistani sources estimate that, during 2005 alone, about 103,100 hectares were cultivated with an estimate yield of 4,100 metric tons of poppy. A profit of US$ 2.8 billion, equivalent to 50 percent of the country's GDP, was generated from the opium crop. A bumper crop during the year 2006 recorded a 50 percent increase over the previous year, indicating trend lines that have remained consistent over subsequent years. Apart from complicating NATO efforts in the war in Afghanistan, the narco factor is a strong obstacle that undermines efforts to curb the cross-border movements. Various warlords with multiple loyalties, criminal gangs, and the Taliban have a convergence of interest in keeping the Afghan hinterland unstable and out of the reach of the LEAs, benefiting immensely from an environment of insecurity and anarchy. The nexus between the drug mafia and the Taliban has been proven, and the amount of money the Taliban is offering to Pashtun defectors cannot be matched by any other organization. Now and in the future, warlords would be able to lure in

Afghan Army and militias that would be a huge challenge for the viability of Afghanistan National Army's future. Afghan–Pakistan issues lead not just to political issues; they also spill into economic tensions, and unofficial trade across the border continues to boom. Unrecorded business is significant in terms of generating incomes and providing employment and access to basic goods, including food, that both governemnts are incapable of providing. The resulting anarchy affects the entire region, in terms of narcotics trade, the flow of financial resources, and the movement of people.[29]

THE PAKISTAN–AFGHANISTAN ISSUES AND THE ROLE OF EXTERNAL ACTORS

The next area that compounds the border problems and relations with Afghanistan is the role of external actors, most notably India. In the military's threat perception, Afghanistan does not loom large, but India remains the primary threat in the long run. Pakistan's greatest fear is the strategic alliance between Afghanistan and India (with logistic supplies and subtle support from Iran) that will put Pakisan into two fronts, entrapping Pakistan into the "jaws of a nutcracker." In addition, competing interests of regional powers and outside actors in Afghanistan continue to contribute to the instability.

Russia continues to remain involved with major warlords in Afghanistan, many of whom have historic ties. Moscow believes it has its own experience and expertise in Afghanistan and must reestablish its interests. Given the history, Pakistan is very uncomfortable with this development and is now trying to reach out to Moscow for strategic dialogue to alleviate its concerns, especially after its relations with the United States came under strain.

Once the British left India, the Soviets sought Afghanistan's alignment with the Soviet bloc through economic penetration.[30] In the 1950s, in reaction to Pakistan joining U.S.-sponsored anticommunist pacts, the Soviet Union declared its support of the Afghan policy in regard to Pashtunistan and challenged the validity of the Durand Line.[31] After withdrawal from Afghanistan, and with the independence of the Central Asian Republics (CARs), Russian interests in Afghanistan have been limited to preventing unstable conditions there to endanger the CARs' ability to develop transit facilities to the Arabian Sea. Moscow is also using the Afghan situation as justification for its military presence in Tajikistan and had been instrumental in forging the Northern Alliance, providing them with substantial material, financial, and military support. Given the history of occupation, this alienated the Pashtuns (Taliban), who saw it as efforts to marginalize them. The ripple effect of such actions along with historical memories runs deep in the tribal areas. Pakistan saw this move as a way to undermine a friendly government in Kabul, marginalize the majority Pashtuns, and, with the support of India, rejuvenate the Pashtunistan movement and embroil Pashtuns in a conflict with Pakistan.

China's geographic proximity has made it a stakeholder in the stability in Afghanistan and Pakistani–Afghan relations. Beijing's historical alliance with Islamabad and competition with Russia and India for a dominant position on the Asian continent affect its policies in the region. China has expressed concern over the Pashtunistan demands made by the Kabul regime, as it directly affects the Karakoram Highway, the symbol of Pakistani–Chinese friendship. Beijing has also condemned any such nationalist and separatist movements, due to apprehensions and sensitivity to China's neighboring Xinjiang province, often volatile due to Uyghur separatist movement. In the 1970s and 1980s, Beijing perceived the Soviet invasion of Afghanistan as purposeful encircling of China.[32] Beijing supports the integrity of Pakistan's western border security as derivative to its own security because many Uyghur had sought refuge and fought with the Taliban. Peaceful coexistence between Pakistan and Afghanistan is significant for China. It is building the deep-sea hub port of Gwadar in Pakistan and has keen interests in Central Asia's energy resources and, thus, supports a moderate government at Kabul. China's strategic interests are mirrored by the security of its lines of communication and potential energy corridors, which runs counter to Afghanistan's fresh rhetoric on Pashtunistan.

Iran and Pakistan have been close partners through most parts of the Cold War. Any instability in the tribal areas, especially in Baluchistan, has been of key interest to them.[33] Any territorial collapse of Pakistan, or domestic instability that threatens to draw in Afghanistan or other external actors, has and will always remain of key interest to Iran. It has always feared nationalistic developments of Pashtunistan and Baluchistan spilling over into neighboring Iran, destabilizing its Baluchi population, or activating greater Baluchistan. Iranian Baluchis are culturally, ethnically (Sunnis), and politically (liberal), thus totally different from the majority of (Shiite) Iran.[34] To protect its interests, Tehran has always urged Pakistani–Afghan rapprochement on Pashtunistan and Baluchistan, and Iran helped to bring it about with events in 1963 and 1975–1976.[35] Iran since the revolution, however, has had major issues over Afghanistan. Pakistan and Saudi support to Taliban and the massacre of the Hazara (Shias) in Hazarajat, as well as wars against Persian-speaking

Panjsheris (Northern Alliance) in the 1990s, have left bitter memories and distrust of each other. Since President Ahmednijad's reign, Iran and Pakistan have moved in tandem to support the Karzai government, which both states continue to maintain as manifest in organizations like the Organization of Islamic Conference (OIC) and the Chinese-sponsored Shanghai Cooperation Organization (SCO). However, hard-liners in Iran still support warlords and factions opposed to Pakistan and are still suspicious of the Saudi role.[36] On balance, however, improved Iranian–Afghan and Pakistani–Iranian relations have a positive affect on Pakistani–Afghan relations with regards to Pashtunistan and the border dispute.

But Iran has yet another issue with Pakistan, that of competing energy and access corridors to and from Central Asia. Iran has joined hands with India. For the past several years an Indian–Iranian–Afghan economic nexus has been growing, with the building up of trade routes to Central Asia, from Chabhar Port via Zahidan to Delaram-Herat in Afghanistan, then up to Turkmenistan. All the roads and related infrastructure are being built by India, Iran, and Afghanistan, providing free passage for Indian goods in transit to and from Central Asia. With such developments, Iran would not like to see any nationalistic movements in the areas bordering Pakistan and Afghanistan, from where this trade route is developing. But for the Pakistani perspective, it is the designs of India that affect its security.

Pakistani sensitivity to India's involvement in the Pakistan–Afghanistan imbroglio goes back to the days when the British were contemplating partition of the Indian subcontinent and formulation of the nexus between Pashtun nationalists and the Indian national Congress. In the 1970s, a synergy among Moscow, Kabul, and Delhi made both the NWFP and the Baluchistan provinces volatile with separatist trends, especially when the Pakistan Army was involved to quash a Baluch insurgency. But over time India's influence was lost as the Pashtunistan movement died down with major political shifts in the region.

India's support for "Pashtunistan" is based on simple logic. It undermines the idea of Pakistan and has the potential to destabilize its nemesis Pakistan. Louis Dupree describes Indian involvement by saying, "I was among those who were in Pakistan and Afghanistan almost immediately after partition in 1947, and I looked into what was happening in Kabul. There was a group of Indians there controlling Kabul Radio, and they are the ones who even invented the term Pashtunistan."[37] In 1951, a Pashtunistan *jirga* was held in Delhi, and All India Radio (AIR) was made available to Sardar Najibullah Khan, later president of Afghanistan, for the making of anti-Pakistani speeches in 1951.[38] AIR has regularly alleged that Pakistan has suppressed the Pashtunistan freedom movement, while broadcasting over the Kabul Radio network.[39]

In 1967, the United Pashtunistan Front (UPF) was formed in New Delhi, under the chairmanship of Mehr Chand Khanna, former minister of Works, Housing and Rehabilitation in the government of India. The political purpose of the Front was made clear in a resolution passed on July 16, 1967, which endorsed the demand for Pashtunistan as a homeland for the Pathans. India, it said, "owed a debt of gratitude to the people of the Frontier who had been among the leaders in the battle for freedom, which for the Pathans had only resulted in their being 'thrown to the wolves' in Pakistan."[40] The Indian Foreign Minister Swaran Singh also told the Indian Parliament that "we are fully aware of the fundamental freedoms and natural aspirations of the brave Pashtuns have been consistently denied to them, and their struggle has got our greatest sympathy and we will certainly support the efforts that Khan Abdul Ghaffar Khan might undertake in that direction."[41]

During the Soviet invasion of Afghanistan, later in the 1990s period of civil war, and even later during the Taliban regime, Indian influence was limited to supporting the Northern Alliance from Dushanbe in Tajikistan. Since 2003, with the dominance of pro-Indian Northern Alliance, New Delhi has dramatically increased its involvement in Afghanistan.[42] India has reopened four consulates in war-ravaged Afghanistan, along the Pak–Afghan border, in Jalalabad and Kandahar, and Mazar-e-Sharif and Herat, seeking trade routes and the rehabilitation of Afghanistan. But these soon became a hub of intelligence activities. Indian covert activities—under the guise of intelligence gathering and sharing information with the Coalition Forces—have been rampant along the Durand Line in Pashtun-dominant areas. Influential political figures and Afghan government functionaries have been joined to instigate anti-Pakistan sentiments among Afghans, particularly the Pashtuns.

The Pakistani strategic community has discerned India's objective as threefold: to destabilize Pakistan as a quid pro quo for Kashmir, forcing it to regress on its Kashmir policy; to create a two-front threat scenario for Pakistan; and to deny Pakistan the economic, trade, and energy linkage to the CARs. In pursuit of its objectives India has structured a five-pronged strategy: to destabilize Baluchistan/FATA using Afghanistan (and Iran) as their base for operations; to subvert the Baluch people to launch a freedom struggle, leading to instability in Pakistan; to create a gulf between the federal government of Pakistan and the tribes by funding notables from Baluchistan and FATA, for antistate and covert activities; to neutralize the Gwadar and Ormara naval ports through terrorist activities; and finally to wean the CARs outlet from Pakistan toward Iran by constructing the requisite infrastructure.

These areas where Indian missions and intelligence are now operating have been the backyard of Pakistani sensitivities. It is a near certainty that such activities will evolve a countervailing response from Pakistan. Afghanistan, once again, could well become a pawn on the chessboard of proxies between India and Pakistan, if not great powers in the new great game.

THE BORDER LANDS AND PAKISTANI STRATEGY IN FATA

Initially, the environment created after September 11, 2001, and the GWOT allowed Pakistan for the first time to seek formal integration of the tribal areas into Pakistan. President Musharraf, at a joint conference on June 24, 2003, at Camp David with President George W. Bush, stated that "Pakistani forces had for the first time in over a century entered the tribal areas in search of Al Qaeda members."[43]

The initial moves of the Pakistan Army into the FATA area were smooth and without much resistance. In the first phase, the Army moved into the Kurram and Tirah Valleys in Kurram and Khyber Agencies in December 2001, establishing a safety net through the active cooperation of the tribes. The immediate returns were apprehension of about 200 al-Qaeda. The second phase began in June 2002 when the Army and Frontier Corps (FC) moved into the Shewal area of the North and South Waziristan Agencies (NWA and SWA) and remaining parts of tribal areas (except the Mahmond Agency) in June 2002. The tribal chiefs cooperated, and the Army's entry was managed without firing a single bullet. In the third phase, the Army entered Mahmond Agency with the cooperation and coordination of U.S. forces.[44]

The Musharraf government used a carrot-and-stick policy, blending the British strategy of forward policy and masterly withdrawal into an operational strategy interspersed with political and economic instruments. The operations can be divided into three stages. In the first stage, from December 2001 to March 2004, the policy was to keep the Maliks/influential leaders co-opted for the military operations. The next stage was from March 2004 to October 2005. The initial period saw a number of operations in SWA and negotiations and agreements with local facilitators (local leaders). This allowed the Frontier

Corps to remove some established check posts. As a result of this vacuum, facilitators took advantage and emerged as commanders and enhanced their influence in the area, and many foreigners were reported in Waziristan area. Two major Army operations were conducted in Shakai (June through August 2004) and in Dila Khula (September 9, 2004) in SWA. This allowed the foreign fighters to run away from South to North Waziristan. The hub of militant activities was reported in Mir Ali/Jani Khel. In the spring of 2005, the Army started search operations in and around Mir Ali. Military operations were now resulting in local resentment.[45] From October 2005 to May 2006, the Army took the backseat and allowed the political administration and FC to remain in the forefront. But the political administration was weak. As the military remained less engaged, foreign fighters (al-Qaeda and the Taliban) received support not just from the facilitators but also from the general public in the NWA and SWA areas. Militants found security and movement within the areas, and it facilitated their operations.

Soon the Taliban formed a parallel government and even started dispensing justice summarily. The political administration failed to establish the writ of the government. The Taliban were emboldened and began attacking isolated posts despite suffering tremendous losses.

After considerable deliberations, the government of Pakistan structured a three-pronged strategy for tribal areas: political process, selective use of force, and development projects in tribal areas.

The political process was directed to deny local support to foreign fighters in FATA. On July 20, 2006, the Grand Tribal Jirga, comprising forty-five members, was formed to implement the governor's peace initiative process. The Jirga was informed that the Army would continue to stay in the area until the situation was stabilized to ensure that there were no more safe havens for foreign fighters and al-Qaeda elements. Under a peace agreement signed on September 5, 2006, at Miran Shah, the federal government pledged to stop military operations in North Waziristan and compensate those who suffered human and material losses while tribal militants committed not to harbor non-Pakistanis or launch cross-border attacks into Afghanistan. The two sides also agreed to form a ten-member committee, comprising officers of the political administration in North Waziristan, tribal elders, and religious scholars, to monitor and ensure implementation of the peace agreement.

Salient aspects of the 2006 agreement include:

- No attacks would be launched against law enforcement agencies, armed forces, and government installations. Also, there would be no target killings.
- No parallel administration would be set up in North Waziristan, and the writ of the government of Pakistan would be accepted.
- Nobody would be allowed to cross the border to take part in military operations in neighboring Afghanistan.
- All non-Pakistanis would leave North Waziristan.
- Military action would promptly commence if there were evidence or actionable intelligence regarding presence of high-value targets or the conducting of any type of training activity.

President Musharraf, during his visit to Kabul in September 2006, clarified that Pakistan did not distinguish between al-Qaeda and the Taliban. He clarified to the Afghanistan government about the agreement between the government of Pakistan and the tribal elders (Maliks) of North Waziristan Agency and reiterated that the deal was with the tribal *jirga* and not with the Taliban, as some media have speculated. President Karzai was apprehensive that the Pakistan military was being recalled from North and South Waziristan, which was not the case because only some military check posts were moved out from villages and towns. Meanwhile, Pakistani security forces continued to patrol and monitor the border as best as they could.

Under the agreement, foreign militants were to leave the agency. However, there were many foreigners who were former warriors of the Afghan War in 1980s and were living with families. Such elements were required to give up arms, live peacefully, and abandon militancy, specifically not to cross into Afghanistan. The tribal elders gave guarantees in this regard. By then, the local population was tired of the conflict and thus amenable to a political approach. By seeking renunciation of militancy from tribes, Pakistan thought it was providing space to the people—hitherto ignored and involved in fighting for decades—to give peace and development a chance. In the process, the Pakistan government sought to elicit cooperation of moderate tribal elders and moderate religious leaders (*ulema*). This strategy eventually failed. Al-Qaeda and the Taliban were much more deeply entrenched in tribal areas; soon al-Qaeda decimated cooperative tribal *jirgas* and cooperative moderates, resulting into a formation of Tehrik–Taliban Pakistan (TTP) by December 2007. Since then, Pakistan military and security services are in a constant state of war, with the

TTP on the one hand and controlling Baluch insurgency on the other, that turned ugly after tribal leader Akbar Bugti was killed in a military operation. Meanwhile, President Musharraf, who ruled with authority, was ousted from power after a civil society movement and political forces that returned to power in elections.

CONCLUSIONS AND RECOMMENDATIONS

"Following the events of September 11, 2001, the political landscape" of the region has "transformed dramatically," with Pakistan and Afghanistan, once again, returning to the mainstream of the international system, this time due to the global war against terrorism (GWOT).[46] Another period of intense instability has begun along the Durand Line. After a "decade-old forward policy" toward Afghanistan, Pakistan decided on a hands-off policy on Afghanistan, but the dynamics in its western provinces and borderlands have exacerbated national security concerns, particularly the role of external actors.[47]

The Taliban disintegration from power that began in November of 2001 did not lead to its destruction; instead, the operations allowed it to melt away into familiar territories of the Pashtun belt and across Afghanistan's porous border with Pakistan. The Pakistani government assisted the United States in its hunt for al-Qaeda and Taliban members and succeeded in capturing or killing many and suffering many casualties as a result. However, either its inability or lack of resources, harsh geographic or local operational environment, and clever asymmetric strategy by al-Qaeda and the Taliban to exploit those conditions combined in ways that prevented Pakistan from achieving enough progress to satisfy American objectives. Though the United States officially recognized and praised Pakistani contribution, it was common to hear criticism of Pakistani intentions, wobbly support, and impatience with Pakistan's performance. In turn, Pakistan authorities have bristled at the American criticism, saying they have had a well-thought-out operational strategy respecting their public opinion.[48] In the wake of the ongoing combat operations by U.S.-led coalition forces in Afghanistan in hunting the Taliban and al-Qaeda who live astride the border, and by the Pakistani forces in Pakistan, distress and misconceptions relating to different aspects of the border are again sprouting.

The Afghan–Pakistan border should no longer be referred to as the Durand Line, at least in deference to the memory of the Pashtuns. It is an inhospitable, long-stretched, and porous border (2,430 kilometers). Militarily it is impossible to be sealed; it is politically unacceptable to do so—and historically a sore point for the locals. In practical terms, the restricted nature of the terrain and the favorable troops ratio in the north (NWFP) make prevention of cross-border movement relatively easy. To the south (Balochistan), the vast and trackless terrain facilitates undetected crossings of even large groups.

For effective surveillance and assured prevention round the clock, a great deal of additional personnel and resources are required. Capacity building of the border forces is imperative, and operational forces need communication, monitoring and surveillance equipment (satellite phones, ground surveillance radar, unmanned aerial vehicles (UAVs), night vision equipment, and reconnaissance vehicles.

Insurgency and guerrilla wars have been experienced in the region (Afghanistan, Kashmir, and the like) for the past three decades, and large forces from all modern armies in the world as well as local forces have operated in the regional environment. But, despite all these resources, cross-border movement continues unabated. These are operational conditions that will be time consuming and require close coordination from all; they cannot be done by one side alone.

The local tribes do not accept restrictions and insist on their right to move across the border. This results in uncertainty of the political boundary between two sovereign states. It is about time for the issue of the border to be settled once and for all.

There is no stated policy with regards to easement rights of the tribes. Cross-border movement under the garb of traditions and culture is being exploited. An undemarcated border with a historical violability by common tribes living on either side poses serious challenges. A large number of border tribes from Balochistan and NWFP/FATA have their agricultural land on Afghan territory and regularly visit for cultivation, business, and interaction; hence, such sociopolitical ramifications prevent strict enforcement of checks. Active deployment of FC and LEAs is not a permanent answer. For effective border control, movement will have to be enforced through established frequented routes. Any border control mechanism is never foolproof, as the U.S. border enforcement agencies are learning in their own backyard. This would require a multitiered progressive strategy involving political leaders, administration, local influential notables of the areas, and the local populations to work jointly. Finally, the elimination of drugs and repatriation of all Afghan refugees will help reduce cross-border movement.

At the geopolitical level, Pakistan and Afghanistan relations have three clear and simple demands of each other: that both states should have friendly governments that recognize the territorial boundaries and jurisdiction of each other; that neither should allow hostile powers to have sanctuaries for activities against each other's security; and that both should proactively engage and facilitate trade, transit, and energy routes between Central and South Asia for the benefit of people on both sides of the border. For regional powers, China, India, and Iran all have economic stakes in the stability of the Pakistan–Afghan borderlands and their healthy mutual relations. The United States is the only power that can provide the leadership to bring together diverse stakeholders into an agreement for regional stability and prosperity and defeat extremism.

NOTES

The author is grateful to the Pakistan Government for providing inputs, data, and briefings for this project. Special gratitude goes to Major General Shaukat Sultan Khan, Director General Inter Services Publication, The Pakistan Army, for his briefings on June 19, 2006, and September 17, 2006. Special thanks are due to the Pakistan Embassy, Washington, D.C., for briefing and notes on September 15, 2006. Views expressed in this chapter are that of the author alone and do not represent those of Pakistan or the U.S. government or any agency.

The author wishes to acknowledge the master's thesis of Lt. Col. Tariq Mahmood, Pakistan Army, and Wing Cdr. Khawar Hussain, Pakistan Air Force, who both graduated from the Naval Postgraduate School in June 2005 and whose research work on a similar topic was extensively helpful in this chapter.

1. Mahomed Ali Jinnah, *Jinnah: Speeches and Statements 1947–1948* (New York: Oxford University Press, 2000), 4.

2. George Curzon, 1st Marquess Curzon of Kedleston, *Frontier, the Romance Lecture,* Oxford, November 2, 1907 (Oxford, UK: Clarendon Press, 1907), 7 as cited by Tariq Mahmood, "The Durand Line: South Asia's Next Trouble Spot," Naval Postgraduate School Master's Thesis, June 2005, 3, n.5; available at www.dtic.mil/dtic/tr/fulltext/u2/a435574.pdf.

3. Rashid, 2001, 7, as cited by Khawar Hussain, "Pakistan's Afghanistan Policy," Naval Postgraduate School Master's Thesis, June 2005, 2, n.7; available at www.dtic.mil/cgi-bin/GetTRDoc?AD=ADA435525.

4. Nation Master Encyclopedia, "Durand Line," Nationmaster.com, as cited by Tariq Mahmood, "The Durand Line: South Asia's Next Trouble Spot," Naval Postgraduate School Master's Thesis, June 2005, 13, and referenced in n.16 in the same page;

available at www.dtic.mil/dtic/tr/fulltext/u2/a435574.pdf; retrieved by Mahmood on June 19, 2004 from www.nationmaster.com/encyclopedia/Durand-Line.

5. *Pashtunistan, Pakhtoonistan, Pukhtunistan,* and *Pathanistan* are variants of the same word, adopted form the words *Pashtun, Pakhtoon, Pukhtun,* and *Pathan.* The hard sound is used in the north, whereas the soft one in the south. The word *Pathan* is the Indian variant adopted by the British.

6. Leon B. Poullada, "Pushtunistan: Afghan Domestic Politics and Relations with Pakistan," in Ainslie T. Embree, ed., *Pakistan's Western Border Lands: The Transformation of a Political Order* (Delhi: Vikas Publishing House Ltd., 1977), 127–128.

7. In March 1955, mobs attacked Pakistan's embassy in Kabul and ransacked Pakistani consulates in Jalalabad and Kandahar, prompting a trade blockade of landlocked Afghanistan. Mob attack against the Pakistan Embassy was a pattern repeated at various times until recently. As described by Tariq Mahmood, "The Durand Line: South Asia's Next Trouble Spot," Naval Postgraduate School Master's Thesis, June 2005, 1; available at www.dtic.mil/dtic/tr/fulltext/u2/a435574.pdf.

8. George Grafton Wilson. *Handbook of International Law* (St. Paul, MN: West Publishing Co., 1939); cited by Poullada, 1977, 135–136.

9. Ainslie T. Embree, *Pakistan's Western Borderlands: The Transformation of a Political Order* (Durham, NC: Carolina Academic Press, 1977), 136.

10. Olaf Caroe, *The Pathans* (New York: Macmillan, 1958), 358.

11. Poullada, 1977, 139.

12. Paragraph 2a of Article 62 of the Vienna Convention on the Law of the Treaties, 1969, states that "a fundamental change of circumstances may not be evoked as a ground for terminating or withdrawing from treaty: a) if the treaty establishes a boundary"; Afghanistan tried to get this clause removed from the treaty at the time of debate in 1968 and 1969 but failed. It however made a declaration at the end of conference that Afghanistan interprets this article not applicable to treaties that are unequal and illegal. Ijaz Hussain, "Is the Durand Agreement Dead?" in Perviaz Iqbal Cheeema and Maqsudul Hasan Nuri, eds., *Tribal Areas of Pakistan: Challenges and Responses* (Islamabad: Islamabad Policy Research Institute, 2005), 162.

13. Ibid., 160.

14. Noor-ul-Haq, "Pak–Afghan Relations," Islamabad Policy Research Institute (IPRI), Fact File no. 44 (2003); available at http://ipripak.org/factfiles/ff44.shtml, as cited by Tariq Mahmood, "The Durand Line: South Asia's Next Trouble Spot," Naval Postgraduate School Master's Thesis, June 2005, 24 and referenced in n.46 on the same page; available at www.dtic.mil/dtic/tr/fulltext/u2/a435574.pdf; retrieved by Mahmood on March 26, 2005, from http://ipripak.org. .

15. Paragraph 8 of the SEATO communiqué:

The members of the Council severally declared that their governments recognized that the sovereignty of Pakistan extends up to the Durand Line, the international boundary between Pakistan and Afghanistan, and it was consequently affirmed that the Treaty area referred to in Articles IV and VIII of the Treaty includes the area up to that Line." As cited by Tariq Mahmood, "The Durand Line: South Asia's Next Trouble Spot," Naval Postgraduate School Master's Thesis, June 2005, 24, and referenced in n.47 on the same page; available at www.dtic.mil/dtic/tr/fulltext/u2/ a435574.pdf, citing Noor-ul-Haq, "Pak–Afghan Relations," Islamabad Policy Research Institute (IPRI), Fact File no. 44 (2003), retrieved by Mahmood on March 26, 2005 from http://ipripak.org/factfiles/ff44.shtml.

16. Declassified Documents Reference System, Background Information for President Ayub's U.S. Visit July 1961, Pak–Afghan Relations, CK3100270550; available through Dudley Knox Library at http://galentgroup.com/servlet/DDRS?vrsn=1.0& view+etext&slb+KE&locID+naval (May 5, 2004). As cited by Tariq Mahmood, "The Durand Line: South Asia's Next Trouble Spot," Naval Postgraduate School Master's Thesis, June 2005, 25, n.48; available at www.dtic.mil/dtic/tr/fulltext/u2/a435574.pdf; the declassified documents were retrieved by Mahmood on May 5, 2004 from http:// galentgroup.com. Also see Dennis Kux, *The United States and Pakistan 1947–2000: Disenchanted Allies* (Washington, D.C.: The Woodrow Wilson Center Press, 2001), 42–43, also cited by Tariq Mahmood, "The Durand Line: South Asia's Next Trouble Spot," Naval Postgraduate School Master's Thesis, June 2005, 25 n. 48; available at www.dtic.mil/dtic/tr/fulltext/u2/a435574.pdf.

17. The author is grateful to Major General Shaukat Sultan, Director-General of the Pakistan Army's Inter Services Public Relations, for a personal briefing over the phone on September 17, 2006.

18. Briefing notes from Major General Shaukat Sultan, September 17, 2006.

19. Khan Wali Khan, leader of opposition in Pakistani parliament in his affidavit to the Supreme Court of Pakistan, 1975. Quoted by Selig Harrison in "Ethnicity and Political Stalemate in Pakistan," in Ali Banuazizi and Myron Weiner, eds., *The State, Religion and Ethnic Politics* (Syracuse, NY: Syracuse University Press, 1986), 285.

20. Harrison, 1986, 285.

21. Poullada, 1977, 149.

22. Caroe, 1958, 435–436. Also see Poullada, 1977, 150–151.

23. A large number of vehicles in the Frontier and Baluchistan Province are not registered, as many have been smuggled from across the border in Iran and Afghanistan. Because they have been in use for a long time, it is a very complicated exercise for LEA to ensure documentation. Many vehicles stolen from cities in Pakistan ply around these areas with tribes and warlords.

24. Author's meeting with Pakistani government officials on June 15, 2006.

25. Ibid.

26. The author is grateful to the Pakistani government for providing these data.

27. There is a total of forty-four registered camps (thirty-one are in NWFP, twelve in Baluchistan, and one in Punjab).

28. Under the United Nations High Commission for Refugees (UNHCR) Assisted Repatriation Program, so far 4.727 million refugees have been repatriated to their homelands. Factually, the issue should have been resolved after the repatriation of these estimated figures, yet, according to recent census data in Pakistan, 2.6 million refugees are still present in the country. The main reasons for this disparity are that not until February 2005 was any census taken; further, the annual birthrate of approximately 4 percent is not accounted for, and extensive cross-border movements continue, making refugee censuses complicated, especially those Afghan refugees who have dual homes in Afghanistan and Pakistan but stay mostly in Pakistan for better economic conditions.

29. World Bank Watching Brief for Afghanistan, "Afghanistan's International Trade Relations with Neighboring Countries," February 2001, http://lnweb18.world bank.org/SAR/sa.nsf/Attachments/8/$File/intltrade.pdf, as cited by Tariq Mahmood, "The Durand Line: South Asia's Next Trouble Spot," Naval Postgraduate School Master's Thesis, June 2005, 70, n.139; available at www.dtic.mil/dtic/tr/fulltext/u2/a435574 .pdf; retrieved by Mahmood on March 7, 2005 from Worldbank.org. Mahmood further writes, "Afghanistan's unofficial exports to Pakistan totaled $941 million in 2000, while official exports were only $98 million, whereas unofficial imports from Pakistan totaled $82 million." Tariq Mahmood, "The Durand Line: South Asia's Next Trouble Spot," Naval Postgraduate School Master's Thesis, June 2005, 70; available at www .dtic.mil/dtic/tr/fulltext/u2/a435574.pdf.

30. Afghanistan was subjected to trade blockade by Pakistan during crises, which Afghanistan saw as a lever to give up demand of Pashtunistan. Afghanistan went to the Soviet camp to open another economic bloc. See Kux, 2001, 108, 109, 124.

31. Larry P. Goodson, *Afghanistan's Endless War: State Failure, Regional Politics and the Rise of Taliban* (Washington, DC: University of Washington Press, 2001), 49.

32. Gerald Segal, "China and Afghanistan," *Asian Survey* 21, No. 11 (1981): 1158–1174.

33. The shah of Iran actively supported Pakistan during the Baluch Insurgency in the 1970s. The shah leased Iranian helicopters fearing spillover into Iran's Baluch.

34. Syed Saleem Shahzad, "Pashtunistan Issue Back to Haunt Pakistan," *Asia Times*, October 24, 2003, as cited by Tariq Mahmood, "The Durand Line: South Asia's Next Trouble Spot," Naval Postgraduate School Master's Thesis, June 2005, 52, n.103; available at www.dtic.mil/dtic/tr/fulltext/u2/a435574.pdf; retrieved by Mahmood on June 18, 2004, from www.atimes.com.

35. Shirin Tahir-Kheli, "Iran and Pakistan: Cooperation in an Area of Conflict," *Asian Survey* 17, no. 5 (1977): 479–483.

36. Mohsen Milany, remarks made in a presentation on seminar on Afghanistan at Woodrow Wilson Center seminar, Washington, DC, November 15, 2002.

37. Quoted in Stephen Ian, *Pakistan: Old Country, New Nation* (London: Penguin, 1964), 265.

38. Kamal Matinuddin, *The Taliban Phenomenon: Afghanistan 1994–1997* (Karachi: Oxford University Press, 1999), 3.

39. Paul Wolf, "Pakistan: Partition and Military Succession," Pashtunistan Documents from the U.S. National Archives (Afghanistan–Pakistan Relations, Declassified Airgram of the U.S. Embassies to the Department of State from 1952 to 1973, as cited by Tariq Mahmood, "The Durand Line: South Asia's Next Trouble Spot," Naval Postgraduate School Master's Thesis, June 2005, 54, n.110; available at www.dtic.mil/dtic/tr/fulltext/u2/a435574.pdf; retrieved by Mahmood on March 23, 2005, from www.icdc.com/~paulwolf/pakistan/pashtunistan.htm.

40. Ibid., 8.

41. Owen Bennett Jones, *Pakistan in the Eye of the Storm* (Islamabad: Vanguard), 139.

42. Aly Zaman, "India's Increased Involvement in Afghanistan and Central Asia: Implications for Pakistan," *Islamabad Policy Research Institute (IPRI) Journal* 3, no. 2 (Summer 2003), as cited by Tariq Mahmood, "The Durand Line: South Asia's Next Trouble Spot," Naval Postgraduate School Master's Thesis, June 2005, 54, n.113; available at www.dtic.mil/dtic/tr/fulltext/u2/a435574.pdf; retrieved by Mahmood on July 19, 2004, from www.ipripak.org/journal/summer2003/indiaincreased.shtml.

43. Rahimullah Yusufzai, "Pakistan's Army in the Tribal Areas," *BBC NEWS World Edition*, June 25, 2003, as cited by Tariq Mahmood, "The Durand Line: South Asia's Next Trouble Spot," Naval Postgraduate School Master's Thesis, June 2005, 19, n.9; available at www.dtic.mil/dtic/tr/fulltext/u2/a435574.pdf; retrieved by Mahmood on February 25, 2005, from http://news.bbc.co.uk/1/hi/world/south_asia/3020552.stm.

44. Shaukat Sultan, "Government Initiatives in FATA before and after 9/11," in Pervaiz Iqbal Cheema and Maqsud-ul Hasan Nuri, eds., *Tribal Areas of Pakistan: Challenges and Responses* (Islamabad: Islamabad Policy Research Institute, 2005), 170.

45. Maulvi Sadiq Noor emerged as commander of local Taliban, and his forces spread into the area and actively started engaging the army and other law enforcement agencies. The president then directed the army to adopted a pragmatic approach, engaging but avoiding collateral damage and minimizing local resentment.

46. Khawar Hussain, "Pakistan's Afghanistan Policy," Naval Postgraduate School Master's Thesis, June 2005, 1; available at www.dtic.mil/cgi-bin/GetTRDoc?AD=ADA435525.

47. Ibid.

48. Pamela Constable, "Pakistan's Uneasy Role in Terror War; Conciliatory Approach to Tribal and Foreign Fighters Leaves U.S. Officials Frustrated," *Washington Post*, May 8, 2004, A8, as cited by Tariq Mahmood, "The Durand Line: South Asia's Next Trouble Spot," Naval Postgraduate School Master's Thesis, June 2005, 61, n.62; available at www.dtic.mil/dtic/tr/fulltext/u2/a435574.pdf; accessed by Mahmood on August 8, 2004, from the *Washington Post*.

7 THE MANEUVER COMPANY IN AFGHANISTAN

Establishing Counterinsurgency Priorities
at the District Level

Michael R. Fenzel

> *The basic unit of counterinsurgency warfare is the largest*
> *unit whose leader is in direct and continuous contact with the*
> *population. This is the most important unit in counterinsurgency*
> *operations, the level where most of the practical problems arise,*
> *where the war is won or lost.*
>
> —David Galula[1]

THE SHIFT IN NATIONAL CONCERN from Iraq to Afghanistan and the initial increase in forces committed by the Obama administration directed greater attention to the current problems in Afghanistan. U.S. forces and Coalition partners are working on many fronts to secure a stable future for the country, but they face more than a few obstacles. At the macro level, the Afghan central government is weak and plagued by corruption and indifference to the plight of its rural constituency; yet, without tribal accord, the government has no real chance of extending its reach to the rest of the country. The Afghan National Army, police, and border police are increasing their numbers and improving their skills, but, with the exception of a few exceptional Afghan National Army battalions, they are not yet capable of operating on their own. The poppy fields and drug trade in southern and eastern Afghanistan continue to flourish. The border with Pakistan remains porous enough for a resurgent Taliban to use it as its primary and most unfettered means of infiltration into remote rural sections of the country. These are just a few of the many problems for the government of Afghanistan and the U.S.-led Coalition.

Many authors, strategists, and politicians have offered measured opinions and recommendations on how to improve the situation, but most agree that to fix these problems and allow Afghanistan to develop without the constant pressure of an insurgency, we must establish and maintain security and develop governance in the rural districts.

Completing these tasks may appear impossible to a casual observer of the conflict. Indeed, while fighting a growing insurgency, Coalition casualties mount. Historically, the rural population in modern Afghanistan has rejected all large-scale reforms attempted by a central government. Unfortunately, change acceptable to the tribes will simply not come from the center. Establishing security in this war-torn land is achievable only if we focus our efforts and resources at the district level, where the subtribes are culturally dominant.

Nowhere in Afghanistan is this more pressing than along the border of Pakistan's Federally Administered Tribal Areas (FATA). It is commonly accepted that the Taliban, al-Qaeda, and other foreign fighters use the FATA as a safe haven from which to plan, resource, stage, and launch attacks in the border districts and deeper into Afghanistan's interior. Since 2006, the number of foreign insurgents involved in the border fight has substantially increased, which strengthens the insurgency and decreases security. The struggle to secure this area has become the front line in the counterinsurgency fight and the Coalition's most important strategic task.

If we can establish security and stabilize the border provinces and districts in southern and eastern Afghanistan, the accompanying momentum may guide the rest of the country to a sustainable peace.

The problem is that the insurgents are most effective in these rural areas, and limited troop levels make on a wider scale a confounding proposition.

I propose a fundamental shift in the way we think about fighting the counterinsurgency in Afghanistan. To set the conditions for success, we need to engage tribal leaders and establish a district-level security architecture in which the district governor is the key leader elected by the *shura*. In conjunction, we need a bottom-up focus that places the Coalition maneuver company commander where he can work closely with the district governor. Next, we need to redistribute critical assets now located at the provincial level down to the district level. Afghan security forces should be redistributed to districts and rural areas, and we should dismantle entities like the provincial reconstruction teams and reassign those assets to the maneuver battalions for use in the maneuver companies at the district level. Finally, we need to integrate native Afghan intellectual capital into our maneuver company operations to improve cultural engagement and provide expertise in critical development skills.

TRIBAL INFLUENCE

To create the environment for such advances, we begin by reinforcing the role of the tribes. We've taken the first steps toward establishing security when we recognize and embrace the prestige and broad power base of tribal elders and accept the influence of the mullahs. Invading armies throughout history have failed to understand the tribal structure that has always defined this nation. Breaking this troubling paradigm is the first challenge for a refocused U.S.-led Coalition. We cannot engage just a handful of tribes for this mission. There is no one ruler in Kabul who can consolidate the loyalty of all tribes in Afghanistan. Rather, we must reach out to every subtribe in each of the 400 or so districts across the country. The real power and potential in Afghanistan exists among the local tribes in the rural areas.

Developing governance capacity at the district level is a low-level affair, but hugely important. Currently, provincial governors appoint district governors, often favored friends and acquaintances, not men of the people or even of the local tribes. The vast majority of provincial council members do not live in the provinces they represent. For this reason, provincial councilmen are almost entirely irrelevant to their constituencies. The current flawed process of selection, rather than election, almost guarantees that the appointed district governor will be irrelevant as well. This method rarely yields a close connection with the elders—it must be changed to meet the cultural threshold of what is acceptable and suitable.

Everything of intrinsic value to Afghans is rooted in honor, reputation, and familial pride. The current method of selecting district governors is arbitrary and antithetical to the tribal culture and Pashtun traditions of selecting leaders. There should be no quibbling with a method that meets the demands of democratic traditions, eschews the noninclusive self-selection modes of warlordism, and reinforces the real power and influence of Afghan communities—the *shura* of elders.

Setting Conditions for Success

Counterinsurgency forces routinely engage the leaders of the district subtribes, or *shura* elders, throughout Afghanistan. Once legitimate governors take office, the Coalition must integrate them into the counterinsurgency effort. The key component for successful counterinsurgency efforts is the Coalition maneuver company and its commander. A company commander is, in effect, the counterpart to the Afghan district governor. The tribal elders are not his counterparts; indeed, it is the responsibility of the company commander to ensure that the district governor maintains a close relationship with the elders and acts as the immediate interlocutor between them and the provincial government.

Figure 7.1. Akram Khapalwak, then provincial governor of Paktika Province, addresses a grand shura of elders and villagers in Naka district, Paktika Province, August 2007.

SOURCE: U.S. Army Chaplain Major Kevin Guthrie, in Michael R. Fenzel, "The Maneuver Company in Afghanistan: Establishing Counterinsurgency Priorities at the District Level," Military Review (U.S. Army Combined Arms Center, Fort Leavenworth), March–April 2010; available at http://usacac.army.mil/CAC2/ MilitaryReview/Archives/English/MilitaryReview_20100430_art007.pdf.

When these young commanders have proper direction and focus, they can identify where to channel resources and effort in a way no other counterinsurgent leader can replicate. Much of their insight comes from the weekly *shuras* in the district centers where they are often guests. District centers are the focal point for all government and economic activity and clearly places where counterinsurgent forces must have a significant presence. Coalition forces that have spent considerable time among the people understand that these district centers are the places that must become well-defended Afghan National Security Force bastions and political centers from which the district governors function. A district governor should conduct business with the full backing and strength of a sizeable Afghan police and security force operating from the district center. Where better to position Afghan forces in a rural Afghan counterinsurgency than among rural Afghans?

The vision for effective local government administration in Afghanistan includes the district center as the point of initiation for all Afghan-led political, development, and security operations. The district center is already a local nerve center—it must also become the security epicenter. This is the first fundamental change to effect across the country. There are six important steps to take in every district in every province:

- Tribal elders within a district *shura* must elect a district governor they trust.
- A well-trained police chief must be appointed, and he should have no fewer than thirty police officers to maintain order.
- District centers must be reinforced with Coalition support and funds for governance and economic activity (with a designated development stipend to facilitate reconstruction programming).
- Each Afghan district must have no less than one company of the Afghan National Army garrisoned at the district center; their mission must be to conduct counterinsurgency operations, and their primary task must be to engage daily with the population.
- A point security force must be emplaced (an Afghan public protection force of thirty guards) in each district that reports directly to the district governor and guards the district center and other sites at risk of Taliban attack (that is, girls' schools, bazaars, and the like).
- A district-level and native Afghan National Directorate of Security chief must be assigned and, through appropriate Coalition oversight, a robust informant network developed to counter Taliban human intelligence efforts and provide early warning.

These six critical steps would set the stage for an immediate counterinsurgency advance because they focus exclusively on the protection of the Afghan people, the center of gravity in this war. The adoption of this district-centric approach places the execution of the war at the appropriate level.

Blended Security Architecture

Putting this strategic approach into operation demands a security architecture with an appropriate blend of command, control, coordination, and crosstalk among the key players. Figure 7.2 illustrates how the district-level structure might look. Establishing these baseline capabilities would empower district governors to move beyond their understandable preoccupation with self-preservation and begin working for the people in the villages that comprise each district. The direct link between the district governor and the district *shura* is deliberate. The district governor should be answerable to the *shura* of

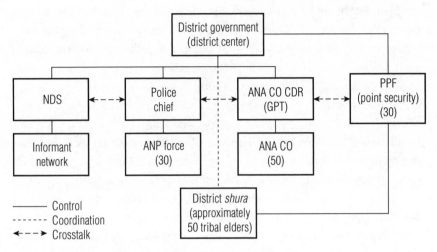

Figure 7.2. Optimal Afghan district security structure.
SOURCE: Fenzel, 2010.

elders who elect him to the office. This will require a paradigm shift and support for this method at the national level in Kabul.

Once these changes are in place in the districts, the governors will be in a much better position to counter Taliban intimidation. A great deal of credence is paid to the importance of governance and development in Afghanistan, but until there is an environment where the average Afghan feels empowered to resist the armed thugs that fill the ranks of the Taliban, the insurgency will continue to grow. We must integrate the district governor into the security architecture and support him over time to ensure sustained advances. Until this type of structure exists at the local level, no political official will enjoy credibility among the tribes. Stability in Afghanistan will emerge at the district level through a structure that reinforces cultural traditions and provides an armed force to underwrite the authority of district governor elected by the district's tribal elders.

OPTIMIZING AFGHAN NATIONAL SECURITY FORCES

The current number of Coalition Forces available in Afghanistan, even with the original 2009 surge of 21,000 soldiers and marines, is insufficient to combat the Taliban's district offensives. The coming surge of 30,000 additional U.S. troops should address this shortfall, but it is not likely to change insurgent tactics or what up until now has been an effective strategy. Despite what the high number of Coalition casualties since 2008 reflects, the Taliban and foreign fighters focus more on preventing cooperation and severing the link between the Coalition Forces and local Afghans than they do on direct action against Coalition Forces. This adjustment in insurgent strategy was a matter of necessity. Because U.S. and other Coalition Forces have continually dealt significant blows to the insurgents in direct contact, the insurgents have turned to coercion, intimidation, and terrorism to send a clear message to the Afghan population—"Coalition and Afghan security forces cannot protect you." The insurgents reiterate this message in night letters with accompanying threats to the local population. Historically, the Taliban has targeted district governors, contractors, and Coalition Force base employees and their families. The Taliban has displayed a knack for attacking targets of opportunity. Increasingly, these targets have become Afghan security forces and Afghan Public Protection Force personnel. As an insurgent strategy, this approach is very effective in keeping counterinsurgent forces off balance and preventing the population from believing that things have somehow improved.

The center of gravity of this mission is protecting the Afghan people and assisting them in meeting their basic needs. This requires robust Afghan security resources at the local and district level, not at the regional level. This comprehensive effort should start with a more optimal distribution of Afghan National Security Forces. The Afghan National Security Forces living on large forward operating bases need to move into the rural districts where the population is at risk; the forces will position themselves in the best locations to facilitate constant engagement with the people. Only then can we effectively cross the pronounced cultural divide into the tribal areas of rural Afghanistan. For Afghan National Security Forces to become capable enough to meet this challenge, every single unit and detachment must formally partner with Coalition Forces. This will only lead to positive effects. Some of these changes are already underway.

Afghan National Army

With the current top-down approach, Afghan National Security Forces are often in general support at the provincial level with specific fixed site security responsibilities. We must change this relationship to make the district level the ascendant strategic focus. The Afghan National Army is growing steadily in capability. However, its soldiers are typically deployed in battalion-sized elements and centrally located. In fact, the rural areas generally do not benefit from the existing array of these forces in Afghanistan. We need to consider where they can achieve the most positive effects in counterinsurgency terms.

Optimally, one company of the Afghan National Army should be in each district, and one Coalition maneuver company should partner with it. These partnerships are necessary among the district governor, the district police chief, the Afghan National Army company commander and battalion commanders, and the Coalition Force company commander. Depending on the level of violence in a given district and the district's size, it may well be feasible for one Coalition Force company to manage security in more than one district. In fact, in some cases one maneuver company could handle up to three districts, though there are obvious exceptions in larger districts. The commander would become the liaison to the district governors and have regular dealings with his counterparts. He would become the subject matter expert responsible for overall security and development in the districts. In this scenario, the primary task for Coalition Forces would be to achieve and maintain security, apply resources, help in reconstruction and development, assist the district governors in matters of governance, and increase capacity with partnered Afghan security forces. This would continue until the Afghans are able to do the work themselves. Until they reach that point though, Coalition Forces must take the lead to establish a secure environment and foster growth.

Each Afghan National Army battalion currently deploys to a major forward operating base intended as a launching pad to project force. However, these forward operating bases have essentially become shields from insurgent forces and impediments to maintaining contact with the rural populations. Ideally, one brigade-sized element of the Afghan National Army should deploy to each province in Afghanistan. In certain larger provinces (with more districts) or where the threat is substantially higher, up to two Afghan National Army brigades may be appropriate. Afghan National Army battalions should be distributed over a series of districts and address security in no more than three districts. At least one Afghan National Army company should have a headquarters in each district. A "company per district" strategy should drive refinements to the Afghan National Army battalion and brigade battle space. Every Afghan National Army element—whether company, battalion, or brigade—should have a Coalition Force counterpart unit to facilitate training, drive combined operations, and provide reinforcement in extremis. The logical formula is Coalition maneuver companies paired with Afghan National Army battalions and Coalition battalions paired with Afghan National Army brigades.

At the district level, Afghan National Army companies should conduct counterinsurgency operations partnered with Coalition Forces based out of district centers, rather than from forward operating bases. This partnership must encompass all operations, from patroling to training to regular engagement and standard counterinsurgency operations. Although this proposal may appear overly prescriptive, it is the only effective means to build a genuine and lasting capacity in the Afghan National Army and to strengthen the Afghan National Security Force's connection to the Afghan people. Both of these goals are imperative to success.

The Afghan National Police

The Afghan National Police suffer from a similarly poor distribution of forces. Often the provincial police chief has only a small pool of dependable Afghan police under his control. This makes clear the dearth of well-trained police available at this stage in the war. The police also suffer from insufficient re-sourcing, ineffective recruiting, and poor local training compared to the army. Ideally, the police would have no less than a platoon-sized force (thirty police officers) in each district to back up the district governor and provide a credible deterrent to insurgents.

The appointment of an effective district police chief is critical to this process. In many ways, the mission of the Afghan National Police is more complex than that of the Afghan National Army because the police are responsible for enforcing Afghan law. The police need to focus on maintaining order, rooting out crime, and protecting the district center. Indeed, they should serve as the governor's police force and operate out of a police station adjacent to the district center to facilitate their subordinate relationship to the governor and his priorities.

The demand for personnel is a significant issue. In larger districts, there might be a need for satellite district centers and police stations, with multiple checkpoints in between them and the district center. Securing all these locations is an incredible personnel drain. This role should be shouldered by the Afghan Public Protection Force, or a point security force, a brilliant innovation already in place that keeps the Afghan security force focused on its core counterinsurgency mission.

Innovation is an incredibly effective tool in a counterinsurgency unless it distracts from fundamentals. However, when it comes to establishing an overarching security structure, we must keep in mind that interactions through representatives, by either proxy or the Afghan Public Protection Force, cannot substitute for direct and constant contact with the population. The Afghan National Police must partner with other forces to optimize effectiveness and ensure direct contact with the Afghan people as the conflict continues. The Afghan National Police and Afghan National Army must routinely work together. At a more fundamental level, the seat of district-level government and focal point of counterinsurgency efforts must be both secure and dynamic.

Afghan Border Police

In districts along the border with Pakistan, the Afghan border police are charged with disrupting infiltration by the Taliban and foreign fighters. However, the border police are currently the most disorganized and least supported component of the security forces. Yet, in some districts, the border police are supplementing the Afghan National Police. The border police should focus exclusively on operating border combat outposts and checkpoints, or they will lose their relevance as a part of the larger national security network. When Coalition Forces construct a combat outpost, a joint team of Coalition Forces and Afghan border police should initially operate the outposts along the border. When the border police are trained and strong enough, the Coalition Forces can pull back and let them handle it. The very nature of their mission requires that they work closely with the Afghan National Army to develop a sense of partnership and solidarity in the counterinsurgency fight.

The last refinement to the development of Afghan National Security Force capacity is the command relationship of the Coalition Force trainers to the maneuver battalion task force. Trainers must be responsive to the maneuver battalion and company task force priorities, instead of either developing their own independent priorities or following those of a distant headquarters detached from ongoing operations. Indeed, the Coalition Force trainers must be woven into a direct support relationship with the maneuver company to reinforce the already existing lines of control. For the training mission to be effective, Coalition Force trainers must be answerable to the maneuver battalion task force commander. Otherwise, there will always be the potential and even likelihood to work at cross-purposes. Coalition training teams not directly responsible to a maneuver battalion task force commander may plan and conduct independent operations completely unaware of the threat picture or ongoing operations that may have an impact on their plans. This is the complex reality of the training mission as it is carried out in the midst of a violent counterinsurgency. Training the Afghan security forces will always be a task that is carried out inside the combat mission, and it should be subordinate to that mission, given the consequences of failure. Partnership with the Afghans must be constant (both on patrols and in training)—we need to build their capacity and take the requisite and valuable time to coach, teach, and mentor. The combat mission is led by the maneuver force, and it is only logical that the training mission not ever be separated from it. The relationship of all security enablers to the maneuver task force must be clear and direct. It follows then that the reconstruction teams should fit into the same command structure.

PUSH DOWN CRITICAL ASSETS

Most important to this concept of reorganization in Afghanistan is empowering the company maneuver unit. We must meet the challenges unique to the Afghan counterinsurgency environment with new capabilities to lessen insurgent influence and provide a powerful advantage to the counterinsurgent. Key enablers and assets that perform more complex functions in the development realm have historically been distributed to the provincial and regional level. The value of these enablers at the district level is far greater, and the tactical impact is often immediate. These enablers have the potential to dramatically improve security and even achieve transformational effects.

To develop capacity at the district level we should consolidate certain critical assets at the maneuver company level. A maneuver company commander is the Coalition lead at the local level for security, development, and governance. He is responsible for synchronizing the efforts of Afghan security forces and Coalition enablers. If we keep development and security assets separate, efforts will be uncoordinated and fleeting at best and damaging to district- and provincial-level counterinsurgency efforts at worst.

The provincial reconstruction team concept remains sound and still addresses a need that counterinsurgent strategists widely agree is imperative—building capacity and proceeding steadily along the development and governance lines of operation. Yet, more than a decade into the conflict, we must adapt the concept to the changed situation on the ground. The inefficiencies of the provincial reconstruction team model have become more apparent in recent years. These teams need to be disassembled and the assets distributed to the district level to support counterinsurgency efforts in the rural areas and improve unity of command.

Figure 7.3. A paratrooper from Easy Company of Task Force Eagle (1-503d, 173d Airborne Brigade) on patrol in Orgun District of Paktika Province, February 2008.
SOURCE: U.S. Army CPT Christopher Weld in Fenzel, 2010.

Provincial reconstruction teams are ill equipped to address broader development and district-level governance challenges. Nearly all reconstruction teams are geographically separated from the rural sections of their assigned province, and they do not possess the capability to venture far beyond the population centers unless they plan their movements well in advance and operate in tandem with the maneuver battalion task force. This is certainly no fault of theirs and would be the case regardless of how well a provincial reconstruction team functioned. Regardless of the wealth of talent infused into the teams, circumstances and conditions will always challenge them and put them at a disadvantage. The reality is that a provincial reconstruction team's infrequent contact at the district level has the potential to render the concerted efforts it makes a distraction from the development plan a maneuver company may already be in the midst of implementing.

Provincial reconstruction team architecture and location is not the only problem with the teams. One imperative that we must address is the absence of true unity of command. By definition, establishing the hierarchy of command in a conflict environment requires clear lines of responsibility and authority that are not open to interpretation or dispute in the field. Units that fall outside of these command lines are often "orphans on the battlefield" and far more vulnerable to enemy attacks than a cohesive force that works through one commander. In a postconflict environment, this may evolve to a looser structure where the objective is to achieve a cooperative—if not harmonious—effort, but when an enemy is actively threatening all lines of operation, the responsibility must be that of one military commander at the appropriate level in each battalion-level sector.

To address the existing problems of cooperation and coordination, we must abolish the stand-alone provincial reconstruction team and integrate its assets into the maneuver task force at the battalion level. This should remain a joint and interagency effort, given the unique talents and perspectives each service and department brings to it.

In this case, a major or lieutenant commander, rather than a lieutenant colonel or Navy commander, would be the commander. Under these conditions, the existing civil affairs B-Team (the provincial reconstruction team project management section focused on brigade priorities) would then become part of the battalion civil affairs section to expand the maneuver battalion task force governance and development staff capabilities. The senior major would then become the seventh organic company-level commander in the task force and the interagency representative adviser to the commander.

Instead of one internal civil affairs field team, there would be five developed for the maneuver battalion task force. One would work directly for each company-level commander and become a formal part of their "company team," while the senior major and civil affairs company commander would consolidate and be responsive to their requirements with the dual hat of battalion S9. This system would create an organic capability to draw on during company-level maneuver operations and engagements with the district governors.

Integrating these assets would require significant development funding, but as General David Petraeus said early on in Operation Iraqi Freedom, development dollars are as important as bullets in a counterinsurgency. Adopting this decentralized and maneuver-fused approach to development would dictate that all provincial reconstruction team funding earmarked for a given Afghan province be diverted to the maneuver task force at the battalion level and subsumed into its overall development budget.

This integration would empower the battalion level commander to focus on areas of concern, synchronize the mission with maneuver priorities without additional coordination or competition (with a provincial reconstruction team), and push the funds down to the company level for development in the districts. This new capability at the maneuver company level would become one of the two cornerstone initiatives for the counterinsurgency in rural Afghanistan. The other and more potent initiative would be adding native Afghan staff officers with critical expertise to the maneuver company.

INTEGRATING AFGHAN INTELLECTUAL CAPITAL

Recent policy discussions about the need for a civilian surge of U.S. government agency personnel with development expertise overlook a central point—suitable candidates already exist in Afghanistan. We must reverse the flight of intellectual capital from rural areas to the cities. It is the rural areas where agricultural and innovative engagement expertise is most needed. Native Afghan cultural, agricultural, and communications experts are a powerful resource in this type of war. Each district requires certain assets and capabilities that native Afghan experts are in the best position to provide. Although these experts would work for Coalition Forces, they would also be valuable for the district governor to use for governance and development purposes. In an agrarian society, these advisers would have a positive effect on the overall agricultural output in the district and help to develop a closer relationship between the population and local government.

Adding these key Afghan positions to a maneuver company headquarters would ideally have two predictable effects. First, it would produce a far superior product because these positions demand an in-depth understanding of cultural nuances that Coalition Forces can never possess. Second, the population's negative perception of the Afghan government would ideally diminish as a direct consequence of the increased responsiveness to the people's concerns and needs. And these effects would be felt none too soon, because most Afghans currently feel little connection with their government and lack confidence in its capabilities.

We should add three key Afghan positions to a company commander's counterinsurgency team—a native cultural adviser, an agricultural adviser, and an information operations specialist. The addition of these three Afghan professionals has the potential to transform a plodding counterinsurgency

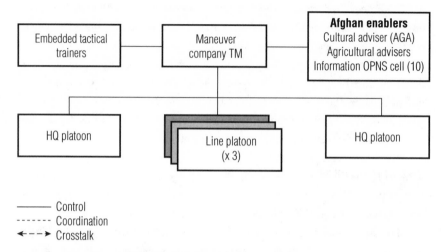

————— Control

------- Coordination

◄ – – ► Crosstalk

Figure 7.4. Expansion of coalition maneuver company assets.

SOURCE: Fenzel, 2010.

effort at the district level into one that is vibrant and connected to the Afghan people. This small group of Afghan professionals would eventually become permanent members of the district governor's staff. In the end, this effort would focus on what the local community and tribes value and would build capacity. The creation of these three key Afghan positions at the district level would provide the capacity for substantial counterinsurgency progress and set the stage for development of a district governor's professional staff to sustain that progress after we leave. Figure 7.4 depicts how these three key positions and the Afghan National Security Force embedded tactical trainers would fit into the existing Coalition maneuver company structure.

Afghan Cultural Adviser

In light of how critical culture awareness is in any counterinsurgency, and the vast challenge of grasping the nuances of tribal culture in Afghanistan, it is a wonder that the concept of assigning a native cultural adviser at the company level has not yet become formally established. A cultural adviser who is well educated and familiar with the subtribal structure and key elders network in local areas of operation can work directly with a Coalition company commander to prevent missteps that have negative effects on the operation.

The cultural adviser should advise the company commander on all matters concerning culture. In this capacity, the adviser would help Coalition Forces avoid pitfalls, understand cultural mores, and engage the population. Moreover, he could facilitate a close working relationship between the company commander and the district governor. A strong cultural adviser can help develop information operations messages to connect the district governor with the Afghan people. The adviser can take the governor's vision and a commander's intent; weave in Islamic principles, tenets of the *Pashtunwali* code, and tribal history; and communicate with the population.

When I commanded Task Force Eagle in Afghanistan from 2007 to 2008, we found ourselves tapping into the experience of the Afghan cultural adviser continuously. For example, in March 2008, an improvised explosive device killed four Afghan guards in the Bermel district of Paktika Province. The Afghan cultural adviser quickly created an information operations message condemning the attack. The message was so compelling that, for the first time, members of the local population conducted their own investigation, discovered the culprits and their location, and informed the Afghan district police chief, who arrested the terrorists responsible for the attack. This was not the first message crafted by the Afghan cultural adviser in the district, but it showed that consistent, compelling communication with the population can transform the environment. Developing civic pride is one thing, but working to improve every Afghan citizen's quality of life is quite another.

Afghan Agricultural Adviser

The vast majority of Afghans in the rural areas, where the Taliban have historically enjoyed freedom of movement, are farmers. An enabler who possesses agricultural expertise has the potential to be a powerful counterinsurgent weapon. The most important economic indicators in most areas of rural Afghanistan relate to agriculture. Because Afghanistan is a largely agrarian society, an adviser with a degree in agriculture should work with the company commander at the district level to develop, plan, and carry out agricultural initiatives.

Such an adviser can be a useful tool for the district governor and Coalition Forces in developing a close relationship with the population. He may run seminars and courses for the local farmers to help them produce larger crops, conduct assessments, advise local farmers on irrigation projects, and distribute agricultural humanitarian assistance. Participants in agricultural seminars may improve their farming operations and perhaps receive a tool kit, wheat and corn seed, or fruit tree saplings on graduation.

Task Force Eagle arranged agricultural seminars to help improve agricultural production. The seminars became so popular in Paktika province that we hired an additional agricultural adviser for each company in our battalion task force. In addition, locals requested that an agricultural radio program be broadcast on the local radio station. Farmers began asking advisers questions by mail and during visits to the district center. Clearly, such seminars and other initiatives can help the local government win over the population. Creating an institutionalized Afghan capability that focuses exclusively on developing and distributing this sort of critical information is the next logical step to make this approach systematic.

Afghan Information Operations Specialists

The most effective information operations in the Afghan war are conducted by Afghans and supported by Coalition Forces. For best results, we need to fuse Coalition Force and Afghan information operations. The company headquarters platoon should have an Afghan information operations cell com-

Figure 7.5. Afghan cornfields in Northern Bermel district of Paktika Province. Agricultural productivity increased substantially with a focused investment in subsidizing seed, fertilizer, and saplings, through formalized agricultural training and workshops in Eastern Paktika.

SOURCE: U.S. Army in Fenzel, 2010.

posed of native Afghan experts familiar with the districts in question. One of the experts should be the adviser for the maneuver company commander, offering insights and proposing methods to "reach" the people most effectively. Another should work at the battalion level to coordinate battalion support for the company under the coordinating hand of the battalion fire support officer. At the company level, at least one Afghan specialist should program and announce radio material. The battalion-level cell should help create messages that resonate with the population and demonstrate that the Afghan district government (district governor) and Coalition Forces (company commander) speak with one voice to the population. The district governor would have the lead in these efforts, and the Coalition Force commander would play a supporting role, offering ideas, pressing for action where appropriate, and adding a degree of quality control to the system.

The Afghan information operations specialists can produce leaflets, run the radio station (if available), and ensure that all communications with the populace are well thought out and effective. These Afghan professionals can play a critical role as they inevitably become the voice of the district government to the population and help break the cycle of rumors and lies propagated by the Taliban through night letters and other forms of intimidation. They could conduct interviews with the district police chief, Afghan National Army commanders, or the district governor to assist in getting important messages out to the people. Local mullahs, loyal to the Afghan government, could run radio shows coordinated by the Afghan information operations team to challenge the inflammatory rhetoric put forth in radical madaris and mosques across the border in Pakistan. In Paktika province, the Afghan workers who ran the mobile radio station (called a "radio in a box") typically received over 500 letters a week from the local population in an overwhelmingly favorable response to the programming. The letters ranged from requests for programming to both progovernment and anti-Taliban poetry, essays, and songs designed to be read or sung on the air. Adding positions for a native Afghan cultural adviser, an agricultural adviser, and an information operations specialist has the potential to provide formidable expertise to a counterinsurgency force. These Afghan experts might also advise on the best way to invest the development resources crucial to success in counterinsurgency operations. The possibilities to favorably shape the environment and create even greater opportunities to exploit are innumerable. Figure 7.6 illustrates relationships across a maneuver

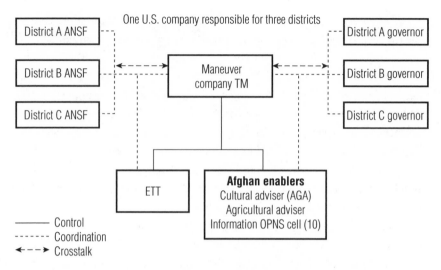

Figure 7.6. Proposed maneuver company counterinsurgency structure in Afghanistan.

company's sphere of influence. This model optimizes all assets and creates an atmosphere to unify effort at the company level.

THE POWER OF THE PEOPLE

With the ongoing policy debate surrounding the war in Afghanistan, it is easy to lose sight of the fact that, in the end, the success of the mission is not dependent on the actions of the Taliban. The mission depends first on the people of Afghanistan contributing to a more secure environment, then on a dramatically improved performance of the Afghan National Security Forces, and only then on our efforts as a Coalition Force. The mission to establish a secure environment in Afghanistan can succeed, but with modifications to the distribution plan for Afghan national security forces and refinements to the command structure of enablers and tactical assets already in the fight, the momentum will swing toward greater stability.

We must make President Hamid Karzai and his provincial governors see the value of empowering the tribal *shuras* to elect their own district governors. The voice of rural Afghanistan would then emerge. Indeed, district centers must become the security epicenters where Afghan National Army and Afghan National Police colocate and support a district governor in the daily business of engaging the people and addressing their needs and concerns.

Longer-term stability in Afghanistan depends on the creation of a district-level structure built around the leadership of district governors partnered with Coalition maneuver company commanders and a full complement of Afghan security forces.

The more urgent proposition is to redistribute Afghan National Army forces from forward operating bases into Afghan communities and rural areas to live among the people and partner with the Afghan National Police. This move alone would send a powerful message to the people and to the Taliban that the stability and future of the nation is in the hands of the Afghan people and protected by a unified security force. Although the signature elements of this reorganization proposal are Afghan led, Coalition maneuver company commanders must partner with district governors and their Afghan National Army battalion commander counterparts to coordinate governance and security efforts.

Structures that worked well through the first several years of the war must evolve to this decentralized approach to countering the insurgency. An important feature of this restructuring plan is disassembling provincial reconstruction teams in favor of a company-level construct that focuses on distributing robust development assets to the maneuver company and interagency advisers to the battalion task force level. We must expand the battalion-level development function to address the distribution of development teams to every maneuver company and empower them to manage more development funds and projects. The cornerstone of this new tactical realignment of assets will be the integration of Afghan intellectual capital into maneuver companies to assume roles as both conduits and primary staff to their district governor counterparts as native Afghan cultural and agricultural advisers and information operations team specialists. They can provide a stronger capability to wage the counterinsurgency than has yet been at our disposal. Afghans must win this war, but an appropriate cross-fertilization of assets and capabilities will facilitate that victory.

NOTES

This article is reprinted with the permission of *Military Review, the Professional Journal of the US Army*, Combined Arms Center, Fort Leaveanworth, Kansas. It was originally published in the March–April 2010 issue of *Military Review*.

1. David Galula, *Counterinsurgency Warfare: Theory and Practice* (Westport, CT: Greenwood, 1964), 78.

8 DEVELOPING AN IO ENVIRONMENTAL ASSESSMENT IN KHOST PROVINCE, AFGHANISTAN

Information Operations at Provincial Reconstruction Team Khost in 2008

Robert J. Bebber

INFORMATION OPERATIONS (IO) TRADITIONALLY SUFFER from a lack of available metrics by which planners can assess their environment and measure the effectiveness of their programs. This often places IO practitioners at a distinct disadvantage when attempting to gain the confidence of unit commanders, who are tasked with allocating scarce battlefield resources and who are often skeptical of information operations as a whole.

The goal of IO is to "influence, corrupt, disrupt or usurp adversarial human and automated decision making while protecting our own."[1] But how does one know whether the decision process—either human or automated—has actually been influenced in some way? We can assume or surmise that, based on the actions of the target of the IO campaign, some desired effect was achieved or not achieved (but how much of that was based on our IO campaign and how much on other factors, perhaps unknown even to us?). We can also, if given the opportunity, ask the target after the fact whether campaign activities influenced their decision making.

Commanders conducting counterinsurgency operations should have two primary IO targets: the insurgents and the local population. Nagl notes that "persuading the masses of people that the government is capable of providing essential services—and defeating the insurgents—is just as important" as enticing the insurgents to surrender and provide information on their comrades.[2]

The provincial reconstruction team (PRT) is not charged with directly targeting insurgents. Instead, its mission is to build the capacity of the host government to provide governance and development to the local population—to show the people that the government can indeed provide "essential services," as Nagl notes.

Information operations traditionally suffer from a lack of available metrics by which planners can assess their environment and measure the effectiveness of their programs. It may be impossible to show direct causation—or even correlation—between information operations and actual effects (that is, did my PSYOP program actually have its desired effect?) in all cases. This often places IO practitioners at a distinct disadvantage when attempting to gain the confidence of unit commanders, who are tasked with allocating scarce battlefield resources and who are often skeptical of information operations as a whole.

This project developed an information operations environmental assessment tool that can be utilized and replicated at the unit level (battalion or less) for use by planners to establish an initial benchmark (where am I?) and measure progress toward achieving the IO program goals and objectives (where do I want to go?) The provincial reconstruction team in Khost province, Afghanistan, needed a tool by which the leadership could benchmark current conditions and evaluate the information environment under which the population lived. It was hoped that such a tool could help provide clues whether our IO (and overall PRT) efforts were having the intended effect.

KHOST PROVINCE, AFGHANISTAN

Khost Province itself is situated along the eastern border with Pakistan, adjacent to the notorious Federally Administered Tribal Areas (FATA) Kurram Agency and North Waziristan—areas that have recently been subject to a number of U.S. drone strikes. The major ethnic groups are Pashtun tribes who share the common tribal tradition of *Pashtunwali*. Recent estimates put Khost's population at 639,849. There are 87,199 households each of which has, on average, eight family members. Almost 98 percent of the population lives in rural districts, with the remaining 2 percent in the urban core of Khost City. Nearly half (46 percent) of households rely on agriculture as their source of income, and over half (54 percent) own or manage farmland or plots. Overall literacy is projected at around 28 percent (44 percent of men versus 7 percent of women), though 52 percent of men age fifteen through twenty-four are literate. There are 157 primary and secondary schools and 2,205 teachers working to educate 107,732 boys and girls in Khost. Khost is also home to a university—Shaik Zayed University—which had 687 students as of 2005. The vast majority of villages do not have health care facilities readily present.[3]

IO ENVIRONMENT ASSESSMENT TOOL

To create a user-friendly IO assessment tool, the decision was made to use a Likert scale approach. The Likert scale is a psychometric response scale where respondents provide a level of agreement to a statement or question. It uses a bipolar scaling method, measuring positive and negative on the extreme ends (that is, "strongly agree" to "strongly disagree"). Likert scales are subject to distortion, such as central tendency bias, acquiescence bias, and social desirability bias. However, they are readily comprehensible and easy to understand for the novice researcher and present a good start from which to develop a simple information operations environmental assessment tool.

The tool used would ask participants open ended question or questions. Based on the response and follow-up questioning, the interviewer would categorize the participant's response on a scale of 1 to 5, with 5 being the "best" and

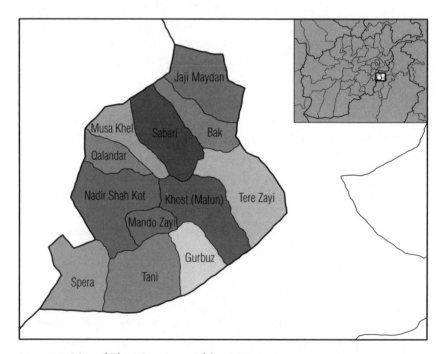

Figure 8.1. Map of Khost Province, Afghanistan.

SOURCE: Adapted from http://upload.wikimedia.org/wikipedia/commons/1/11/Khost_districts.png.

1 being the "worst." One important difference between traditional Likert scale methodology in survey research and this methodology is that the interviewer, not the respondent, is the one who quantifies the response. This is mostly due to issues of participant literacy and the hazards of having to translate between English and Pashtu, the dominant language spoken in Khost Province, Afghanistan. Another difference is that the assessment tool does not directly ask the interviewer or participant to "strongly agree" or "strongly disagree" with a specific statement. Rather, the scaling methodology provides examples to get an idea of what a security condition valued at "2" might be compared to "4," and the interviewer marks the appropriate value (a judgment call, to be sure). Table 8.1 provides an example. "ANSF" refers to Afghan National Security Forces, such as the Afghan National Army and Afghan National Police. "AAF" means "Anti-Afghan Forces," which was the nomenclature used at the time to refer to the insurgents. (Note that, during the author's stay in Afghanistan, that nomenclature changed from "ACM"—Anti-Coalition Militia—to "AAF" to "EOA," or "Enemies of Afghanistan." A series of three name changes over a nine-month period says more about us than it does about the insurgents, but that is the subject for an entirely different chapter.)

The instrument is designed to gather data on five main domains: security, development, governance, economic conditions, and the view of the future. In

Table 8.1. Sample assessment tool question.

			Age *Gender*	*1*	*2*	*3*	*4*	*5*
Category	*Question*	*Scale/Example*						
Security	In general, describe the security situation in your village.	1 ANSF ineffective, seriously corrupt, nonexistent; AAF operate freely and dominate						
		2 ANSF limited effectiveness, moderately corrupt; AAF activity significant						
		3 ANSF moderately effective, some corruption, AAF moderate presence						
		4 ANSF effective, little corruption; AAF activity small/limited effectiveness						
		5 ANSF very effective, barely to no corruption; AAF nonexistent or extremely small						

this way, IO planners can see if their programs had an impact on any or all of the major categories that are the emphasis of international efforts in Afghanistan. Using the tool, planners might give insight into the relationship among the categories. They can also gauge whom the population "trusts" to provide truthful information and what the primary source of information is (such as publicly available sources or newspapers, radio, television, and so on).

QUALITATIVE VERSUS QUANTITATIVE RESEARCH

It is important to distinguish the use of the IO environmental assessment tool from pure survey research or *quantitative analysis*. At the unit level, formal survey research, including random selection of participants, stratification, scaling and regression analysis, would be impractical. IO planners at the unit level do not have the resources or the time to conduct such endeavors. Therefore, these results should not be taken to be an accurate reflection of public opinion in the same way we would suggest a public opinion poll in the United States might be (as much as can be said for that in any case!). This is an instrument that was designed and used under wartime conditions in an area of the world that can barely be said to be at a Third World level and with more than two-thirds of the population being illiterate.

The tool was also crafted so that, with a little training, IO planners at the unit level could train squad leaders and troops on its use and purpose, so that other members of the team might also be in a position to collect data for the IO effort. Its use can best be described as *qualitative research*, rather than quantitative.

Qualitative research has its strengths and weaknesses. While it is subjective in nature, it seeks to understand and gain insight into the thought process of respondents. It relies on inductive logic to generate hypotheses and conclusions. If the goal of information operations is to change the decision-making process by actors to influence their actions, then qualitative research attempts to gain insight into that thought process, recognizing that "how people think" influences their behavior.

Reliability is also an issue in qualitative research because it relies on the interviewer (in this case, the author) to measure the data and therefore can become "personal" in nature. However, it can capture more dimensions of concepts that we seek to explore.

The reader may also ask whether it is possible to make generalized statements about a population of approximately 700,000 based on a little more than

200 interviews. The goal of all surveys is to be able to say something about a population based on interviewing a sample. The raw data itself are "correct" in the sense that they are an accurate reflection of what the respondent said. Problems arise when statisticians and pollsters attempt to use statistical methodology to say that within a given degree of confidence *an entire population* shares a certain opinion or point of view. That methodology—random selection of a sample, stratification, and so on—was not possible under the operating conditions in Khost province at the time. That being said, more than 200 interviews is a significant undertaking (especially for a one-person operation), and the data are consistent in their findings. Indeed, just the mere fact that we were conducting interviews on such a large scale in and of itself is extremely useful for units involved in counterinsurgency and reconstruction effort. But they are not data that can be generalized to the entire population and should not be confused as such.

CONDUCTING THE ASSESSMENTS

The PRT conducted missions almost daily during the time frame it was stationed in Khost (March through November 2008), and the IO officer traveled on the missions most of the time to collect data and conduct the assessment. The data were updated regularly and reported to the leadership team during the battle update brief (or "BUB"), which was held three times per week. The IO officer was aided by a cultural adviser assigned to the IO unit, a local national working directly for Coalition Forces.

During the more than 200 interviews, several practices were adopted to elicit more "honest" responses. That being said, it is important to acknowledge up front that interviews are being conducted by an individual in an American uniform, wearing body armor and carrying weapons, and with other American and Afghan military and police in the area. Despite the presence of a cultural adviser who was interpreting for the IO officer, some results may have been skewed, but how much or often is unknown.

There is a Pashtu saying that "A single 'no' is worth a thousand 'yeses.'" This means that whenever questioned by someone, a "yes" response will tend to elicit follow-up questions while a "no" response might end the questioning. After decades of brutal Soviet occupation, civil war and the repressive rule of the Taliban, most Afghans are understandably wary when approached and asked if they would mind "just answering a few questions." We must also acknowledge this limitation.

Every attempt was made to conduct each interview separately, away from groups of civilians and military personnel. This was done not only to mitigate the presence of security personnel but also to separate the individual away from his or her group of friends, who might influence the subject. However, this was not always possible.

The reader will note immediately that very few females were interviewed. Tribal customs in this area of Afghanistan do not permit interaction between foreigners (or even other nonfamily tribal males) with postpubescent females. Not surprisingly, when a PRT convoy would arrive in the area of any village, any females outside their compound returned indoors.

DATA AND RESULTS

The original benchmark study was conducted from April 29 to June 16, 2008, and consisted of ninety-eight interviews gathered in eleven of the thirteen districts of Khost Province. The follow-up study was conducted June 29 to October 26, 2008. During this period, Coalition and Afghan Security Forces conducted a series of operations along K-G Road (Khost to Gardez Road) and in the several districts of Khost province. This provided us the opportunity to evaluate the effect of not only these operations but continued operations of the PRT and local government on the information operations environment.

Tables 8.2 and 8.3 are the frequency tables showing the location distribution, age range, and gender of interviews conducted. (Note: The author used

Table 8.2. Benchmark study frequencies (April 29–June 16, 2008)

Count of district		Count of age range		Count of gender	
District	Total	Age range	Total	Gender	Total
Bak	5	17 or under	6	Female	5
Gorbuz	5	18 to 35	54	Male	93
Jaji Maidan	8	36 to 50	26	Grand total	98
Mando Zayi	1	51 to 75	10		
Matun	15	76 and over	2		
Musa Khail	9	Grand total	98		
Nador Sha Kot	10				
Shemal	14				
Spera	7				
Tani	12				
Tera Zayi	12				
Grand total	98				

Table 8.3. Follow-up study frequencies (June 29–October 26, 2008).

Count of district		Count of age range		Count of gender	
District	*Total*	*Age range*	*Total*	*Gender*	*Total*
Bak	19	17 or under	19	Female	3
Gorbuz	5	18 to 35	39	Male	101
Jaji Maidan	5	36 to 50	34	Grand total	104
Mando Zayi	9	51 to 75	12		
Matun	14	Grand total	104		
Musa Khail	23				
Nador Sha Kot	5				
Shemal	5				
Spera	1				
Tani	10				
Tera Zayi	8				
Grand total	104				

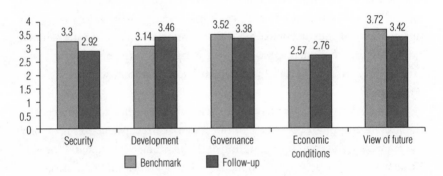

Figure 8.2. Average responses.

Microsoft Office Excel 2007 for data collection and analysis.) Even though operational needs dictated the location and number of interviews, the sample size permits us to conclude that the data are fairly reliable.

The summarization of both studies in Figure 8.2 shows a remarkable consistency in the findings. Two measures show a slight improvement—development and economic conditions—although three measures show a moderate decline—security, governance, and the view of the future. This reinforced the general understanding of facts on the ground during the time period the PRT was operating and seems to show that the situation in Khost had been following the same general trajectory as Afghanistan as a whole.

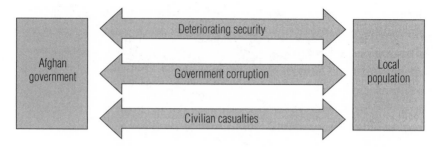

Figure 8.3. Factors driving the Afghan people and the government apart.

Several factors are likely in play. A significant increase in insurgent activity in the region—well reported in open source both in the international media and locally in Khost—plays largely into the insurgents' goal of separating the population from the government by showing that the government is unwilling and/or unable to secure the population.[4] At the same time, a number of civilian killings by Coalition Forces, including a popular national cricket player in Khost,[5] has made the population feel uncomfortable with the international military presence. Endemic government corruption at the national and provincial level has also certainly contributed to frustration with the Afghan government.

At the same time, there has been some improvement in development in the province through the efforts of the provincial reconstruction team and the maneuver units and the beginning of the yearlong effort to build the K-G Road, a U.S. Agency for International Development project. Food prices had fallen; the price of eighty kilos of flour, as high as 5,000 afghani in July, had fallen to about 2,600 afghani by November 2008. While this is still high by Afghan standards, the decrease in food prices has helped mitigate some economic fears.

Figure 8.3 best summarizes what was believed to be the general situation. It should be noted, however, that two of the three main factors driving a wedge between the local population and the government are not directly tied to the insurgents but are rather related to the Afghan government and the Coalition.

DISCUSSION OF FINDINGS

Security

At the conclusion of the benchmark study, joint operations began to attempt to improve security conditions in Khost Province. According to McCreary,

Khost Province had only thirteen clashes with Afghan and Coalition forces in October—a drop from twenty-two in September and the lowest since the May 2008 total of fourteen.[6] This also coincided with the traditional lull in cross-border infiltration and attacks due to the onset of winter, as well as the increase of U.S. unmanned aerial vehicle attacks into Pakistan. It remains to be seen whether the reduced violence is permanent or simply a pause as the insurgents regroup, reorganize, and make another push.

Perception of security in Khost declined from 3.3 to 2.92, an 11.5 percent decline.[7] The vast majority of interviews were conducted during the ongoing security operations and extensive public coverage of the deteriorating security conditions in Khost and Afghanistan at large. It is possible that this is a lagging indicator and that, should significant activity in Khost continue to decline, we would see an improvement of public perception of the security environment.

That being said, there were some indications of a great deal of frustration with the Afghan National Police (ANP). "They hide behind 'hescos' during the day and are thieves at night," according to one interview respondent. ANP staff currently receive inadequate training, poor equipment, and low pay and are behaving accordingly. Improving their situation and increasing their presence in the outlying villages and districts may go a long way toward improving public confidence in the Afghan government. The Afghan National Army (ANA), on the other hand, is well liked and respected (as well as being better trained, equipped, and paid). In areas where there are ANA units, respondents' security perception was typically much better. It should be noted that members of the ANA are drawn from the national population and assigned nationwide, whereas ANP are drawn from the local community and assigned locally. One possible effect of this policy might be that ANP are more susceptible to bribery, intimidation, and corruption because the criminals and insurgents can easily find them and their families, whereas a member of the ANA might be from a province and tribe on the other side of the country.

There seemed to be an increase in complaints about Coalition Forces conducting searches—especially at night—and the growth in civilian casualties. Locals complained that only Afghan security forces should be permitted to conduct searches and that they could be conducted during the day. They wondered why the Coalition could not just surround a house at night to prevent anyone from escaping and then wait until morning so the entire village could see who was being arrested and why. (Note: The author is not criticizing Coalition military tactics, merely reporting what the common complaints were.) It should be noted that villagers said they had no problem with arresting those who aid the Taliban in any way. They also said that if villages permitted insurgents to use their village to stage attacks on Afghan and Coalition Forces, it was appropriate for the Coalition to respond, even if civilians are killed. This follows the *Pashtunwali* tradition of attacking those who permit their homes to be used as a base to conduct attacks on others. In that same vein, most locals were extremely pleased with American efforts to step up UAV cross-border attacks on Taliban and al-Qaeda safe havens in Pakistan.

For the local population, it is clear that despite the tens of millions of dollars of investment by the government and international community in public goods and services, security remains the paramount issue. As was expressed in many interviews, "What good is a school when we live under threat each day? The government does not take security seriously. At least under the Taliban, we had security."

The frustration with Afghan National Security Forces (ANSF) to effectively react to and counter insurgent actions appears to be the driving force behind the anxiety expressed about security. The local sentiment that the government "does not take security seriously" was reinforced when it was pointed out that, even when insurgents are arrested, they are soon released because of government corruption (that is, bribing judges or village elders being coerced or bribed into vouching for the perpetrator's innocence) or ineffectiveness. Afghan forces—primarily ANP—are suspected of being easily intimidated, unwilling to fight, and largely corrupt. (It should be pointed out that the ANP do take the highest casualties among the ANSF.) The lack of confidence on the part of the population, coupled with the intimidation tactics of the insurgents and inability of Coalition and Afghan Forces to clear and hold large land areas may create a "perfect storm" in terms of a growing psychology of fear.

Development

Respondents' perception of development improved by more than 10 percent, from 3.14 to 3.46. There was a significant increase in the number of projects and development, and with the beginning of construction on the Khost to Gardez (K-G) Road project by USAID—a long-awaited national development goal—improvement was expected. Development remains one of the most positive aspects of the Coalition presence in Khost province. However, despite widespread public support for international assistance, there seemed to be mounting frustration at the perceived slow pace. Compared to other provinces, Khost is actually one of the more developed in terms of road infrastructure, schools, cell phone availability, and industrial production.[8] In spite of this, the vast majority of the population live in poor conditions.

It appears that previous Coalition units might not have been effective in managing expectations on the part of the local population in terms of development. One common refrain is, "You have been here for six years. How come you have not done more? How come we still live like this?" While there has been much publicity on the fact that the local government and Coalition Forces have spent approximately $50 million on reconstruction and development in Khost in 2008 and 2009, it might as well have been $50 *billion* if the vast majority of the local population does not see a tangible benefit in their daily life.

To be sure, there are tangible benefits that are a direct or indirect result of the international presence. During the Taliban regime, there were no cell phones or televisions, barely any paved roads, few schools and even fewer clinics, and hardly any personal automobiles. The local population seems to recognize this.

Continued emphasis on reconstruction and development by the local government and Coalition Forces will further legitimize the current Karzai regime and maintain popular support, but it is important to remember that this probably has a *diminishing* utility with the passage of time. Taken in context with the other measures of the environment (that is, a deteriorating security environment), its effect is further compromised.

One mitigating factor in this is that Afghanistan has just emerged from decades of war and tyranny. The massive social upheaval has helped undo many of the cultural and traditional bonds that were the "glue" of the Afghan people. Coming out from under the shadow of Soviet occupation, civil war, and the radical despotic rule of the Taliban, it is unsurprising that people's expectations are easily inflated as to the capability of highly developed and wealthy nations to radically transform and improve the infrastructure and standard of living. This was true in Iraq (a more developed nation than Afghanistan), whose population was initially frustrated with the pace of reconstruction after the U.S. invasion of 2003. It was also true of Russia after the fall of communism, where expectations failed to meet the reality of the daunting task ahead. Therefore, from an IO perspective, we should not be surprised at some level of disappointment being a constant factor.

Governance

On the eve of elections in Afghanistan, governance saw a marginal decline of 3.52 to 3.38 (nearly 4 percent). It is somewhat surprising that there was not a more noticeable drop due to recent national and international news reports of systemic corruption within the Afghan government. Part of this might be explained away by most Afghans' tendency to accept some level of corruption as a normal conduct of government business, so long as public needs were being generally met. However, it should remain a concern for Coalition Forces operating in Khost, since nearly all local nationals believe that, without Coalition presence, the government would collapse. Therefore, the Coalition becomes an enabler of corruption by supporting the government. Local villagers' knowledge of who their district subgovernor was remained poor, and most villagers reported having never even seen a representative of the Afghan government (national or local) visit.

Economic Conditions

Respondents' satisfaction with the local economy seemed to marginally improve, going from 2.57 to 2.76, a 7.4 percent increase. This might have to do with the decline in food prices; during the benchmark study, the price of eighty kilos of flour had reached more than 5,000 afghani ($100). Since then, the price of flour moved to between 2,600 afghani and 3,000 afghani ($52 to $60). Many locals continue to travel to foreign countries to work and support their families back home in Khost. A concern from the benchmark study was the public complaining that, under the Taliban, food prices were not as bad. This concern subsided somewhat.

Average View of the Future

Not surprisingly, anxiety about Afghanistan's future seemed to grow. The average response fell from 3.72 to 3.42, an 8 percent drop. A hopeful sign was that, again, no one responded that he or she believed life would be better under the Taliban. (Again, we note that interviews were conducted in the presence of Coalition and Afghan security forces, which might have influenced those responses.)

Table 8.4. Benchmark.

Trust	
Government	32.65%
Taliban	0.00%
Elders	13.27%
Mullahs	12.24%
Coalition Forces	5.10%
No one	36.73%
Total	100.00%

Table 8.5. Follow-up.

Trust	
Government	29.41%
Taliban	0.00%
Elders	33.33%
Mullahs	7.84%
Coalition Forces	3.92%
No one	25.49%
Total	100.00%

Source of Trust

There appeared to be some movement on who local nationals trusted to tell them the truth and help them with their problems. (See Table 8.4 and Table 8.5.)

Trust in the government declined from 32.65 percent to 29.41 percent, although trust in elders rose from 13.27 percent to 33.33 percent. Those responding "none of the above" or "no one" fell from 36.73 percent to 25.49 percent. (Note that "no one" and "none of the above" were never provided as options for the respondent. Therefore, this is a measure of free response.) Again, in another hopeful sign, no one said that he or she trusted the Taliban to tell them the truth or help them with problems.

After the benchmark study, we thought that Coalition Forces might place more emphasis on the local government rather than tribal elders because tribal authority had been so undermined by decades of civil war and corruption. Although locals still complained about elders expecting bribes to help their villagers, there did seem to be a general improvement in the satisfaction with the elders. This may be because, although the population would prefer to have a government presence in their area (namely in the form of security forces), the fact that the government was unwilling and unable to do so meant that villagers had to turn to their elders to resolve disputes and protect them from insurgent activity. Many elders, seeing that Afghan and Coalition Forces were inadequate to provide effective security, made informal agreements with insurgents in their areas to keep them at bay. This probably had some impact on their standing, perhaps at the expense of the trust in the government. However, this is only speculation.

Table 8.6. Benchmark.

Source of information.	
Radio	77.55%
Television	20.41%
Newspaper	0.00%
Elders and mullahs	1.02%
Family and friends	1.02%
Total	100.00%

Table 8.7. Follow-up.

Source of information.	
Radio	80.39%
Television	16.67%
Newspaper	0.00%
Elders and mullahs	0.00%
Family and friends	2.94%
Total	100.00%

Source of Information

The benchmark and follow-up study both show that radio remained the dominate medium as a source of news and information (see Table 8.6 and Table 8.7).

IO practitioners are quick to rely on radio as the primary means to shape public opinion in Afghanistan. Television is a distant second, and the use of the Internet (not included in the IO assessment tool) and newspapers were nonexistent. However, almost all the interviews were conducted among villagers living outside the urban area of Khost city. Within the city, dozens of newspapers and magazines are published and Internet cafes can be found, so we can reasonably assume that such media are used. What might be a critical area of future study is to determine what *key leaders* use primarily to obtain their news and information. Future IO campaigns might seek to "influence the influencers" to create a multiplier effect.

USING THE IO ENVIRONMENTAL ASSESSMENT TOOL

Collecting data is one thing, while using them is quite another. We noted in the beginning that IO practitioners often suffer from a lack of reliable metrics, which often leads to difficulty in encouraging battlefield commanders to allocate scarce resources toward full-spectrum information operations. Like it or not, "what gets measured, gets done," as the old engineering saying goes.

An assessment tool can have a variety of uses in counterinsurgency and poststabilization operations. (See Table 8.8.) First, it can give a commander a quantifiable view of where the population might be in terms of broad domains—domains that are critical in such operations. Second, it can give clues to possible nonkinetic tactical options that might support the overall strategy of improving popular belief in the legitimacy in the host government. For example, our initial benchmark study showed substantial concern over economic conditions. During the interviews, we understood that was primarily tied to the rising price of food. At the time, the Taliban just across the border in Pakistan had announced locally that they would kill any truck drivers they found to be carrying food from Pakistan into Afghanistan. Taliban and criminal gangs operating openly in FATA would stop trucks bound for Khost and extract "taxes" from the drivers, which also had an inflationary pressure on food prices. Of course, the worldwide food shortage was a major contributor to rising food prices as well. However, people expected that their local and national government would act on ensuring that food remained available and affordable. A major coordinated effort to inform the population that the Taliban was partially responsible for rising food prices, coupled with a concerted effort by the national and local government (supported by the Coalition) to bring in more food supplies to at least stabilize food prices might have served the twin strategic purposes of separating the local population from the insurgents as well as building popular legitimacy—all without firing a single bullet. This is obviously a simplistic example, and it is not meant to suggest that such an undertaking would have been easy to accomplish. However, it does show how the use of the IO environmental assessment tool might provide alternate paths toward accomplishing strategic objectives.

Third, the regular, consistent use of the tool can give a glimpse into understanding possible variations in why specific tribes, villages, or districts might have different perceptions on conditions or where they obtain their information and whom they trust most. It might serve as part of the tool set used to look for indicators and warnings of potential conflict and concerns.

Finally, it could provide the IO practitioner and commanders with data on how the conditions within the information environment have changed over time, which could be used to measure whether overall strategic goals are being met.

These are probably just a few of what might be other uses for the tool. The goal was to provide IO practitioners at the unit level with an easy-to-use tool by which they might measure the effect of their information operations campaign strategy and tactics and perhaps something to use to buttress their request to their commanders for more support and actions. No doubt that this tool is crude in its refinement and application, and it is hoped that, if found useful, it can be replicated and improved on.

Table 8.8. IO environmental assessment tool.

District	Average of security	Average of development	Average of governance	Average of economic conditions	Average of view of the future
Bak	2.80	2.60	3.40	2.20	3.40
Gorbuz	4.40	4.20	4.00	3.60	4.40
Jaji Maidan	4.63	3.63	4.50	2.00	4.50
Matun	4.07	4.20	4.40	3.80	4.00
Musa Khail	3.22	2.89	2.89	2.00	3.56
Nador Sha Kot	2.90	2.80	2.70	2.60	3.30
Qalandar					
Sabari					
Shemal	3.00	2.57	3.07	2.36	3.79
Spera	1.86	2.71	2.57	1.57	2.57
Tani	3.25	3.25	3.92	2.58	3.83
Tera Zayi	2.83	2.58	3.50	2.33	3.67
Mando Zayi	3.00	3.00	3.00	3.00	4.00
Grand Total	3.30	3.14	3.52	2.57	3.72

Count of district

District	Total
Bak	5
Gorbuz	5
Jaji Maidan	8
Mando Zayi	1
Matun	15
Musa Khail	9
Nador Sha Kot	10
Shemal	14
Spera	7
Tani	12
Tera Zayi	12
Grand Total	98

Count of IO source

District	RADIO	TV	Family and friends	Elders and mullahs	Grand Total
Bak	80.00%	0.00%	20.00%	0.00%	100.00%
Gorbuz	40.00%	60.00%	0.00%	0.00%	100.00%
Jaji Maidan	87.50%	12.50%	0.00%	0.00%	100.00%
Matun	40.00%	60.00%	0.00%	0.00%	100.00%
Musa Khail	100.00%	0.00%	0.00%	0.00%	100.00%
Nador Sha Kot	50.00%	40.00%	0.00%	10.00%	100.00%
Shemal	100.00%	0.00%	0.00%	0.00%	100.00%
Spera	100.00%	0.00%	0.00%	0.00%	100.00%
Tani	83.33%	16.67%	0.00%	0.00%	100.00%
Tera Zayi	91.67%	8.33%	0.00%	0.00%	100.00%
Mando Zayi	100.00%	0.00%	0.00%	0.00%	100.00%
Grand Total	77.55%	20.41%	1.02%	1.02%	100.00%

Count of IO Trust

District	IO Trust Governance	ELDERS	MULLAHS	CF	NOA	Grand Total
Bak	20.00%	0.00%	20.00%	0.00%	60.00%	100.00%
Gorbuz	40.00%	40.00%	0.00%	0.00%	20.00%	100.00%
Jaji Maidan	50.00%	25.00%	0.00%	12.50%	12.50%	100.00%
Matun	33.33%	0.00%	6.67%	0.00%	60.00%	100.00%
Musa Khail	44.44%	0.00%	33.33%	0.00%	22.22%	100.00%
Nador Sha Kot	0.00%	0.00%	10.00%	0.00%	90.00%	100.00%
Shemal	35.71%	28.57%	0.00%	14.29%	21.43%	100.00%
Spera	0.00%	28.57%	28.57%	0.00%	42.86%	100.00%
Tani	58.33%	8.33%	33.33%	0.00%	0.00%	100.00%
Tera Zayi	33.33%	16.67%	0.00%	16.67%	33.33%	100.00%
Mando Zayi	0.00%	0.00%	0.00%	0.00%	100.00%	100.00%
Grand Total	32.65%	13.27%	12.24%	5.10%	36.73%	100.00%

NOTES

This chapter originally appeared in the November 1, 2009, edition of *The Culture and Conflict Review* and appears here with permission from the publisher.

1. Department of Defense, *Joint Publication 3-13: Information Operations* (Washington, D.C.: Joint Chiefs of Staff, 2006), ix.

2. John A. Nagl, *Learning to Eat Soup with a Knife: Counterinsurgency Lessons from Malaya and Vietnam* (Chicago: University of Chicago Press, 2002), 93.

3. Program for Culture and Conflict Studies, *Khost Provincial Profile*, 2007; retrieved on June 27, 2008, from www.nps.edu/programs/ccs/Khost.html.

4. John McCreary, "Nightwatch Special Report: October 2008 in Afghanistan," *AFCEA Intelligence*, December 15, 2008; retrieved on January 2, 2009, from www.afcea.org/mission/intel/nightwatch.asp.

5. Radio Free Europe/Radio Liberty, "Afghan Cricket Star Reportedly Killed in U.S.-led Raid," *RFE/RL.org*, August 27, 2008; retrieved on January 2, 2009, from www.rferl.org/content/Afghan_Cricket_Star_Reportedly_Killed_/1194358.html. Note that questions remain regarding the cricket player's affiliation with insurgents, and to this author's knowledge, no classified data have been released.

6. Official military reports of significant activities in Khost province, or "SIGACTS," remain classified.

7. The author will note the change in the benchmark to the follow-up study as a percentage increase or decrease; however, he recognizes that this is not an exact measurement in a statistical sense. The environmental assessment tool can perhaps give us an idea of direction, but not an exact measure of variation.

8. Program for Culture and Conflict Studies, 2007.

9 IMPLEMENTING A BALANCED COUNTERINSURGENCY STRATEGY IN NORTHEAST AFGHANISTAN, MAY 2007–JULY 2008

Nathan R. Springer

THIS CHAPTER WILL EXAMINE the successful implementation of balanced counterinsurgency strategy in northeastern Afghanistan through the lens of my experiences executing it in my area of operation as an army troop commander from May 2007 through January 2008 and as the squadron Fire Effects Coordination Cell (FECC) officer in charge, responsible for the squadron's application of nonlethal effects in the northern Konar provincial districts of Naray and Ghaziabad and the eastern Nuristan provincial district of Kamdesh.[1] I define a balanced counterinsurgency (COIN) strategy as the appropriate level of effort applied to killing and capturing the enemy versus partnering with and protecting the Afghan population and enabling the Afghan National Security Forces (ANSF) to operate independently. The weighting of this effort is determined by the unique local conditions of each area of operation (AO), including the status of the local population; the insurgent force's influence with respect to the local population; the enemy's disposition, composition, and strength; and the effectiveness of the ANSF in the area. Local conditions constantly change. An effective counterinsurgency strategy changes with it.

I will recount how my unit, the 1st Squadron, 91st Cavalry, 173rd Airborne Brigade Combat Team (ABCT), arrived at the decision to apply a balanced strategy. I will outline how we combined an enemy-centric and population-centric strategy by line of operation. Finally, I will describe the time, patience, and personal relationships required to at once empower the traditional Afghan leadership and population, from the village and the tribal levels on up, while marginalizing and isolating the insurgency.

Table 9.1. Determining the appropriate strategy.

Enemy centric	Population centric
Conditions	Conditions
• Enemy is foreign or external influence; ideologically, ethnically, religiously, culturally separated from people • Enemy unwanted in area • Popular desire for kill-capture options to free population • People connected with government • Developed area; enemy disrupts economy, functional activities of daily life	• Fighters mostly local; related to elders and villagers • Traditional society; elders = local government • Little popular desire for kill-capture; popular tolerance for fighters as individuals • Immature environment; economic deprivation; fractured society • Little connection with central government
Method	Method
• Focus on kill-capture; lethal (–) HVI targeting • Other LLOs as able; especially as follow-on to kinetic strike	• Marginalize and isolate insurgent leaders through focus on strengthening traditional leaders, governance, jobs, development, co-option (lethal and nonlethal [+/–] HVI targeting • Kill-capture isolated enemy after deliberately setting conditions

SOURCE: Lt. Col. Christopher Kolenda and 1-91 Cavalry Staff strategy comparison list devised in October 2007, Conn Barracks, Schweinfurt, Germany.

Over the past twelve years of war in Afghanistan, a philosophical debate has emerged as to which counterinsurgency approach most readily produces favorable outcomes: population centric or enemy centric. Population-centric counterinsurgency (COIN) emphasizes partnering with and protecting the population from the enemy, whereas enemy-centric COIN emphasizes the importance of focusing all effort on killing and capturing the enemy.[2] A third school of thought deems neither approach appropriate when executed in isolation but advocates a balanced strategy customized for each area of operation's dynamics. The debate over adopting a population-centric versus an enemy-centric strategy is multidimensional and not remotely black and white. It is gray. Each approach contains critical elements necessary to success. We called our approach population centric, which, unfortunately, some analysts have come to associate with the absence of traditional warfare methods. Table 9.1 clearly delineates how we viewed population-centric counterinsurgency. Note that kill-capture is clearly listed as an element of that approach.

In the current political climate I have taken to referring to our approach at that time as a "balanced" one, but it is important to understand we all called it population centric back then. In my head, I still do. We favored the approach that would preserve the lives of the most people and propel us toward our goals. Period. But the implementation of our strategy likely scared some of the naysayers out there. Our war was a personal one. We spent time in the villages, getting to know the people, so we could learn how best to liberate them and defeat the insurgency. At first, we executed our mission each day with twice the force we needed because we were cautious and unsure. I soon discovered that rumbling through town with weapons drawn and sunglasses gleaming tended to discourage locals from confiding much of anything in me, much less remaining in the streets as we approached. We knew we needed to work together. But how? My commanding officer, Lt. Col. Christopher Kolenda, was instrumental in guiding us to the approaches that worked. It was risky. We cautiously met with tribal leaders regularly. At first, I'll admit, I brought everybody with me. We set up a perimeter of vehicles and soldiers, surrounding the home I was visiting, to deter the insurgents from attacking. But, over time, as my leadership team dined in the tribal leaders' homes, seated cross-legged on their living room rugs, discussing the tremendous issues facing Afghanistan, we developed a mutual respect. We all began to relax. The tribal leaders sometimes walked us to the edge of the village or even back to our FOB afterwards, as a show of support and to protect us from anyone who might be hiding in the trees. I think that was the most surprising element of my time there. I was frequently protected, and several times saved, by the villagers and leaders I had originally feared. It is much easier to be brave from behind a desk safely tucked behind the wire. Wise or not, I stopped wearing my helmet when I would walk through the villages. I scaled back my entourage. I learned to listen and detect whom I could trust and whom I could not. While I met inside the homes, my soldiers played soccer in the streets with the village children. Everyone was encouraged to develop a relationship with a villager. We put ourselves out there. And if you look back at the statistics, our time in that AO was the least violent, with the fewest casualties. It took effort and so much time and many, many meals.

Make no mistake, we suffered casualties and horrible losses at the hands of the insurgency several times. The squadron lost soldiers during our time there. We were certainly at war, fighting and dying. But when we would leave our weekly meetings, the tribal leaders would place their hands over our hearts, as a show of solidarity. In those moments I knew we were succeeding with our strategy. I understand our former AO became far more dangerous in the years after we left. I also understand that a strategy much more tilted toward the enemy centric was implemented by the unit that directly followed ours. I concede that the situation on the ground has changed radically. The Ghaziabad and Naray Districts I primarily operated in and our forward operating base, now named FOB Bostick, after a fellow troop commander killed in action on July 27, 2007, during our deployment, is being handed over to the ANSF. But the fact is that our balanced approach yielded progress at the time my unit occupied that AO. As we draw closer to the end of the war in Afghanistan, COIN is becoming a subject of derision. I find that unfortunate. We cannot talk the successes of this approach out of existence. The history of what happened cannot be changed by political swings in sentiment. The facts remain. We made strides.

I have had the privilege of deploying to both Iraq and Afghanistan (twice), where I witnessed the implementation of two disparate strategies within the context of the War on Terror. My first deployment, OIF II in 2004–2005, was set in Iraq's Sunni Triangle within a squadron AO that stretched from Samarra north to Tikrit. My squadron implemented an enemy-centric strategy. The enemy-centric strategy worked well in the most volatile central and southern portions of our expansive AO, but we failed to recognize the situation was different in our northern AO. I didn't know it then, but our squadron missed a potentially game-changing "transition point" in this portion of our AO. A transition point is a key juncture where the operating environment necessitates the implementation of a new strategy or the adaptation of an existing strategy to accommodate the fluid conditions on the ground. It would take a deployment to Afghanistan in 2007–2008 and the implementation of a balanced strategy for me to digest this fact and to assign full relevance to transition points, whether they represented a 180-degree shift from a wholly enemy-centric strategy to one that also focuses on the population, like our missed opportunity in Iraq, or the simple recognition of the transition points within our balanced strategy in Afghanistan.

Lt. Col. Christopher Kolenda, the commander of 1st Squadron, 91st Cavalry during our deployment, devised the comparative checklist seen in Table 9.1 to visually depict the operating environment necessary for the appropriate implementation of an enemy-centric versus population-centric strategy. As the table clearly delineates, the squadron's initial assessment of our area of operation overwhelmingly demanded a strategy focused on the population. Still, a powerful insurgency existed in our AO, and we had to deal with them. The key was to understand the nature of the war we would be fighting, the nature of the people, and the nature of the enemy. Conventional wisdom suggested this was a cross-border insurgency; actually it was a local insurgency and an insurrection in the Kamdesh district. We had to analyze the relationships among multiple sets of actors, including the fighters and the people and the drivers of the insurgency and instability. This approach was critical in enabling us to develop an appropriate balanced strategy.

Our area of operation was set in rural northeastern Afghanistan where there was little to no perceived connection between the local population and the Afghan central government. Local tribes and community leaders had been powerful, while local governance operated efficiently at the village level, which included every male in the village/tribe taking part in a Greek-style tribal participatory democratic system. The village and community elders had watched their power wither over the past thirty years of fighting, while radical mullahs and "commanders" had steadily gained power. An active local insurgency existed. The twist was that many of the fighters were the sons and grandsons of the village elders and mullahs, making our military's kill-capture operations often counterproductive. With over 70 percent of the Afghan population under the age of twenty-five, we were not going to kill our way out of this. Finally, severe economic and social deprivation existed, with a near 90 percent illiteracy rate, while infrastructure was nonexistent.

DETERMINING THE RIGHT BALANCE

Our squadron had a balanced strategy that was weighted toward our local population. The strategy was neither popular nor was it the conventional wisdom of the day in the months preceding our deployment in May 2007. The decision to implement a balanced strategy versus a wholly enemy-centric strategy came after months of careful preparation, consideration, and research on our operating environment. Most of the leaders and soldiers in the squadron had completed a deployment to Iraq, where an enemy-centric strategy had been applied. Changing mind-sets in the squadron took fifteen to eighteen months of preparation, study, analysis, and dialogue. The decisions about which strategy to implement or which methods within a particular strategy are tenable to execute in one's AO are critically important to success. Choose the correct strategy, or, in the case of Afghanistan today, choose the right balanced population- and enemy-centric approach appropriate tailored to your unit's AO, and you have a chance at success. Choose the wrong approach, and no matter how much blood, sweat, or treasure is poured in, success will be limited.

The critical point is to understand the nature of the environment—the people, the insurgents, the factors that drive instability. Once you achieve a level of understanding, you can employ the right approach. Because a myriad of actors is adapting constantly, so must your approach. Unfortunately, there are no easy, pat answers or cookie-cutter solutions for any unit. In Afghanistan the overall goal of all units, ranging from troop to brigade, should be the implementation of a balanced counterinsurgency strategy; however, our forces will not always find themselves in an area of operation ripe for its immediate, full, outright implementation. To complicate things further, you will find, as my squadron did in Afghanistan, that each troop or company AO demanded a different approach. In the northern portion of our squadron's AO in Afghanistan, it was B Troop and B Company, set in Kamdesh district, Nuristan Province, who experienced the heaviest fighting. In our squadron's center AO, the Troop I commanded, HHT, set in Naray and Ghaziabad Districts of Konar Province, contended with significantly less fighting and violence than B Troop and B Company in Nuristan. C Troop, set in the squadron's Southern AO and headquartered in Asmar district, Konar Province, dealt with the least amount of fighting. Each troop or company in the squadron would implement a balanced strategy; however, the approach was different for each AO based on the enemy situation, the operating environment, and where each unit found itself in time and space using the Army's standard clear, hold, build methodology, as seen in Figure 9.1.

IDENTIFYING TRANSITION POINTS

Identifying transition points within a balanced COIN strategy has not been afforded the generous mental capital it deserves. In the early planning stages of our mission to Afghanistan in 2007, we recognized the need for an overt shift in strategy from an enemy-centric to a more balanced strategy focused on partnering with and protecting the population and determined it should be employed on our arrival. In Afghanistan today, a shift in strategy has taken effect beginning with the president's announcement of the new policy to the American people on March 27, 2009.[3] As we draw closer to 2014, our focus again shifts to enabling the ANSF as our primary task. This does not eliminate the need for the critical study of transition points within a unit from the troop to the brigade combat team. Recognizing transition points within a specific area is critical to success but can be easy to overlook. A commander must

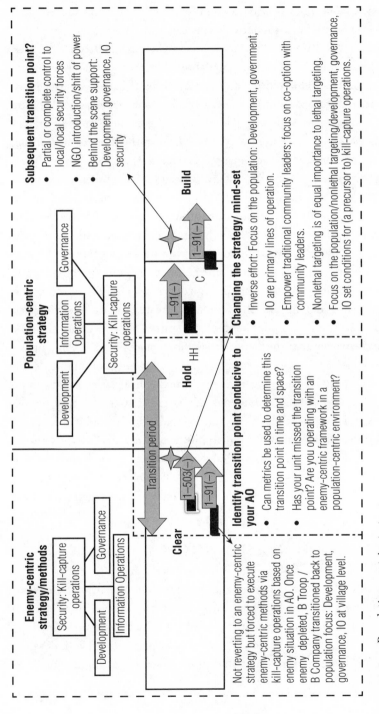

Figure 9.1. Population-centric strategy.

analyze where his unit exists in time and space within that strategy and what combination of methods is required for success.

Every unit will find that its AO is unique, possessing its own nuances, challenges, enemy situation, and population. Recognizing where we are, realistically, in relation to our dictated strategy is battlefield calculus we cannot afford to disregard. I chose the most dramatic time frame, summer 2007, of my deployment to Afghanistan to illustrate this point. Figure 9.1 graphically represents this dichotomy. As already stated, the three cavalry troops and infantry company in the squadron arrived at their respective AOs executing a population-focused strategy. But, in early summer 2007, heavy, protracted enemy contact constantly occupied B Troop and B Company, our infantry company attached to the squadron in Nuristan. Both commanders, while forced to concentrate on fighting the enemy, were still setting the conditions through building relationships with the local elders and coordinating development. Once B Troop and B Company's kinetic activities had sufficiently handed the insurgency enough of a blow to limit its effectiveness, the work they had done with the population created critical opportunities. Once this occurred, the commanders recognized they faced a transition point and changed their focus back to the local population, employing development, governance, and IO directly at the village and community levels. The conditions they had set enabled them to make the transition and sustain momentum. Meanwhile, throughout the entire summer fighting season, HHT and C Troop continued to execute a population-focused strategy, each using a different combination of methods to best achieve progress within their respective AOs. As shown in the figure, within a squadron/battalion-sized formation the three cavalry troops and infantry company were executing the same strategy, but their tactical methods were adapted to local conditions.

LINES OF OPERATION: CONCEPTUAL SHIFT FROM CONVENTIONAL WISDOM

To operate within the parameters of the population-centric strategy my squadron took the standard lines of operation (shown in Figure 9.2) and upended them. Previous conventional wisdom, to include my deployment to Iraq, had kill-capture operations as the number one priority, with development, governance, and information operations serving as supporting func-

How I conceptualized the fight in the past

Security: Kill-capture operations and SFA
Development, governance, IO as supporting lines of operation

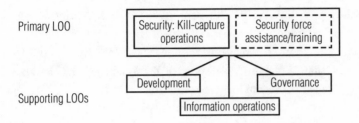

How I conceptualized the fight in Afghanistan:
Strategy implemented in OEF2007–2009

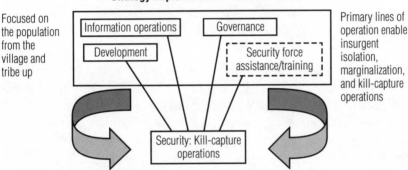

Figure 9.2. Lines of operation.

tions. In Afghanistan we made development, governance, and information operations our primary lines of operations, with a heightened focus on the village and district levels. This strategy hinged on empowering local leaders, specifically village elders; lifting up and protecting the local population; and improving local infrastructure. Our unwavering focus on the population's well-being necessarily isolated the insurgency, making kill-capture operations more precise with less collateral damage. Often we had both the cooperation and support of local leaders. We quickly found that by placing development, governance, and information operations as our primary lines of operation, they, in turn, created the right conditions to conduct kill-capture operations. Governance, development, and information operations enabled security, not the other way around.

IMPLEMENTING THE LINES OF OPERATION IN KONAR PROVINCE, NARAY AND GHAZIABAD DISTRICTS

The version of the population-centric strategy I used in my AO was to leverage my primary lines of operation—development, governance, and information operations—in an effort to reempower traditional tribal and village elders. Daily, we asked one another, "What asset, knowledge, technique, or training do we possess that can be used to elevate tribal and village elders to take charge of their villages and regain the respect, reverence, and obedience of the young men living there?" We believed if we could accomplish this at the village level while providing security, improving the infrastructure, enhancing the standard of living and daily life, and reestablishing a sense of normalcy, the population would reject the insurgency, ban them from their villages, and demand an end to violence. We were right. Once the village and tribal elders began to restore their power and villages were empowered to reject the insurgency, the insurgency became isolated. Once the insurgency was isolated, they were easier to target, engage, and destroy. The focus on the population using development, governance, and information operations set these conditions. An analysis of the implementation of balanced (population-centric) strategy and associated methods is given in the following sections by line of operation.

DEVELOPMENT

In my area of operation one fact was clear; the insurgency could not compete with our development dollars. Development and the dollars associated with it served as the most influential and successful weapon I possessed. The ability to bring construction and social projects into my rural communities empowered local elders, while engendering the local population and marginalizing the power and control of the insurgency over that population paid off. That said, from our first day in country we began working against organizational norms, conventional wisdom, and the established in-country processes to best utilize this very potent asset. The development money was not being spent in a way that maximized its impact. I discovered I could easily get a project approved, but directing the implementation of that project was incredibly time intensive. In almost typical American fashion, development projects were awarded to the large companies, with the best equipment and material, who often were not from the local area. Further, many of the projects in progress were American, rather than local, ideas. Because of this, Americans were "building projects," but the local elders and community neither gained the monetary benefit nor were committed to the quality, security, or success of the project. Sure, the company hired some locals for unskilled labor; however, they couldn't have cared less about the quality of the project once the ribbon was cut and they received their last paychecks. They would leave town soon enough, but the community had to live with it.

Achieving Long-Term Gains with Development Dollars: Changing the Way We Did Business

The first idea we outright dumped was the notion that each project needed to be of a certain American quality, built with the finest of materials. Who better to know what their village needed than the village elders? Our development dollars became a primary accelerant to reempower traditional community and village elders. We stopped telling the communities what they needed or by what standard it should be built. We started listening. We told the village elders they now possessed the power to bring prosperity to their villages. The elders would take full credit for the prosperity to come, and they would be responsible for hiring the engineer to design the project, hiring the local village skilled and unskilled labor; finally, the elders took it on themselves to provide security and quality control. The power, money, and employment the project would manifest did not leave the confines of the village. At countless village *shura* meetings across the Naray and Ghaziabad districts, heated Greek-style democratic debates soon began between the elders over what projects the villagers most needed. Projects were nominated, voted on, and agreed on at the village *shura* meetings with no American interjection. Once the project was decided, the village elder or elders responsible for its future success or failure attained a piece of the puzzle that had been missing in the previous way we were doing business. Their reputation and honor were now on the line to ensure the project was successful and to ensure their people were pleased with the results.

This process was the same at the district level, where larger-scale infrastructure projects were proposed. The projects often benefited our larger villages comprised of multiple tribal ethnicities. The most powerful village elders from the major ethnic groups and tribes[4] of each district would attend their respective weekly district *shura* meetings. In both Naray and Ghaziabad, the elders voted on and created development and infrastructure priority lists for their districts. We were completely cognizant that disagreements could arise as to the execution of the cross-tribal district projects. To ensure equitability and trust between the tribes, we had the elder-hired project engineers attend the weekly *shura* meetings, give a progress report to the elders on the project, and answer any questions they might have. Additionally, the project engineer would receive payment for the project at the 25 percent, 50 percent, 75 percent, and project complete stages at the district *shura* meeting after the tribal elders had inspected the project's progress and approved payment. We used this method at the village level when necessary. This technique worked well and possessed the same positive incentives for the elders to have a stake in the outcome because the elders themselves, the most powerful and respected in the district, had initiated these projects. They had a vested interest in seeing the project succeed.

Development as the Catalyst to Establishing a
Relationship with an Antigovernment Village

Development dollars opened the door to a large number of antigovernment areas and villages in my AO. Personal relationships kept those doors open. The village of Saw, a key Kohistani village of around 3,000 people, located very near the boundary between the Naray and Ghaziabad districts, was such a village. A younger elder from Saw attended my weekly Naray district *shura* meetings every week.[5] He was sent to the *shura* meeting to keep the powerful elders in Saw up to date on the movements of the Americans based just seventeen kilometers to their north. They weren't actively fighting U.S. presence; however, they did not support the presence of U.S. forces. Many months later I would discover the reason from the town's head elder and mullah. In the winter of 2005, Saw was a village friendly to the United States. One night, a U.S. Army unit acted on what turned out to be bad intelligence and raided the village. The unit was searching for a high-value target (HVT) that had been responsible for rocket attacks against the American Forward Operating Base to the north. While the unit did not find the HVT, they diligently searched each house, kicking in a number of doors, and departed as abruptly as they had arrived. The village elders felt dishonored and decided to withdraw from contact with U.S. forces after that day.

In August 2007, after a couple months of weekly district *shura* meetings in Naray, the elder and I had become friends. I often told him I hoped to bring projects to Saw and establish a connection with their village. He would graciously listen to me, but because he remained unsure of American motives and agendas he remained noncommittal. The Afghan National Army (ANA) would prove critical in our building a relationship with the village, making strides where I could not. The ANA went to Saw village and began building relationships with the elders, soon discovering their desire to bring education to their children. The ANA shared this with us, and our unit responded with truckloads of school supplies for Saw. The next day the elders, accompanied by the senior village elder, traveled to our outpost with 100 thank-you notes written in Pashtu from the kids. I was introduced to the head elder and the village mullah. We immediately began discussing potential development projects for Saw. I knew I had to get a project approved quickly to reestablish trust and confidence with both men. I knew the head elder had taken a personal chance on meeting me in the first place. He reminded me often that "when they had openly talked with Americans in the past, lots had been promised and nothing had ever been delivered."

The development projects became a priority for Saw and were approved quickly. Between August and November 2007 we began construction of a clinic, a bridge, and a school in the village. Contact with the people of Saw, and the head village elder himself, increased exponentially over these months as we hashed out project-related issues and progress reports. The Afghan National Army began to make regular trips to Saw, executing medical missions, humanitarian assistance, and simply social visits with the people. I introduced the head elder to my boss, and he immediately became a key ally and advisor for not only my troop but the entire squadron. Saw village completely turned from red to green because of the combination of the Afghan Army, development dollars, and a commitment to the traditional leaders and the people of Saw to maintain a positive, active, personal relationship.

GOVERNANCE

I had the wrong impression of how governance would work as I entered Afghanistan. I'll never forget sitting through one of my first village-level *shura* meetings and thinking what an amazing, advanced, effective system was in place. The Greek-style, participatory tribal *shura* is a more pure form of democracy than we experience in our own country and provided each Afghan man a voice, opinion, and stake. The system's structure yields a drastically higher participation in Afghanistan than that of our Jeffersonian system at home. The district-level meetings were another story and required a lot of my time and patience.

The district-level *shura* meetings were run by the troop commander when I arrived in my AO. I worked hard to end this practice quickly and pass authority along to where it belonged, with the subgovernor. I fell in on what would be the best set of subgovernors I would work with during my time in Afghanistan. In Naray, Samshu Rochman, Kohistani, was accepted by the elders, was respected, and was the best district administrator in my AO. After just a couple of months in Naray, July 2007, I created a district governor premeeting with Samshu Rochman. The day before each *shura*, Rochman and I would meet. I typically passed him all the relevant information I had at my disposal, including project approval statuses, information on my troop's operations, and news stories, both positive and negative, the district elders needed to hear. After the exchange of information, I would practice with Samshu Rochman, and he would provide a brief back to me and share any concerns he might have had. The next day at the *shura* meeting, Samshu was in charge. He ran the meeting and made the decisions, while I assumed the role of spectator. This turned out to be a great technique in the Naray district, and Samshu Rochman became more adept at running these meetings with time.

Ghaziabad was my most challenging district. The district subgovernor, Haji Gul Zimon, a Mushwani, had control of four of the five tribes that lived in Ghaziabad. The weekly *shura* meetings were comprised of Kohistani, Mushwani, Salarzi, and Gojars; however, the Nuristani tribe refused to participate in the Pashtun-run "criminal *shura*." The Nuristani tribe of Ghaziabad also provided me with my largest insurgent population, often complicit in attacks on both coalition and local convoys in my AO. The Nuristani villages in Ghaziabad were one of the few tribal areas in my AO that were clustered. They were located in the high elevations, off the main road (the only road in my AO) in the Helgal, Marid, and Darin Valleys. After establishing a good relationship with Haji Gul Zimon, beginning the district governor prebriefs, he took charge of his district *shura* meetings, and I reached out to the Nuristani population. In July 2007, I began to send word through the local population in Ghaziabad that I wanted to start a Ghaziabad Nuristani *shura*. I was interested in talking about neither the past nor their heavy participation in the local insurgency. I wanted a solid working relationship with them and to provide an equal opportunity for the development dollars and humanitarian assistance the other four tribes were soon to receive. After a couple of weeks of sending requests for meetings, the Ghaziabad Nuristani *shura* came to the forward operating base. They first sent a couple of lower elders to feel me out and make sure I wasn't setting a trap. After a couple of iterations of this, the head mullah and elder of the *shura* came to see me with a *shura* of thirty men. We met for the first time in late August, immediately following a deadly insurgent attack on a U.S. convoy in Ghaziabad for which their tribe was responsible. The mullah was Mohammad Shamshu, and the spokesman and second in charge was the senior elder Haji Mohammad Jon.[6]

Haji Mohammad Jon was the spokesman of the Nuristani *shura* for a reason; he was smart, educated, and wise. I always suspected, as I was speaking with him, that he knew more than he let on. It was rumored that he understood English but hid the fact to gain an advantage when communicating with Americans. My relationship with the Ghaziabad Nuristani *shura* was tenuous at first. Some onlookers initially questioned me about why I would meet with a group known to have fought Americans in the past. My boss, Lt. Col. Kolenda, had the best answer for this. He would say, "Do we want vengeance, or do we want to win?" Well, I wanted to win.

The Ghaziabad Nuristani *shura* issued forth a number of demands in exchange for establishing a working relationship with us. They desired recognition as official representatives of their communities, possessing the same power as their rival Pashtun *shura* in Ghaziabad. They wanted access to development projects and humanitarian assistance, and they wanted to administer it all through their newly formed *shura*. These conditions were easy for us to meet if only they, too, would bend a bit to accept our terms. The local insurgent leader in their area of Ghaziabad was Mullah Juma Khan. He had been complicit in a number of deadly attacks on coalition and Afghan forces in the past. We wanted the attacks to stop. Mullah Mohammad Shamshu and Haji Mohammad Jon did not agree to deliver Juma Khan to us; however, they agreed to marginalize him and stop his attacks. It quickly became clear that if we would recognize their legitimacy and come through on our end of the agreement, a relationship that would benefit all of us, while further isolating and marginalizing the insurgency, was possible.

The *shura* met every two weeks from late August 2007 on. It was our intention to eventually combine the Ghaziabad Nuristani *shura* with the Ghaziabad Pashtun *shura*. This would prove too difficult to accomplish; however, we had achieved something—we were in direct contact with the Ghaziabad Nuristanis, which we had not been before this *shura*. We quickly infused development dollars into their area. The proverbial carrot of development had brought them to the table while the relationships we built, and our nonstandard governance arrangement with their tribe kept them there. Attacks in Ghaziabad declined drastically from September 2007 on.

INFORMATION OPERATIONS (IO)

Forward Operating Base Naray possessed one of the most unusual radio station capabilities in all of Afghanistan. The radio station had a range of around fifty kilometers; it worked on an FM band and was fully staffed by Afghans. Wind-up radios were provided to the local population in huge quantities through humanitarian assistance initiatives. The Afghan radio staff played traditional Afghan music, Afghan poetry, and national and local news; finally, they served as a command information medium for the squadron. This was a huge asset for the task force and a capability that enabled our squadron to quickly put out important information, dispel rumors, and tell both good and bad news pertaining to the squadron before the insurgency had a chance to put a negative spin on it.

The radio station provided me an excellent medium to empower local leaders. This was a limitless capability that was stifled only by lack of imagination. After village- or district-level *shura* meetings, I would often invite the head elder of the meeting to the radio station to talk to his people. This was a great way to announce new project initiatives in villages or good news stories while at the same time elevating the elder making the broadcast. It also provided a great unintended consequence for us by staking the elders' reputation on the success of the project or whatever good news he announced. No elder wanted to announce good news to a few thousand of his people and then not come through. Additionally, the radio was a great way to connect the local population to its government. We would often have the commander of the Afghan National Army (ANA), the commander of the Afghan Border Police (ABP), and the commander of the local uniformed police talk about their organizations and how they were assisting the local population in the area. The radio station was extremely popular in the surrounding communities, and it was, by far, our most effective communication medium.

We also employed a local, fully staffed newspaper crew at Forward Operating Base Naray. The Afghan journalists produced a weekly newspaper, which was widely distributed from Asmar to Kamdesh covering the local news in the area, upcoming events, and good news stories such as the kick-off of a new project or special event. It was not uncommon to be on a patrol in a local village and find a young man reading the newspaper to a group of people in the village center. The newspaper staff also completed special projects for the squadron. We relied on the newspaper staff to poll the local population so we might gauge the success or failure of squadron policies or practices. The newspaper staff created handbills for distribution to the local population that both my soldiers and the Afghan National Army soldiers would distribute while on patrol. The handbills ranged from information announcing U.S.-sponsored events in the AO to warnings of insurgent activities.

SECURITY: KILL-CAPTURE OPERATIONS

The focus on development, governance, and information operations within our population-centric-tilted strategy did not preclude kill-capture operations; it made them more accurate and focused, while setting the conditions for success. We fought hard and punished the enemy when we were forced to do so. I was quite vocal at my *shura* meetings when asked about an engagement. I would always tell the elders, "I may not fire the first bullet, but I promise you I'll be firing the last." The day after each fight, however, we refocused and got back on track with the more population-focused aspects of our strategy. The best illustration of how the execution of a population-centric strategy can affect a major kill-capture or terrain seizure operation is the squadron's final operation. In Nuristan's Kamdesh district, the easternmost village of Gowerdesh possessed a key bridge that had become an insurgent strong point in a relatively unpopulated area on the outskirt of the village. Geographically, it was located at a key point on the only road in the district, serving as the southern boundary for both the Nuristan Province and the Kamdesh district. Gowerdesh was the furthest sizable eastern village before the Pakistan border. Locals called it the "Gateway to Nuristan." At the beginning of our deployment, Gowerdesh served as a security station for the Afghan border police. The insurgency threatened the border police, who frequently ran away from their position. This opened the east–west corridor from Pakistan into Afghanistan, giving the insurgency virtually free rein to move supplies, weapons, and materials. The months to follow entailed an uptick in combat within the area. We had to devise a new approach if we were to gain, maintain, and reestablish government presence in the Gowerdesh area.

Lt. Col. Kolenda, the squadron commander, and Captain Joey Hutto, the B Troop commander, had established a powerful *shura* comprised of the most influential elders in Kamdesh in February 2008. As they had with the Ghaziabad Nuristani *shura*, they sought official recognition and access to the associated development and governance initiatives that came with it. We desired an end to the violence in Kamdesh district and to reestablish Afghan government presence in Gowerdesh. All that was asked of the elders was to marginalize the local insurgency in their districts so we could bring them the lucrative development projects their population so needed. The *shura* had the power to do so. Many of the local fighters were relatives of the elders and would not go against them if they were united. The Kamdesh *shura* was huge. Often over 100 members would attend, and Lt. Col. Kolenda did everything he could to elevate their power in the eyes of their people. Tons of humanitarian assistance were distributed through the elders to the people. They coordinated all aspects of the development projects being infused into the area. The squadron began to push information operation themes to the elders, outlining the critical importance of government presence in the Gowerdesh bridge area. Project proposals for Gowerdesh bridge and surrounding areas were approved and waiting. Meeting by meeting, the elders slowly warmed to the idea of reestablishing the Afghan border police at the Gowerdesh bridge. The conditions were set. Development and humanitarian assistance were standing by. Information operation themes were out continuously in every channel we possessed, from the radio to the local police to citizens on the street, for weeks prior to the operation. Everyone had heard the good news of the American help that would soon come to Gowerdesh.

Despite the condition setting we had achieved, Operation Mountain Highway II was planned as a kill-capture operation. After all, we had fought there multiple times before, and there were known targets of value in the area. The operation was executed, after months of painstaking preparation, in April–May of 2008. The elders of the Kamdesh Nuristani shura agreed that the operation should proceed; they had been co-opted. They agreed on the need for the border police to establish a strong position at the bridge. Development projects began immediately on our arrival. Information operations were aggressive and effective. Humanitarian assistance was distributed to the local population in the area within hours. Our unit's history with the Gowerdesh area was one of constant fighting and enemy contact, but this time we conducted our operation without incident. We had done the hard work of correctly setting the conditions. A few hours after arriving at the Gowerdesh bridge and immediately starting construction on the new border police building, the Nuristani *shura* walked together along the road to greet us at the bridge. There would be no bullets fired that day.

AFGHAN NATIONAL ARMY, AFGHAN BORDER POLICE,
AND UNIFORMED POLICE

Inherent to the success of our strategy was the success of the national-, regional-, and district-level Afghan security forces. I made it a rule to integrate with at least one of the three Afghan security forces in my AO on every operation, even if we were simply conducting a daily patrol. I felt comfortable operating with the Afghan National Army and was delighted to have a tactically and technically proficient counterpart, Capt. Hyuddien Uddin. I did not feel as comfortable operating with the local uniformed police. The border police gave me even greater pause, but I had committed myself to work with them from the very beginning and soldiered through my misgivings.

To adhere to my rule of including Afghan security forces in every operation, I had to get inventive. Other than what I had learned from the previous commander, I was not acquainted with the personalities in the police force. Depending on what district I was operating in that day, I would call or send for the police chief or his representatives about an hour before our operation. Once they arrived I would brief him or them on the operation and then execute it. Nine times out of ten, even with late notification, they would be happy and honored to participate. The other technique we used often when we didn't have the Afghan Army with us was to stop at the police station in each respective district and run the same drill as already described. Once we got accustomed to the area of operation and figured out who was who, those standards were relaxed slightly for specific individuals. Inclusion was the key. People support operations that value them and include them. This simple idea was transformative to our time in Afghanistan.

Because training the Afghan National Security Forces (ANSF) was a top priority, the squadron had two embedded training teams (ETTs) focused on the Afghan National Army (ANA) and the Afghan Border Police (ABP) respectively. The Afghan Uniformed Police (AUP) were trained by the local U.S. troop or company that possessed the area of operation in which the AUP resided. Our Afghan Army training team was Marine led. They focused on integrating the Afghan National Army into every operation we conducted in the squadron. We integrated the Afghan planning staffs and supporting functions with their counterparts within our squadron headquarters. The ANA was a critical component of every major operation we conducted.

A U.S. Army ETT was brought in to train the Afghan border police. They performed magnificently, taking an inexperienced ABP battalion comprised largely of new members and turning them into a viable police force. The ABP's efforts were critical to the planning, execution, and success of the squadron's last operation to reestablish an ABP post at the Gowerdesh bridge. Finally, the AUP gained trust and respect quickly in my area of operation. The Naray AUP, led by their able commander, Haji Yousef, would accompany me on nearly every patrol I conducted in the district. It would not be long until Yousef was leading his police force on independent operations. Haji Yousef led the squadron to its largest insurgent weapons cache in September 2007. The Afghan National Security Forces were critical to our success and critical to the success of a population-focused strategy. An overt effort was made to include, train, and mentor the Afghan Security Forces with every asset we had. They are the future of their country, not us.

EXTERNAL FACTORS KEY TO SUCCESS: THE IMPORTANCE OF PERSONAL RELATIONSHIPS

Inherent to the successful population-centric/balanced strategy I've described are the external factors that served as its foundation. Time, patience, compassion, empathy, and a desire to form lasting relationships with the local population are critical. Ninety percent of my time each day was spent building relationships with locals, learning about the tribes, clans, and subclans of the area and having tea or meals with elders, business leaders, farmers, and mullahs. Only 10 percent of my time was spent planning operations to kill or capture members of the local insurgency. Greg Mortenson's famous quote from his friend Haji Ali in the book *Three Cups of Tea* is right on: "The first time you share tea you are a stranger. The second time you take tea, you are an honored guest. The third time you share a cup of tea, you become family, and for our family, we are prepared to do anything, even die."[7] This describes the cultural situation that existed in my AO perfectly. What Mortenson failed to emphasize is once that relationship is established, the context of your relationship and future meetings from that point on are almost wholly skewed to the social side with usually just a tiny sliver of the time addressing business. Even if there is an important, pressing issue we feel is critical to discuss, this fact does not change, ever. There was no such thing as a quick question or a rushed meeting. Our American cultural tendency to get to the point in a conversation or attain information quickly because we are in a hurry did not exist in my AO. We were guests in their country; we respected their customs. We did it their way.

The most important external aspect of the population-focused strategy I executed was time spent on developing personal relationships. If I had not been willing to put in the countless daily hours at the social level, I would not have been able to gain the trust and confidence of the elders in my area, which would, in turn, hobble progress. What I have said sounds simple, but it is not. I encountered plenty of leaders who understood it was important to form these relationships, but they did not possess the compassion, empathy, and patience to do it. If I had not been willing to let down my social barriers and form lasting relationships and friendships, the strategy would not have ever been successful. We cannot execute this strategy from the safety of our desks within our forward operating base. It must be executed in the countless village centers, living rooms, district centers, and police stations we are trying so desperately to protect.

DISTRIBUTION OF SPHERE OF INFLUENCE (SOI) RESPONSIBILITIES AND FEEDBACK LOOP

I assigned each of my subordinate leaders with their own sphere of influence in Naray and Ghaziabad districts. My squadron commander had his SOI comprised of the senior leaders of the districts in the AO. My main SOI was the interaction with the district subgovernors, senior Afghan security force leaders, and head elders. My lieutenants interacted with the senior and midrange security force leaders, elders, and local business leaders. The assignment of SOI went down to the youngest person on the patrol. It amazed me how much information I received from a private who had just spent five hours in a village talking to the people and kids. SOI assignment is another thing we all know to do, but few take the time to specifically assign each soldier. It is not natural for many leaders and soldiers to initiate such contact. It is critically important to assign our soldiers a name, face, or area for SOI and then create a feedback loop and talk to each other.

The feedback loop associated with SOI can be formal or informal. I connected more dots, devised more strategy, and learned something new about my AO every night by simply taking twenty or thirty minutes and smoking a cigar with my boss. His SOI and mine overlapped in numerous ways, just as the SOI of my subordinates overlapped with mine. Each of us had met with various elders or local leaders for hours of our day. It amazed me how often I would find out that these meetings dealt with the same issues; however, they were delivered in completely different contexts and possessed altered agendas.

These informal discussions often provided me with the missing piece of the puzzle I had yet to decipher. I was a big fan of the informal leader discussions and often had the same success in similar situations with my subordinates. I found that if our feedback loop required work or was painful, it probably wouldn't happen, and an opportunity would be lost.

UNDERSTANDING TRIBAL COMPLEXITIES: NARAY AND GHAZIABAD DISTRICT, KONAR PROVINCE

The tribal map in Figure 9.3 depicts the complexity of the tribal situation in the Naray and Ghaziabad districts. The map was a work in progress during my deployment and provides a good general idea of the tribal areas of my AO.

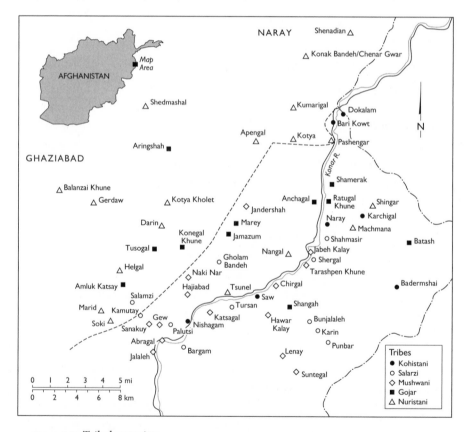

Figure 9.3. Tribal mapping.

SOURCE: This tribal map was a product of the 1-91 Cavalry FECC during OEF 07-09. The author was the OIC of this organization and compiled the data.

It took an overt effort to reach this level, which merely scratches the surface of the complexity involved when you consider the clans and subtribes associated with each of the major tribes of the area. That being said, I studied the tribes daily and was still learning when I left the country. As you can see in Figure 9.3, the tribal mixture by village in my AO was mixed with a few tribal clusters. I had to understand how these tribes worked with each other, what the history between them was, and their likes, needs, and wishes. Additionally, tribal mapping helped me maintain an equitable development scheme so I wouldn't inadvertently make a couple of tribes powerful and rich while unknowingly excluding, marginalizing, and angering a different tribe.

I also learned that the district boundaries in my AO meant little to any of the locals. The district boundaries had been created by the Afghan government and were just flat not recognized by a large majority of people, especially the Nuristanis. Prior to the Ghaziabad and Naray District boundaries being redrawn, clustered Nuristani populations depicted on the map in the north and northeast of the Naray District and the vast majority of the eastern Ghaziabad districts were part of Nuristan. The Nuristanis in those villages still consider themselves part of greater Nuristan and don't recognize the Pashtun district into which they were partitioned. Interestingly enough, the Pashtun district and tribal leaders of Naray and Ghaziabad believe the same thing and make little to no attempt to pull the Nuristani villages caught up in this situation into the fold. After careful research and a lot of time on the ground, the dotted line on Figure 9.3 represents the reality on the ground and what the locals believe. This kind of information can be attained only through hours of interaction with the local people. These tribal dynamics greatly affected how I dealt with the local population in those areas and often led to adjustments in strategy in development procedures, governance, and information operations.

The tribal dynamics and history in my area were fascinating, and my ability to understand them, or attempt to understand them, was critical. If I had not focused my effort here, I would not have been able to break down the invisible barriers of information asymmetry. Locals naturally guarded information for survival reasons. They were not willing to share information until we built a relationship of trust. Even then we had to learn what question to ask because something obvious and self-evident to them might completely escape us if we did not know to ask the question. An example of this is the story of Mohammad Nasir, a Nuristani elder and reliable project contractor who lived in the Naray district, and Mohammad Urallah, the head Gojar elder in the

Naray district. Nasir's father was Anwar Amin, a leader of a popular political organization in the 1980s called the National Islamic Front (NIF). Anwar Amin led the NIF movement in the northern Naray and eastern Kamdesh area. He was also a local hero mujahedeen fighter and a commander in the Afghan–Soviet War. During the Afghan–Soviet War, the other rival political party the Nuristani people had joined in large number was Hezb-e-Islami (HIG).[8] The two political parties were fundamentally opposed to many of each other's beliefs; however, they maintained a marriage of convenience in their fight against the Soviets. Mohammad Urallah's father led the Gojar tribe of Naray during the Afghan–Soviet War. The Gojars at the time, and even today, served as unskilled labor and farmers for the Nuristanis. Urallah's father saw an opportunity, and the Gojars joined forces with the Soviets to attack into Nuristan and establish Gojaristan. The attack into Kamdesh district failed, the Soviets and Gojars didn't make it past the village of Kamdesh, and Urallah's father was killed in the fighting.

After the war, HIG proved more powerful in the Kamdesh district than NIF and expelled the NIF-associated Nuristanis to the south, into the Naray area. Anwar Amin was despised by the HIG and was murdered in 1994 in his home in the town of Bari Kowt in northern Naray district. It was rumored, but never proven, that Amin was murdered by HIG operatives. Mohammad Nasir, his son, would wind up remaining in northern Naray; he is unable to return to Kamdesh even today. Nasir, who proved to be a brilliant contractor in the Naray district, was recommended as the lead contractor for many district level projects while I was in country. Four of the five tribal elder groups would vote for Nasir every time. The Gojar elders, led by Mohammad Urallah, would aggressively oppose Mohammad Nasir. Their history dictated it to be so. The point to this story is important. Tribal dynamics and their histories are complicated, twisted, and hard to follow but are critical to seeing an area of operation within the right historical context. We never want to get involved in someone else's blood feud. If we fail to understand the local histories and relationships, we run a high risk of becoming pawns. There are hundreds of stories like this one and a thousand more I didn't know. We must make the attempt; without an understanding of the historical context, we wind up making decisions in a vacuum, and that can lead to the wrong ones that can have serious security and stability implications.

The northeast Konar and eastern Nuristan areas of operation provided plenty of challenges for my troop and for my squadron. We helped ourselves by adopting the right population-focused strategy. We had the latitude to change, react, and adapt that strategy when necessary. The right mix of training, leadership, an inspired staff, and the courage to sit in homes on ancient rugs and listen delivered us positive results. Ours was one of the only AOs I know of in which senior leaders required all of us to read books like *Heroes of the Age, Islam and the Resistance in Afghanistan*, and other books on Afghan history for reference.[9] Our leadership encouraged us to reach out to the tribal populations in unprecedented ways. Lt. Col. Kolenda actually wrote a letter to Greg Mortensen, author of *Three Cups of Tea* and the president of the Central Asia Institute, commending him on his efforts to build schools for the girls of Afghanistan and Pakistan and requesting advice on how to achieve similar successes in our AO. Within weeks, Mortensen's people were on the ground in our AO, and our first Afghan girls' school was under construction. When leadership has the latitude to focus its military mission on the local population, everyone benefits.

We still have a lot to learn in Afghanistan, but what I internalized the most is that everyone wishes to be respected; so, when troops deploy, it is our responsibility to enter the country with the hearts of both teachers and students. People support what they help to create. The Afghans have a saying, "If you sweat for it, you will protect it." As leaders we must analyze, study, and understand the nature of the conflict and the human environment of our areas of operation. Only then can we select the right approach and apply both the appropriate capabilities for success and the right feedback loops and sensors to enable us to adapt, recognize critical transition points, and seize on opportunities before they disappear.

NOTES

1. I commanded HHT 1-91 CAV in Afghanistan during OIF 07-09. HHT was a maneuver unit comprised of an infantry platoon, a scout platoon, a reconnaissance element, and a 120 mm mortar section.

2. There is no published definition for either population-centric or enemy-centric counterinsurgency in U.S. doctrine. In the absence of these definitions, the following definition is offered: Population-centric COIN focuses on partnering with and protecting the population from the enemy. Although enemy destruction is still important, it is secondary to population protection. Enemy-centric COIN focuses effort on the killing and capturing of the enemy, while population protection is of secondary importance. A balanced strategy takes components of both and applies them to the unique operating environment. The strategy constantly shifts as the environmental

factors in the AO, including friendly and enemy disposition, political context, and the end game goals, change.

3. Barack H. Obama, "A New Strategy for Afghanistan and Pakistan," Prepared Remarks, Washington, DC, March 27, 2009.

4. There are four ethnic groups: Nuristani, Kohistani, Pahtun, Gojar; three Nuristani tribes: Kom, Wai, Gujar; and two Pashtun tribes: Mushwani and Salarzi. There are very few tribal cluster areas, with the exception of both the Ghaziabad and Naray District Nuristani populations. Villages were often comprised of a particular tribe; however, they were interspersed with neighboring villages of different tribal affiliation.

5. I have omitted the names of the village elders from Saw village. The area was handed over to ANSF control in November 2012. I am still in contact with the head village elder today.

6. These names have been changed, as the Nishagam area, including the Helgal Valley, transitioned to ANSF control in November 2012.

7. Greg Mortenson, *Three Cups of Tea* (Chicago: Viking Adult Books, 2006), 78.

8. Hezb-e-Islami is an Islamic organization that significantly increased its membership and grew in popularity for fighting the Soviet occupation of Afghanistan. It is led and founded by Gulbuddin Hekmatyar. The organization started in Pakistan in 1975 from the roots of a Muslim youth organization. The Islamist portion of the organization was founded in Kabul by students and teachers at Kabul University in 1969 for the purpose of defeating communism in Afghanistan.

9. David B. Edwards, *Heroes of the Age: Moral Fault Lines on the Afghan Frontier* (Berkeley: University of California Press, 1996); and Olivier Roy, *Islam and Resistance in Afghanistan* (Cambridge, UK: Cambridge University Press, 1990).

10 CONCLUSION

Thomas H. Johnson and Barry Scott Zellen

"CULTURE" HAS LONG BEEN A CONTROVERSIAL CONCEPT for academics and policy makers.[1] Culture tends to be viewed and treated as an all-encompassing concept that subsumes beliefs and issues that border its boundaries, boundaries that are often viewed as absolute and impenetrable by its purveyors. In addition, cultural "explanations" and narratives have long been used to justify sociopolitical mores and positions that take on moralistic dimensions that can separate "we" from "them." While many often preach the power of "cultural diversity," the lack of tolerance for religious, ethnic, and linguistic differences has often torn societies and peoples apart. Indeed, when one examines the wars and conflicts of the twenty-first century, one is immediately drawn to the cultural as well as sectarian dimensions of these conflicts.

Much of this controversy arises because of culture's value-laden nature as well as the actual definitions used for the concept. Franz Boas, an early twentieth-century German cultural anthropologist, suggested that culture is "the system of shared beliefs, values, customs, behaviors, and artifacts that the members of society use to cope with their world and with one another, and that are transmitted from generation to generation through learning."[2] This definition highlights several important concepts that were central for the assessments presented in this book. First, culture is a shared set of beliefs and values among a self-identified group of people; hence it plays a critical role in the worldview of its proponents. Second, culture has psychological components as well as material manifestations (such as produced artifacts); we often act on impulses that are culturally rather than rationally based. Third, culture is not static but rather dynamic and adaptive and is transmitted through certain processes to others. Cultural artifacts are often conveyed through religion, literature, and societal narratives. For example, as effective communicators, the Afghan Taliban regularly invoke master and other narratives to move audiences in a preferred direction. Taliban influencers rely on their native familiarity with their culture and these narratives to use them effectively. And finally, culture is learned and transmitted through maturation and experience. Here cultural narratives become very important because they represent historically grounded stories that reflect a community's identity and experiences or explain its hopes, aspirations, and concerns. These narratives help groups understand who they are, where they come from, and how to make sense of unfolding developments around them. Understanding culture, narratives, and especially master narratives can be the difference between analytic anticipation and unanticipated surprise for actors involved in the relevant narrative's system. These distinctions are important, especially for military planners.

There is little debate concerning the impact culture has on conflict found in the international system, especially in the form of insurgency and counterinsurgency (COIN)—the foci of this book. Recent history would suggest that the success of a country intending to invade and occupy another is in large part dependent on its knowledge and sensitivity to the relevant cultural processes and dynamics of the targeted country. The U.S. campaigns in both Iraq and Afghanistan have been fraught with problems caused by cultural malfeasance, as evidenced in Afghanistan recently with significant conflicts arising over the burning of Korans and the desecration of the bodies of dead insurgents. If political realities are to change and nations are to be built, or at least reconfigured, then political and social mechanism operatives on the ground in the region in the form of cultural and even sociological processes must be taken into account. This is often not the case, however. The wars in Iraq and Afghanistan are the most recent manifestations of the fact that successful militaries must be culturally informed if they are to be effective in invasion, occupation, and counterinsurgency. And, as is demonstrated throughout this volume, to be effective in such ventures requires that culture is not merely treated reactively but rather approached in a proactive fashion, where cultural factors and dynamics are actually incorporated in the military planning process.

In assessing culture and its impacts, it is instructive to conceive of culture as a "system" consisting of "inputs," "outputs," and "throughputs." Culture is often thought of as merely the social mores that a particular people or region follow; for instance, it's part of American culture to give a "thumbs-up" gesture to show acceptance or appreciation. Such a gesture is an extremely offensive cultural faux pas in the Middle East, West Africa, and parts of South America. Avoiding ethnocentrisms requires understanding and respecting other cultures despite how peculiar they may seem. For instance, when traveling to Afghanistan, it is important to recognize points of cultural etiquette such as "don't eat with your left hand" or "don't show the sole of your foot."

Culture, of course, consists of far more than customs and courtesies, although much of the cultural training given to deploying troops focuses primarily on customs and cultural faux pas. Cultural "worldviews" are much more important and can have a significant impact on counterinsurgency and insurgency. For example, the political and cultural dynamics of Pakistan's Federally Administered Tribal Area (FATA) are closely tied to the continuing insurgency in Pakistan as well as in Afghanistan and narratives associated with both.[3] Widespread political assassinations, terrorist attacks, and periods of intense combat with Pakistani military and paramilitary forces since 2003 have made this region Pakistan's most radicalized and most troubling. The FATA border area is home to dozens of ethnic groups who speak various languages. The largest group by far are the Pashtun tribes that inhabit the center, but the region is also home to Baluchis, Ketranis, Brahui, Savis, Nuristanis, Tajiks, Kalamis, Gujaris, Hazaras, Dameli, Chitralis, Shinas, Wahkis, Munjis, Hindkos, Kowars, Urmurs (who live in the middle of the Pashtun heartland), Gawar-Batis, Burushos, Badeshi, and Khirgiz, among others, each of whom speaks a distinct language, in some cases with dozens of mutually unintelligible subdialects. Of all these ethnicities, however, only the Pashtuns have ever demonstrated any ardent interest in the type of jihad being waged by the Taliban, and it can be argued that this has a strong cultural dimension. The root factor can be traced to their unyielding cultural adherences, and a major reason for this is their professed culture. Historically, the rural Pashtuns have dominated their neighbors and avoided being subjugated or integrated by a larger nation. As one elderly Pashtun tribesman told Mountstuart Elphinstone, a British official visiting Afghanistan in 1809, "We are content with discord, we are content with alarms, we are content with blood . . . we will never be content with a master."[4] This cultural characteristic makes Pashtuns the perfect insurgents. Their unique social code is known as *Pashtunwali*: a set of values and unwritten, but universally understood, precepts that define

Pashtun culture. *Pashtunwali*, literally translated, means "the way of the Pashtun," and to begin to get at the challenges for U.S. and NATO foreign policy, the underlying principles of this cultural value system need to be better understood by policy makers.

Pashtunwali is the keystone of the Pashtuns' identity and social structure, and it shapes all forms of behavior from the cradle to the grave. Its rules have been largely responsible for the survival of the Pashtun tribes for over a thousand years, but they remain little understood in the West. As Charles Allen writes, *Pashtunwali* is "an uncompromising social code so profoundly at odds with Western mores that its application constantly brings one up with a jolt."[5] A Pashtun must adhere to this code to maintain his honor and retain his identity. The worst obscenity one Pashtun can call another is *da'uz*, or "person with no honor." In a closed, interdependent rural society, a Pashtun family without honor become pariahs, unable to compete for advantageous marriages or economic opportunities and shunned by the other families as a disgrace to the clan.

Intrinsically flexible and dynamic, *Pashtunwali* has core tenets that include self-respect, independence, justice, hospitality, forgiveness, and tolerance. Not all Pashtuns embody the ideal type defined by *Pashtunwali*, but all respect its core values and admire—if sometimes grudgingly—those who do. When hillmen come down out of the mountains to buy staples in the bazaar of a valley town, with their long fighting knives visible in their waistbands, the townspeople are likely to sneak admiring glances and eulogize them to their friends about the hillmen's "true Pashtuness."

Pashtunwali imposes on Pashtun society a set of critical restrictions and obligations. In general terms, *Pashtunwali* is the sum total of the tribes' collective expectations of their members to conform to the norms and customs that ensure the group's survival as a distinct sociocultural entity. Most Pashtuns perceive group consensus as the primary source of power, and the *salah-mashwarah*, or "discussion," is the main forum where all important issues are discussed and resolved. For matters of particular gravity or consequence, such as murders or treaty negotiations, a *jirga*—a traditional assembly of all the tribes' adult male members—may be called, but this is not a simple matter. The egalitarian character of the *jirga* and the *salah-mashwarah* are in direct contrast with hierarchical state power structure. They are driven by the consensus of the group, composed of equal individuals. It is understood that representation is a bottom-up structure, operating within a system based on the concept of equality.[6]

Pashtunwali is neither the absence of governance nor summary judgment, nor is it inchoate. Rather, it is an alternative form of social organization with an advanced conflict resolution mechanism that does not involve courthouses, jails, lawyers, law schools, bailiffs, county clerks, prisons, prison guards, judges, or police officers. It has been estimated that *jirgas* resolve about 95 percent of the cases in which they are invoked. Perhaps most important for U.S. security interests in the region, the millions of tribe members who live within this system have no desire to have a new, alien system imposed on them externally. Furthermore, Pashtuns are generally convinced that their system of social order produces men superior to the Western model. While justice and responsibility are collective, however, at the individual level, *Pashtunwali* is about four central personal values: freedom, honor, revenge, and chivalry.

For centuries, these interlocking elements of the unwritten code of the Pashtun—freedom, honor, revenge, and chivalry—have defeated every effort to subdue the Pashtuns and supersede *Pashtunwali* with a more codified and centralized rule of law. Nevertheless, Western policy makers continue to ignore or downplay the primacy of these fundamental cultural values in shaping strategies for southern Afghanistan and northern Pakistan, while the Taliban and al-Qaeda use them for recruitment, shelter, and social mobilization. As with Britain before them, neither Pakistan nor Afghanistan has been able to exert control over the tribal areas along their common border that are inhabited primarily by Pashtuns. The obstinacy of the Pashtun tribes and the inability of the British Empire to control them led to a border policy of "masterly inactivity" that essentially used the tribesmembers as a buffer between India's northern frontier and the approaching Russian empire in Central Asia. Successive Pakistani and Afghan governments were no more successful, and this designation as a kind of tribal no-man's-land over generations created the loose political system of tribal autonomy in the FATA.[7] Indeed, the name for this area is actually a misnomer. It is not federally administered in any sense of the word,[8] and the area has never been under the explicit control of any authority other than the Pashtun tribes who live there.[9]

The intensely social nature of culture, as suggested in the preceding paragraphs, will mean that one way to shift cultures is to enter into the social arena by either *integrating* into a culture or *interacting* with it in a meaningful way; this will often require more people than would otherwise be the case to accomplish more traditional military activities. The adaptive nature of culture means that, in the long run, even if we are not able to change a culture internally, we may be able to get it to change by shifting the environment in which it evolves; cultures change, in large part, to allow peoples to adapt. For instance, one reason why washing hands before meals is such a common cultural practice is because it evolved (at least in part) to ensure that the human desire to live longer by avoiding preventable disease was satisfied. Finally, because culture is learned (and not innate or genetically specified), that means it is part of an *open system*: With appropriate instruments, we can change the inputs and processes so that a different set of cultural norms, values, and beliefs are output. Operation Enduring Freedom was arguably all about shifting a culture so that it embraces democracy and shuns extremist militancy; even if we ultimately conclude we have no business meddling in cultures, understanding why such meddling is pragmatically undesirable or ethically suspect would be very useful for our military planners.

Systems theory serves as the diagnostic model for culture. This approach, derived from the general systems theory of Ludwig von Bertalanffy, conceptualizes a system as an "organized cohesive complex of elements standing in interaction."[10] Interaction refers to two generalized patterns of behavior: (1) the relationships among the "complex elements," or subsystems of culture; and (2) the relationship between the complex whole of culture and its environment (the supersystem in which various cultures exist). The former constitutes the transformational processes of culture, telling us how culture is produced and changed, while the latter draws attention to the reality that cultures are open systems, continually exchanging information and energy with their surrounding environment. Talcott Parsons is perhaps the best-known proponent of the idea that we should treat culture (indeed, all of sociology) as a system. Parsons's work is of uncertain status today; the functionalism that informs it is out of favor in many circles.[11] Still, his work is important, and my intuition is that nascent fields such as evolutionary psychology and cognitive neurobiology will put the teleology back into thinking, and that there will be a neo-Parsonsian renaissance as a result. Even so, systems thinking has advanced since Parsons's time; it is now *biological* more than *mechanical*, with fewer deterministic assumptions and more respect for developmental issues and holistic concerns, as Cummings's list has made clear.

Treating culture as a system involves identifying culture's relationships to the environment, discussing the inputs, transformative processes, and outputs that result in shared beliefs and values in a society; culture is thus both a process and a product, a verb *and* a noun—this is important, as sustainable cultural change will require modification of cultures in both the verb (process) and noun (output) senses. The chapters of this book were organized into two separate but intimately connected sections, one focusing on culture as a *verb*, and the other as a *noun*.

Part I of this volume was thus on "Culture and Conflict: From Theory to Methodology" (*process*) and Part II was on "Culture and Conflict: From Methodology to Practice, Lessons from the War on Terror" (*output*)—with discussion of the wars in Afghanistan, Pakistan, and Iraq. Part I closely examined the nexus of culture, conflict, and strategic intervention and asked the following questions: *Where and how is culture important in a national security and foreign policy context? Is cultural understanding important or is it merely a fad of the day?* After making the case that it was indeed important, that one might argue essential for victory over terrorism, we proceeded to answer the subsequent questions: *What constitutes cultural data? What assumptions need to be made explicit concerning such data? What frameworks should be used to analyze culture? And, lastly, what are the challenges of cultural data collection and application?* Part II then addressed how cultural phenomena and information can best be used by the military, asking: *What has been the impact of cultural understanding on our recent counterinsurgencies? Does it take intimate cultural information/knowledge to effectively counter an insurgency? And, ultimately, what are we good at here, and where must we improve things?* Our authors—who come from a wide diversity of backgrounds and cultures themselves, from the theoretical to the practitioner—enabled us to shine a light on the complex cultural dimensions of this war-torn region and on the many creative efforts by our policy makers, war fighters, and scholars of strategy and conflict to rethink our approach to the War on Terror, charting a viable path to victory. We thus present, in our closing thoughts, a snapshot our authors' responses to the questions set forth at the outset of this project and reiterated in the preceding paragraph.

ON THE ENDURING IMPORTANCE OF CULTURAL UNDERSTANDING

Our authors would be quick to agree on the importance of cultural understanding, both per se and as it relates to conflict behavior and counterinsurgency operations. But the popular rendering of cultural understanding as a fad persists, and it may be precisely this that has engendered such skepticism of and resistance to its relevance within military operations.

Alexei J. D. Gavriel's example, from what he colorfully described as "The Beast," illustrated what he called "the largest misconception of cultural intelligence," namely, that it is "the uncovering of a hidden or secret code" and that it "allows unrestricted control over a population." Such fantastical portrayals of the "magic" of cultural understanding, as Gavriel explained, belong only to "a reality confined to Hollywood." One might argue, nonetheless, that there is some modicum of magic to it. The ability to discern underlying patterns in human behavior and worldview, to understand elements thereof as products of enculturation, and to achieve all this with an open mind free of cultural bias—this ability empowers the wielder to transcend the boundaries and access a foreign culture. Gavriel represented the product of this process as a "comprehensive level of understanding, available only through a culturally relative, nonethnocentric, perspective." The importance of culture in national security and foreign policy contexts is emphasized throughout this journal. It is a matter not only of "knowing the enemy" but also of knowing the impact of culture on the efficacy of security initiatives. It is, as Alexei Gavriel quoted from Benedict, what enables us "to keep ourselves as far as possible from leaping to the easy conclusion that what we would do in a given situation [is] what they would do."

And Marc W. D. Tyrrell's concept of "competing ontologies" served to elucidate the barriers built up by and between incongruent notions of governance, nationality, and the "socially acceptable." Using the example of Iraq, Tyrrell notes that the country's "loose 'national culture' . . . where 'governance' is understood as an institution providing for individual safety" derives from "preexisting tribal and neotribal bases, and not from some ideological assumption in the 'inherent' validity of a liberal democracy." Tyrrell challenged the idealization of a "supposedly 'neutral' political arena" and stresses the implications of cultural differences for the perceived legitimacy of foreign policy objectives. Culture must thus be analyzed relatively and methodically, and the results of such analyses incorporated into foreign policy assessments.

FRAMEWORKS FOR THE EFFECTIVE ANALYSIS OF CULTURE

Frameworks within which to analyze culture were presented in Part I of this book. Alexei Gavriel's chapter provided a comprehensive background, outlining the fundamentals of and relationships between cultural intelligence and ethnographic intelligence and their applications in joint intelligence doctrine. Concepts of note included the distinction between information and intelligence; the "three progressive levels of cultural knowledge" (awareness, understanding, and ultimately intelligence); ethnocentricity and cultural relativism; grounded theory methodologies and the ways they contrast with traditional scientific methods; as well as the steps in processing ethnographic information (evaluation, analysis, integration) into cultural intelligence. Gavriel's framework relied on the data themselves to answer, "What is going on in the social group?" and its subsequent analysis for, "How does the social group's culture affect the operating environment?"

These questions are likewise considered by Marc Tyrrell, whose Darwinian approach identified "the human ability to accept cultural programming [as] an evolutionary survival trait" whose components "operate at an almost 'instinctual' level." Tyrrell explores the aspects of culture that encompass "specific patternings of reality" and explains the difficulty of assigning, like the gene for evolutionary biology, a "unit of analysis [for] the 'coding of the pattern'"—the institution, the meme, and so forth.

When we hear the wisdom of "knowing the enemy," we are reminded that relevant cultural intelligence goes beyond that to include cultural information on the entire battlespace. As Gavriel wrote, cultural knowledge "can benefit operations at the tactical level by . . . minimizing the possibility of turning potential friends into enemies through cultural insensitivity."

Steffen Merten's stance is strong on this: "There can be little doubt that war fighters directly benefit from a deeper understanding of the social context of their operating environment." Of course, in this sense, "social" and "cultural" go hand-in-hand. Thomas J. Barfield provided some specific examples: "The military advantage of [*Pashtunwali*] solidarity was particularly evident in times of conflict. When such groups entered into battle, they were renowned as fierce fighters because individuals would rather die than shame themselves in front of their kin by running away." And, for another: "The Ghilzais do best in times of anarchy because their poor subsistence-based regions cope better with economic or political disruption and are harder to coerce because of their isolation." Clearly the preceding bits of information are relevant, if not absolutely essential, to proper military planning in these regions.

DATA COLLECTION CHALLENGES AND SOLUTIONS

By now we have firmly established the importance of cultural understanding. But there are many challenges to be faced in the collection and application of cultural data. Returning to the exposition on "grounded theory" in Alexei Gavriel's chapter, we note one fundamental challenge in the collection process: "Ethnography takes place in the field, rather than a laboratory, and subsequently the researcher cannot control, manipulate, or recreate the influences that affect the group's environment." According to Gavriel, this aspect binds virtually all cultural data to "a particular point in time and space," that is, cultural data are not universal. This is essentially opposite the case in traditional scientific methods, in which the replicability of data is generally taken as indicative of its veracity. Gavriel also warns of ethnocentric bias on the part of the collector, which can easily contaminate data and render them useless (and even dangerous to use), calling this "the peril of the fine line between an empirical observation and a value-based judgment."

Another major challenge in cultural data collection is identifying proper units of analysis. Culture itself is amorphous, its evolution unstable; and, as Marc Tyrrell wrote, its "coding system is much more subject to 'mutation' both initially and on a day-to-day basis." Thomas H. Johnson's chapter, quoting from Mandaville, provided a modern example of how the selection of one particular unit of analysis over another can influence perception of the data: "The more we stress Islam as a unit of analysis, the more we face the dangers of abstraction and unwarranted generalization. Islam keeps us mired in debates about normativity, where an emphasis on Muslims allows us to appreciate the dynamic nature of Islam as a lived experience." Interestingly, culture itself can be a challenge. And Robert J. Bebber, in recounting a series of interviews conducted in Afghanistan, noted that "very few females were interviewed. Tribal customs in this area of Afghanistan do not permit interaction between foreigners (or even other nonfamily tribal males) with postpubescent females." Thus the "rules" of this society's culture themselves played a role in determining the limits of data collection.

These challenges in the collection process are intertwined with challenges in the application of cultural data. Steffen Merten's chapter considered these latter challenges in depth, focusing especially on the fundamental problem of how to effectively unify data of different types and from different sources. Merten differentiated among various types of data (relational, geospatial, temporal) and asserted the role of data fusion—"the integration of data and knowledge collected from disparate sources by different methods into a consistent, accurate, and useful whole"—as a sine qua non in the production of meaningful cultural knowledge. Merten's proposal relies on visual analytic technology coupled with human cultural and linguistic expertise to map cultural data in ways that are readily applicable to strategic military operations. The significance of data fusion stems from the fact that cultural data take many forms, and defining what constitutes cultural data can be just as difficult as defining culture itself. From an anthropological perspective, an infinite variety of human phenomena—social, political, religious, economic, interpersonal, and so on—can be ascribed to culture. The cultural data set is thus inherently multifarious, and it is therefore no wonder that the methods used in its collection are likewise many in kind.

Alexei Gavriel distinguished between "primary," or "direct," and "secondary," or "indirect," sources in ethnographic data collection. Primary sources include observation, interviewing, surveying, and elicitation methods, while secondary sources include literary, historical, and communications analyses. Together, these sources contribute to the formation of a comprehensive cultural data set whose individual components can be anything from a folktale to an intercepted telephone call. Each of these various types of data carries its own particular subset of challenges in both collection and application, and certain assumptions need to be made explicit regarding their use in producing cultural intelligence. First, as has been discussed previously, there is the basic understanding that cultural data are "fixed" to the time and space in which they were collected. As Gavriel wrote, "This 'time and space' disclaimer does not mean that the information will become 'untrue' at a certain expiration date but rather that ethnographic data are true (accurate) to the time and surroundings they were collected [in,] as the group's culture will inevitably change and adapt over time." The goal of collecting and analyzing ethnographic data is therefore not to compile a set of universals but rather, continuing with Gavriel, "to develop a level of cultural predictability by capturing the patterned behaviors and ideas that are shared by a community." On this, Gavriel alerted us to another important assumption—that cultural predictability is no more universal than the data on which it is based: "although culture is shared, it is not a binding law that all members unfailing[ly] abide and . . . individuals possess their own agency to manipulate outcomes in their favor. Therefore, understanding a society's culture will not provide 100 percent predictability of the actions of all members of a social group, but rather a general level of predictability of the social whole . . ."

Robert J. Bebber made a similar argument: "Problems arise when statisticians and pollsters attempt to use statistical methodology to say that within a given degree of confidence an entire population shares a certain opinion or point of view." In essence, cultural data are neither absolute nor universal—not even within the very culture or community from which they were collected.

A final assumption from Gavriel is that, "Because culture is shared, a group is required for study, as no one individual member can be considered an authority for the entire group." Gavriel allows for the selecting of "key informants . . . to provide insight into certain issues or aspects of the culture" but stresses the fact that culture is inherently a group phenomenon and cannot be tied to a single individual. Gavriel's chapter also considers issues such as source reliability, reminding us that various factors, such as the researcher's access to and rapport with the community, play intimate roles in determining the reliability of data collected from human sources.

Understanding these assumptions and the nature of cultural data is vital to producing accurate cultural intelligence. And, as we have learned from our authors, accuracy is key. But as Alexei Gavriel, citing the example of Abu Ghraib, warned: "Incomplete or inaccurate cultural knowledge can be far worse than the complete absence of cultural knowledge." Feroz Hassan Khan, in his chapter on the Durand Line, explained the historical incongruity between the European notion of "borders" and the more fluid concepts of "zones" or "frontiers" held, in this case, by the Afghans. Nathan R. Springer gave an account of the village of Saw, which turned its back on the United States after "bad intelligence" led to an unnecessary raid on the village. As Springer related, "The village elders felt dishonored and decided to withdraw from contact with U.S. forces after that day."

All of these examples show culture at the heart of the attitudes and behaviors of the people involved. In the history of recent counterinsurgency efforts, the impact of cultural understanding on military operations cannot be underestimated. Indeed, Johnson's chapter provided numerous examples from Afghanistan. It recounted the story of Mullah Omar's rise to power by cultural appeal: "Omar reportedly started the Taliban after a dream in which Allah came to him in the shape of a man, asking him to lead the faithful." Such a claim would mean nothing to non-Muslims; it is relevant only within its cultural context. Johnson also described the evolution of the mullah's role in Afghan culture: "Though they were once primarily apolitical . . . mullahs are now the leading political and ideological figures and voices of the Afghan insurgency." This fundamental shift in the function of the mullah, as Johnson's chapter explains, is of immediate relevance to counterinsurgency operations, as the mullah has become the primary disseminator of information, both religious and otherwise, in rural Afghan populations.

It now seems certain that cultural knowledge is highly useful, perhaps even absolutely essential, in counterinsurgency operations. As Gavriel, quoting from Montgomery McFate, has put it: "Misunderstanding culture at a strategic level can produce policies that exacerbate an insurgency; a lack of cultural knowledge at an operational level can lead to negative public opinion; and ignorance of culture at a tactical level endangers both civilians and troops." Michael R. Fenzel provided us with a concrete example of this: "Historically, the rural population in modern Afghanistan has rejected all large-scale reforms attempted by a central government . . . Establishing security in this war-torn land is achievable only if we focus our efforts and resources at the district level, where the subtribes are culturally dominant." This proposal suggests a plan of action that engages local culture without imposing on it. Fenzel also recommended the appointing of an "Afghan cultural adviser" to provide support for the coalition by producing relevant cultural intelligence.

Cultural knowledge can also be necessary in order to understand the objectives of insurgents and counterinsurgents alike. As Tyrrell advised: "It is important to remember that the goal of warfare for many of the current groups is control over the interpretive framework of a population, not actual, physical control over the geographic area . . . a lesson learned from Vietnam, where the insurgents lost almost all of the battles but won the war."

And this may indeed be the hardest lesson of all to accept: that victory is not determined by body counts alone. In the case of insurgencies, where the disconnect is often political or religious in nature, victories on the battlefield may be less decisive than victories in the cultural sphere. But conventional military training remains focused on combat skills without adequate emphasis on strategies centered around cultural issues, and, where there is cultural training, it is often only superficial at best. This is true not only for the United States; indeed, as Johnson observed critically, the "lack of strategic innovation on the side of the international coalition is striking, and the difficulties in

Afghanistan are in large part due to an intellectual failure to understand the country's social and political dynamics."

And yet, there still remains much hope for cultural understanding. Indeed, as the many conflicts long defined under the rubric of the "Global War on Terror" wind down, and new efforts to restore and maintain order in new and emergent conflict zones take root, research on culture and conflict must be increasingly incorporated into allied and coalition military operations. Thus scholarly works such as this present volume can contribute to our knowledge of the cultural dimensions of counterinsurgencies, strategies for effectively resolving them, and ultimately defining viable pathways for achieving peace.

Indeed, it is our great hope that our combined voices in the preceding pages will help to stimulate a much needed strategic dialogue, here and in the theaters of ongoing counterinsurgency operations in South Asia and beyond, on changing course to ensure that to future generations, "Vietnam" and "Afghanistan" come to represent diametrically opposed metaphors, so that Afghanistan does not become our generation's "Vietnam," with its own lingering syndrome and corrosion of American confidence.

It was this very important goal that undergirded our efforts in the preceding chapters—and that continues to guide us in our ongoing research and counterinsurgency efforts.

NOTES

1. See Robert Welsch and Kirk Endicott, *Taking Sides: Clashing Views on Controversial Issues in Cultural Anthropology* (New York: McGraw Hill, 2003).

2. See Daniel G. Bates and Fred Plog, *Cultural Anthropology, 2nd ed.* (New York: Alfred A. Knopf, 1980), 7.

3. The following section is drawn from Thomas H. Johnson and W. Chris Mason, "No Sign until the Burst of Fire: Understanding the Pakistan–Afghanistan Frontier," *International Security* 32, no. 4 (Spring 2008), 41–77.

4. Quoted in Stephen Tanner, *Afghanistan: A Military History from Alexander the Great to the Fall of the Taliban* (New York: Da Capo, 2002), 134.

5. Charles Allen, *Soldier Sahibs: The Daring Adventurers Who Tamed India's Northwest Frontier* (New York, Carrol & Graf, 2000), 13. See also John C. Griffiths, *Afghanistan: A History of Conflict* (New York: Frederick A. Praeger, 1967), 59; and James W. Spain, *The People of the Khyber: The Pathans of Pakistan* (New York: Frederick A. Praeger, 1962), 46–47.

6. Jolanta Sierakowska-Dyndo, *Tribalism and Afghan Political Traditions* (Warsaw: Institute of Oriental Studies, University of Warsaw, January 2003); available at www.wgsr.uw.edu.pl/pub/uploads/apso4/5Sierakowska-Dydo_Trybalism.pdf.

7. See Peter Hopkirk, *The Great Game: The Struggle for Empire in Central* Asia (New York: Kodansha America, 1992), 285–286; and Martin Evans, *Afghanistan: A Short History of Its People and Politics* (New York: Harper Collins, 2002), 76.

8. As pointed out by Rahimullah Yusufzai in his analysis for BBC, "Pakistani courts and police have no jurisdiction in the tribal areas." See Rahimullah Yusufzai, "Analysis: Pakistan's Tribal Frontiers," *BBC News*, December 14, 2001. For an overview of the political administration and control of the FATA, see the website maintained by the Pakistan government, http://www.fata.gov.pk/index.php?link=3.

9. The obstinacy of the Pashtun tribes combined with the inability of the British to control them contributed to the policy of "masterly inactivity" toward Afghanistan and a very loose system of political activity in the area that now comprises the FATA in Pakistan. See Hopkirk, 1992, 285–286; and Evans, 2002, 76.

10. Ludwig Von Bertalanffy, "An Outline of General System Theory, *British Journal for the Philosophy of Science* I, 2 (1950), 134–165. [0]

11. For an introduction, see chapter 5 of Malcolm Waters, *Modern Sociological Theory* (London: Sage Publications, 1994). For pointed criticisms, see pages 176–187 of Trevor Noble, *Social Theory and Social Change* (New York: St. Martin's Press, 2004).

REFERENCE MATTER

BIBLIOGRAPHY

Abbott, Andrew. *The System of the Professions*. Chicago: University of Chicago Press, 1988.

Ahmed, Akbar. *Pukhtun Economy and Society*. London: Kegan Paul, 1980.

Allen, Charles. *Soldier Sahibs: The Daring Adventurers Who Tamed India's Northwest Frontier*. New York: Carrol & Graf, 2000.

Baeriswyl, Raphaël. "Use and Perception of Violence: A Girardian Approach to Asymmetric Warfare." *Anthropoetics* 13, no. 3 (Fall 2007–Winter 2008).

Baldick, Julian. *Mystical Islam: An Introduction to Sufism*. New York: New York University Press, 1989.

Barfield, Thomas J. "Tribe and State Relations: The Inner Asian perspective," in Philip Khoury and Joseph Kostiner, eds., *Tribes and State Formation in the Middle East*. Berkeley: University of California Press, 1991.

———. "Problems of Establishing Legitimacy in Afghanistan," *Iranian Studies* 37 (2004): 263–269.

———. "Weapons of the Not So Weak in Afghanistan: Pashtun Agrarian Structure and Tribal Organizations for Times of War and Peace." Paper presented as part of the Agrarian Studies Colloquium Series entitled "Hinterlands, Frontiers, Cities and States: Transactions and Identities," Yale University, New Haven, CT, February 2007.

———. "Culture and Custom in Nation-Building: Law in Afghanistan." *Maine Law Review* 60, no. 2 (2008): 358–373.

———. *Afghanistan: A Cultural and Political History (Princeton Studies in Muslim Politics)*. Princeton, NJ: Princeton University Press, 2010.

Barkow, Jerome H. (ed.), *Missing the Revolution: Darwinism for Social Scientists*. Oxford, UK: Oxford University Press, 2005.

Barth, Fredrik. *Political Leadership among the Swat Pathans*. London: Athlone, 1959.

———. *Models of Social Organization*, Occasional Paper no. 23. London: Royal Anthropological Institute of Great Britain and Ireland, 1966.

———, ed. "Pathan identity and its maintenance," in *Ethnic Groups and Boundaries*. Boston: Little Brown, 1969.

Bates, Daniel G., and Fred Plog. *Cultural Anthropology, 2nd ed.* New York: Alfred A. Knopf, 1980.

Bateson, Gregory. *A Sacred Unity*. New York: Harper Collins, 1991.

Baud, Jacques. *La Guerre asymétrique ou la Défaite du vainqueur*. Paris: Editions Du Rocher, 2003.

Benard, Cheryl. *Civil Democratic Islam: Partners, Resources, and Strategies*. Santa Monica, CA: RAND Corporation, 2003.

Benedict, Ruth F. *The Chrysanthemum and the Sword: Patterns of Japanese Culture*. Boston: Houghton Mifflin, 1946.

Berger, Peter L., and Thomas Luckmann. *The Social Construction of Reality: A Treatise in the Sociology of Knowledge*. Garden City, NY: Anchor Books, 1966.

Bernard, H. Russell. *Research Methods in Anthropology: Qualitative and Qualitative Approaches*, 2nd ed. Thousand Oaks, CA: Sage, 1994.

Caldwell, William B., IV. "Changing the Organizational Culture." *Small Wars Journal* [blog], February 2, 2008; available at http://smallwarsjournal.com/blog/2008/02/changing-the-organizational-cu-1/.

Calvin, William H. *The Cerebral Code: Thinking Thought in the Mosaics of the Mind*. Cambridge, MA: MIT Press, 1996.

———. "The Six Essentials? Minimal Requirements for the Darwinian Bootstrapping of Quality." *Journal of Memetics—Evolutionary Models of Information Transmission* 1 (1997); available at http://williamcalvin.com/1990s/1997JMemetics.htm.

Canfield, Robert. *Faction and Conversion in a Plural Society*. Ann Arbor: University of Michigan Press, 1973.

Caroe, Olaf. *The Pathans*. New York: Macmillan, 1958.

CBS News. "Taliban Shadow Gov't Pervades Afghanistan," December 27, 2008; available at www.cbsnews.com/stories/2008/12/27/world/main4687823_page2.shtml.

Cleveland, William L. *A History of the Modern Middle East*, 3rd ed. Boulder, CO: Westview Press, 2004.

Coles, John P. "Incorporating Cultural Intelligence Into Joint Doctrine." *Joint Information Operations Centre* (7-13), 2006.

Constable, Pamela. "Pakistan's Uneasy Role in Terror War; Conciliatory Approach to Tribal and Foreign Fighters Leaves U.S. Officials Frustrated," *Washington Post*, May 8, 2004, A8.

Csikszentmihalyi, Mihaly. *Flow: The Psychology of Optimal Experience*. New York: Harper Perennial, 1991).

Curzon, George, 1st Marquess Curzon of Kedleston. *Frontier, the Romance Lecture,* Oxford, November 2, 1907. Oxford, UK: Clarendon Press, 1907.

Daintith, John, ed. *Oxford Dictionary of Chemistry.* New York: Oxford University Press, 2004.

Dastageer, Ghulam. "Militants Blow Up Rehman Baba's Shrine," *International News,* March 26, 2009; available at http://thenews.jang.com.pk/top_story_detail.asp? Id=20760.

Declassified Documents Reference System. Background Information for President Ayub's U.S. Visit July 1961, Pak-Afghan Relations., CK3100270550; available through Dudley Knox Library at http://galentgroup.com/servlet/DDRS?vrsn=1.0 &view+etext&slb+KE&locID+naval (May 5, 2004).

Department of Defense. *Joint Publication 3-07: Joint Doctrine for Military Operations Other than War.* Washington, DC: Joint Chiefs of Staff, 1995. {moved for chronological order}

———. *Field Manual 2-22.3: Human Intelligence Collector Operations.* Washington, DC: Department of the Army, 2006.

———. *Field Manual 3-24: Counterinsurgency.* Washington, DC: Headquarters Department of the Army, 2006.

———. *Joint Publication 2-0: Joint Intelligence.* Washington, DC: Joint Chiefs of Staff, 2007.

———. *Joint Publication 3-13: Information Operations.* Washington, DC: Joint Chiefs of Staff, 2006.

Department of National Defence, Joint Intelligence Doctrine B-GL-005-200/FP-000. Ottawa: Government of Canada, 2003.

Dewalt, Kathleen M., and Billie R. Dewalt. *Participant Observation: A Guide for Fieldworkers.* Walnut Creek, CA: AltaMira, 2002.

Dodson, John. "Man-Hunting, Nexus Topography, Dark Networks and Small Worlds." *IOSphere,* Joint Information Operations Center, Winter 2006.

Dorronsoro, Gilles. *Revolution Unending: Afghanistan, 1979 to the Present.* New York: Columbia University Press, 2005.

———. "Running Out of Time: Arguments for a New Strategy in Afghanistan." Centre for International Policy Studies (CIPS), University of Ottawa, CIPS Working Paper, no. 3, July 2009.

Dupree, Louis. *Afghanistan,* 2nd ed. Oxford, UK: Oxford University Press, 1980.

Edwards, David. *Heroes of the Age: Moral Fault Lines on the Afghan Frontier.* Berkeley: University of California Press, 1996.

———. *Before Taliban: Genealogies of the Afghan Jihad.* Berkeley: University of California Press, 2002.

Eickelman, Dale F., and James Piscatori, *Muslim Politics.* Princeton, NJ: Princeton University Press, 1996.

Elphinstone, Monsturat. *An Account of the Kingdom of Caubul*. Delhi: Manoharlal, 1998 [1815].

Embree, Ainslie T. *Pakistan's Western Borderlands: The Transformation of a Political Order*. Durham: Carolina Academic Press, 1977.

Encarta World English Dictionary, North American edition. Redmond, WA: Microsoft Corporation, 2009; available at http://encarta.msn.com. Developed for Microsoft by Bloomsbury Publishing Plc.

Enuma Elish: The Seven Tablets of Creation. San Diego: Book Tree, 1998.

Esposito, John L. *What Everyone Needs to Know about Islam*. New York: Oxford University Press, 2002.

Evans, Martin. *Afghanistan: A Short History of Its People and Politics*. New York: Harper Collins, 2002.

Fenzel, Michael R. "The Maneuver Company in Afghanistan: Establishing Counterinsurgency Priorities at the District Level." Military Review (U.S. Army Combined Arms Center, Fort Leavenworth), March–April 2010; available at http://usacac .army.mil/CAC2/MilitaryReview/Archives/English/MilitaryReview_20100430_ art007.pdf.

Fetterman, David M. *Ethnography: Step by Step*, 2nd ed. Thousand Oaks, CA: Sage, 1998.

Firth, Raymond, ed. *Man and Culture*. New York: Routledge and Keegan Paul, 1957.

Fiske, Alan Page. *Structures of Social Life: The Four Elementary Forms of Human Relations*. New York: The Free Press, 1991.

Galula, David. *Counterinsurgency Warfare: Theory and Practice*. Westport, CT: Greenwood, 1964.

Geertz, Clifford. *The Interpretation of Cultures*. New York: Basic Books, 1973.

Glaser, Barney G., and Anselm L. Strauss. *The Discovery of Grounded Theory*. Chicago: Aldine, 1967.

Glatzer, Bernt. "Is Afghanistan on the Brink of Ethnic and Tribal Disintegration?" in William Maley, ed., *Fundamentalism Reborn? Afghanistan and the Taliban*. New York: New York University Press, 1998.

Gomes, Keith. "An Intellectual Genealogy of the Just War." *Small Wars Journal*, August 2008; available at http://smallwarsjournal.com/mag/docs-temp/80-gomes .pdf.

Goodson, Larry P. *Afghanistan's Endless War: State Failure, Regional Politics and the Rise of Taliban*. Washington, DC: University of Washington Press, 2001.

Griffiths, John C. *Afghanistan: A History of Conflict*. New York: Frederick A. Praeger, 1967.

Gurney, O. R. *The Hittites*. New York: Penguin, 1991.

Hamill, Todd J., Richard F. Drecko, James W. Chrissis, and Robert F. Mills. "Analysis of Layered Social Networks," *IO Sphere* (Winter 2008).

Hammersley, Martyn. *Reading Ethnographic Research: A Critical Guide*, Second Edition. Essex, UK: Longmen, 1998.

Hannerz, Ulf. *Transnational Connections: Culture, People, Places*. New York: Routledge, 1996.

Haroon, Sana. *Frontier of Faith: Islam in the Indo-Afghan Borderland*. London: C. Hurst & Company, 2007.

Harris, Marvin. "The Cultural Ecology of India's Sacred Cattle." *Current Anthropology* 7 (1966): 51–66.

Harrison, Selig. "Ethnicity and Political Stalemate in Pakistan," in Ali Banuazizi and Myron Weiner, eds., *The State, Religion and Ethnic Politics*. Syracuse, NY: Syracuse University Press, 1986.

Hartunian, Eric, and Wade A. Germann. "Data Integration to Explore the Dynamics of Conflict: A Preliminary Study," master's thesis, Naval Postgraduate School, Monterey, CA, December 2008.

Hill, Jane H. "Finding Culture in Narrative," in N. Quinn, ed., *Finding Culture in Talk: A Collection of Methods*. New York: Palgrave, 2005.

Holzner, Burkart. *Reality Construction in Society*. Cambridge, MA: Schenkman Publishing, 1968.

Hopkirk, Peter. *The Great Game: The Struggle for Empire in Central* Asia. New York: Kodansha America, 1992.

Hussain, Ijaz. "Is the Durand Agreement Dead?" in Pervaiz Iqbal, ed., *Tribal Areas of Pakistan: Challenges and Responses*. Islamabad: Islamabad Policy Research Institute, 2005.

Hussain, Khawar. "Pakistan's Afghanistan Policy." Naval Postgraduate School Master's Thesis, June 2005, http://www.dtic.mil/cgi-bin/GetTRDoc?AD=ADA435525.

Hussain, Tom. "Pakistani Taliban Target Sufi Shrines." *National*, March 10, 2009; available at www.thenational.ae/apps/pbcs.dll/article?AID=/20090310/FOREIGN/157439541/1002.

Ian, Stephen. *Pakistan: Old Country, New Nation*. London: Penguin, 1964.

Jamali, A. "Taliban Forces Are Now Attacking Sunni Leaders in Afghanistan," Jamestown Foundation, *Eurasia Daily Monitor*, June 2, 2005; available at www.jamestown.org/single/?no_cache=1&tx_ttnews%5Btt_news%5D=30481.

Jinnah, Mahomed Ali. *Jinnah: Speeches and Statements 1947–1948*. New York: Oxford University Press, 2000.

Johnson, Thomas H. "The Taliban Insurgency and an Analysis of *Shabnamah* (Night Letters)," *Small Wars and Insurgencies* 18, no. 3 (September 2007): 317–344.

———. "Religious Figures, Insurgency, and Jihad in Southern Afghanistan," 41–65, in "Who Speaks for Islam? Muslim Grassroots Leaders and Popular Preachers in South Asia," *NBR Special Report*, no. 22, February 2010.

Johnson, Thomas H., and M. Chris Mason. "No Sign until the Burst of Fire: Understanding the Pakistan–Afghanistan Frontier," *International Security* 32, No. 4 (Spring 2008), 41–77.

———. "Refighting the Last War: Afghanistan and the Vietnam Template," *Military Review* (November–December 2009): 4–5.

Jones, Owen Bennett. *Pakistan: Eye of the Storm.* Islamabad: Vanguard, 2002.

Jordan, Ann T. "Organizational Culture: The Anthropological Approach," in Ann T. Jordan (ed.), *Practicing Anthropology in Corporate America: Consulting on Organizational Culture*, NAPA Bulletin #14, American Anthropological Association (1994), 3–16.

Keim, Daniel, Gennady Andrienko, Jean-Daniel Fekete, Carsten Gorg, Jorn Kohlhammer, and Guy Melancon. "Visual Analytics: Definition, Process, and Challenges," in *Information Visualization: Human-Centered Issues and Perspectives*, 154–175. Berlin and Heidelburg: Springer, 2008.

Khaldun, Ibn. *The Muqaddimah: An Introduction to History* (abridged edition), trans. Franz Rosenthal. Princeton, NJ: Princeton University Press, 1967.

———. *The Muqaddimah: An Introduction to History* (3 vol.), trans. Franz Rosenthal. Princeton, NJ: Princeton University Press, 1958.

Kilcullen, David. *The Accidental Guerrilla: Fighting Small Wars in the Midst of a Big One.* New York: Oxford University Press, 2009.

Kipling, Rudyard. "The Ballad of the King's Mercy," 1889; retrieved on July 9, 2013, from www.kipling.org.uk/rg_kingsmercy1.htm.

———. *The Works of Rudyard Kipling.* Roslyn, NY: Black Readers Service, n.d.

Korzybski, Alfred. *Science and Sanity; An Introduction to Non-Aristotelian Systems and General Semantics.* Lancaster, PA: Institute of General Semantics, 1995; 5th edition.

Kux, Dennis. *The United States and Pakistan 1947–2000: Disenchanted Allies.* Washington, DC: The Woodrow Wilson Center Press, 2001.

Laughlin, Charles. "The Cycle of Meaning," in Stephen Glazier, ed., *Anthropology of Religion: Handbook of Theory and Method*, 471–488. Westport, CT: Greenwood Press, 1997; available at www.biogeneticstructuralism.com/docs/cycle.rtf.

LeCompte, Margaret, and Jean J. Schensul. *Designing and Conducting Ethnographic Research.* 7 vols. Volume 1. Lanham, MD: AltaMira, 1999b.

Lee, Dorothy. "Are Basic Needs Ultimate?" in Dorothy Lee, *Freedom and Culture* (Englewood Cliffs, N.J.: Prentice-Hall, 1959), 70-77.

Lewis, Paul. "Inside the Islamic Group Accused by MI5 and FBI." *Guardian*, August 19, 2006; available at www.guardian.co.uk/uk/2006/aug/19/religion.terrorism.

Lindholm, Charles. *Generosity and Jealousy.* New York: Columbia University Press, 1980.

Madhi, Muhsin. *Ibn Khaldun's philosophy of history: a study in the philosophic founda-tion of the science of culture.* Chicago: University of Chicago Press, 1971.

Maffesoli, Michel. *The Time of the Tribes.* London: Sage, 1996.

Magnus, Ralph H. and Eden Naby. *Afghanistan: Mullah, Marx, and Mujahid.* Boulder, CO: Westview Press, 2000, 70–97.

Mahmood, Tariq. "The Durand Line: South Asia's Next Trouble Spot." Naval Post-graduate School Thesis, June 2005; available at www.dtic.mil/dtic/tr/fulltext/u2/a435574.pdf.

Maley, William, ed. *Fundamentalism Reborn? Afghanistan and the Taliban.* New York: New York University Press, 1998.

Malinowski, Bronislaw. *Argonauts of the Western Pacific.* New York: E. P. Dutton, 1922.

———. *A Scientific Theory of Culture.* New York: Oxford University Press, 1960 [1944].

Maloney, Sean M. "A Violent Impediment: The Evolution of Insurgent Operations in Kandahar Province 2003–07." *Small Wars & Insurgencies* 19, no. 2 (June 2008).

Mandaville, Peter. *Global Political Islam.* London: Routledge, 2007.

Marr, J., B. G. Johncushing, and R. Thompson. "Human Terrain Mapping: A Critical First Step to Winning the COIN Fight," *Military Review* 88 (March/April 2008), 37–51.

Marsden, Peter. *Taliban: War, Religion, and the New Order in Afghanistan.* London: Zed Books, 1998.

Mathews, Holly F. "Uncovering Cultura; Models of Gender from Accounts of Folk-tales," in N. Quinn, ed., *Finding Culture in Talk: A Collection of Methods.* New York: Palgrave, 2005.

Matinuddin, Kamal. *The Taliban Phenomenon: Afghanistan 1994–1997.* Karachi: Ox-ford University Press, 1999.

Mauss, Marcel. *The Gift.* New York: W. W. Norton & Company, 2000.

McCreary, John. "Nightwatch Special Report: October 2008 in Afghanistan." *AFCEA Intelligence.* December 15, 2008; retrieved on January 2, 2009, from www.afcea.org/mission/intel/nightwatch.asp.

McFate, Montgomery. 2005a "Anthropology and Counterinsurgency: The Strange Story of their Curious Relationship." *Military Review* (March–April), 2005, 24–38.

———. "The Military Utility of Understanding Adversary Culture." *Joint Force Quar-terly* 38 (third quarter 2005b): 42–48.

MCIA (Marine Corps Intelligence Activity). *Cultural Intelligence: Global Scope, Oper-ationally Focused.* Quantico: Marine Corps Intelligence Activity, 2007.

Metcalf, Barbara D. "'Traditionalist' Islamic Activism: Deoband, Tablighis, and Tal-ibs," Social Science Research Council, 2001, 1–8; available at http://essays.ssrc.org/sept11/essays/metcalf.htm..

Metz, Steven. *Re-Thinking Insurgency*. Strategic Studies Institute, 2007; available at www.strategicstudiesinstitute.army.mil/pubs/display.cfm?pubID=790.

Milany, Mohsen. Remarks made in a presentation in a seminar on Afghanistan at the Woodrow Wilson Center, Washington, DC, November 15, 2002.

Mortenson, Greg. *Three Cups of Tea*. Chicago: Viking Adult Books, 2006.

Nadem, Bashir Ahmad. "Religious Scholar Shot Dead in Kandahar," *Pajhwok Afghan News*, January 6, 2009; available at www.pajhwok.com/viewstory.asp?lng=eng&id=67799.

Nagl, John A. *Learning to Eat Soup with a Knife: Counterinsurgency Lessons from Malaya and Vietnam*. Chicago: University of Chicago Press, 2002.

Najibullah, Farangis. "Can Sufis Bring Peace to Afghanistan?" Radio Free Europe/Radio Liberty, March 5, 2009; available at www.rferl.org/content/Can_Sufis_Bring_Peace_to_Afghanistan/1503303.html.

Naroll, Raoul. *Data Quality Control—A New Research Technique: Prolegomena to a Cross-Cultural Study of Culture Stress*. New York: Free Press of Glencoe, 1962.

Nation Master Encyclopedia. "Durand Line," Nationmaster.com; available at www.nationmaster.com/encyclopedia/Durand-Line.

NATO (North Atlantic Treaty Organization). AAP-6: NATO Glossary of Terms and Definitions. Brussels: NATO Standardization Agency, 2008.

Nazim, Bashir Ahmad. "Religious Scholar, Four Guards Killed in Kandahar." *Pajhwok Afghan News*, March 1, 2009; available at www.pajhwok.com/viewstory.asp?lng=eng&id=70485.

"The Need for Proper [Jihadi] Bloggers," The Ignored Puzzle Pieces of Knowledge, March 16, 2009; retrieved from http://revolution.thabaat.net/?p=1046 (no longer active); available on *MILNews* (*Military News for Canadians*) at: http://milnewstbay.pbwiki.com/f/ProperJihadBloggers-revolution.thabaat.net-172002Mar09.pdf.

Niccoli, Ottavia. *Prophecy and People in Renaissance Italy*. Princeton, NJ: Princeton University Press, 1990.

Noble, Trevor. *Social Theory and Social Change*. New York: St. Martin's Press, 2004.

Noor-ul-Haq. "Pak-Afghan Relations." Islamabad Policy Research Institute (IPRI), Fact File no. 44 (2003); retrieved on March 26, 2005, from http://ipripak.org/factfiles/ff44.shtml.

NPR (National Public Radio). "Special Series: Afghanistan: In Search of Justice," National Public Radio December 12–18, 2008; available at www.npr.org/series/98121740/afghanistan-in-search-of-justice.

Obama, Barack H. "A New Strategy for Afghanistan and Pakistan." Prepared remarks. Washington, DC, March 27, 2009.

O'Reilly, Karen. *Ethnographic Methods*. New York: Routledge, 2005.

Pakistan, Government of. FATA website; retrieved on July 10, 2013, from www.fata.gov.pk/index.php?link=3.

Patai, Raphael. *The Arab Mind*. New York: Charles Scribners and Sons,, 1973.

Perry, Walter L., and John Gordon IV. *Analytic Support to Intelligence in Counterinsurgencies*. Santa Monica, CA: RAND National Defense Research Institute, 2008.

Piddington, Ralph. *Social Forces: An Introduction to Social Anthropology*. New York: The Macmillan Company, 1957.

Pike, Kenneth L. "Emic and Etic Standpoints for the Description of Behavior." In K. L. Pike, ed., *Language in Relation to a Unified Theory of the Structure of Human Behavior—Part I*,

Plett, Barbara. "Can Sufi Islam Counter the Taleban?" BBC News, February 24, 2009; available at http://news.bbc.co.uk/2/hi/south_asia/7896943.stm.

Poullada, Leon. "Pushtunistan: Afghan Domestic Politics and Relations with Pakistan," in Ainsle T. Embree, ed., *Pakistan's Western Border Lands*. Delhi: Vikas Publishing House Ltd., 1977.

Pressfield, Steven. "How to Win in Afghanistan," blog.stevenpressfield.com, 2009.

Program for Culture and Conflict Studies. *Khost Provincial Profile*. 2007; retrieved on June 27, 2008, from www.nps.edu/programs/ccs/Khost.html.

Pullada, Leon B. "Pushtunistan: Afghan Domestic Politics and Relations with Pakistan." In Ainslie T. Embree, ed., *Pakistan's Western Borderlands: The Transformation of a Political Order*. Durham, NC: Carolina Academic Press, 1977.

Quinn, Naomi. "How to Reconstruct Shemas People Share, from What They Say," in N. Quinn, ed., *Finding Culture in Talk: A Collection of Methods*. New York: Palgrave, 2005.

Radcliffe-Brown, A. R. *The Andaman Islanders*. New York: Free Press, 1922.

Radio Free Europe/Radio Liberty. *Afghan Cricket Star Reportedly Killed in U.S.-led Raid*. August 27, 2008; retrieved on January 2, 2009, from www.rferl.org/content/Afghan_Cricket_Star_Reportedly_Killed_/1194358.html.

Raelin, Joseph A. "The Myth of Charismatic Leaders," BNET, March 2003; available at www.findarticles.com/p/articles/mi_moMNT/is_3_57/ai_98901483.

Rappaport, Roy A. *Ecology, Meaning, & Religion*. Berkeley, CA: North Atlantic Books, 1993.

———. *Pigs for Ancestors*. New Haven, CT: Yale University Press, 1968.

Rashid, Ahmed. *Taliban: Militant Islam, Oil, and Fundamentalism in Central Asia*. New Haven, CT: Yale University Press, 2001.

Roy, Olivier. *Islam and Resistance in Afghanistan*. Cambridge, UK: Cambridge University Press, 1990.

———. *The Failure of Political Islam*. Cambridge, MA: Harvard University Press, 1994.

———. "Has Islamism a Future in Afghanistan?" in William Maley, ed., *Fundamentalism Reborn? Afghanistan and the Taliban*. New York: New York University Press, 1998.

Sachs, Susan. "A Muslim Missionary Group Draws New Scrutiny in U.S." *The New York Times*, July 14, 2003; available at www.nytimes.com/2003/07/14/national/14ISLA .html?pagewanted=1.

Sahlins, Marshall. *Stone Age Economics*. New York: Aldine de Gruyter, 1972.

Schensul, Jean J., Margaret D. LeCompte, Bonnie K. Nastasi, and Stephen P. Borgatti. *Enhanced Ethnographic Methods: Audiovisual Techniques, Focused Group Interviews, and Elicitation Techniques*. 7 vols. Volume 3. Lanham, MD: AltaMira, 1999.

Schensul, Jean J., Margaret LeCompte, Robert Trotter, and Merrill Singer. *Mapping Social Networks, Spatial Data, and Hidden Populations*. 7 vols. Volume 4. Lanham, MD: AltaMira, 1999.

Schensul, Stephan J., Jean J. Schensul, and Margaret D. LeCompte. *Essential Ethnographic Methods: Observations, Interviews, and Questionnaires*. 7 vols. Volume 2. Lanham, MD: AltaMira, 1999.

Schimmel, Annnemarie. *Mystical Dimensions of Islam*. Chapel Hill: University of North Carolina Press, 1975.

Segal, Gerald. "China and Afghanistan." *Asian Survey* 21, no. 11 (1981): 1158–1174.

Serafino, Nina M. "Peacekeeping and Related Stability Operations: Issues of U.S. Military Involvement." *CRS Issue Brief for Congress*. Washington DC: The Library of Congress, June 25, 2005.

Shahzad, Syed Saleem. "Pashtunistan Issue Back to Haunt Pakistan." *Asia Times*, October 24, 2003; retrieved on June 18, 2004, from www.atimes.com.

Sierakowska-Dyndo, Jolanta. *Tribalism and Afghan Political Traditions*. Warsaw: Institute of Oriental Studies, University of Warsaw, January 2003; available at www .wgsr.uw.edu.pl/pub/uploads/apso4/5Sierakowska-Dydo_Trybalism.pdf.

Smith, Adam. *An Inquiry into the Nature and Causes of the Wealth of Nations*. London: W. Strahan and T. Cadell, 1776.

Spain, James W. *The People of the Khyber: The Pathans of Pakista*. New York: Frederick A. Praeger, 1962.

Steward, Julian. *Theory of Culture Change: The Methodology of Multilinear Evolution*. Urbana: University of Illinois Press, 1955.

Stewart, Alex. *The Ethnographer's Method*. Thousand Oaks, CA: Sage, 1998.

Sultan, Shaukat. "Government Initiatives in FATA before and after 9/11," in Pervaiz Iqbal Cheema and Maqsud-ul Hasan Nuri, eds., *Tribal Areas of Pakistan: Challenges and Responses*. Islamabad: Islamabad Policy Research Institute, 2005.

Tahir-Kheli, Shirin. "Iran and Pakistan: Cooperation in an Area of Conflict." *Asian Survey* 17, No. 5 (1977): 479–483.

Tanner, Stephen. *Afghanistan: A Military History from Alexander the Great to the Fall of the Taliban*. New York: Da Capo Press, 2002.

Thompson, Grahame F. *Between Hierarchies and Markets: The Logic and Limits of Network Forms of Organization*. Oxford, UK: Oxford University Press, 2003.

Thornton, Robert. "Interview with Colonel Mark Brackney, Deputy Chief Provincial Reconstruction Team," Joint Center for International Security Force Assistance, March 11, 2008. Available in Mosul Case Study: Executive Summary and Interviews, 65, http://marctyrrell.com/wp-content/uploads/2009/02/sfa-case-study-exec-sum-and-interviews-1.pdf.

———. "Interview with Dr. James Knight, Provincial Reconstruction Team (PRT) Chief Ninewa, Mosul, Iraq," *The Colloquium* I, No. 1 (Fort Leavenworth: USA/USMC Counterinsurgency Center, August 2008).

Thornton, Robert, John Fishel, and Marc Tyrrell. "Security Force Assistance Case Study: Mosul, Iraq," *Small Wars Journal*, December, 2008; available at http://smallwarsjournal.com/blog/2008/12/sfa-case-study-mosul-iraq/.

Trimingham, J. Spencer. *The Sufi Orders of Islam*. Oxford, UK: Clarendon Press, 1971.

Turner, Victor. *The Anthropology of Performance*. New York: PAJ Books, 1988.

———. *From Ritual to Theatre: The Human Seriousness of Play*. New York: PAJ Books, 1991.

Tyler, Edward B. "On a Method of Investigating the Development of Institutions; Applied to Laws of Marriage and Descent." *The Journal of the Anthropological Institute of Great Britain and Ireland* 18, (1889), 245–272; available at http://galton.org/essays/1880-1889/galton-1888-jaigi-tylor-remarks.pdf.

Tyler, Stephen. *Cognitive Anthropology*. New York: Holt, Rinehart, and Winston, 1969.

Tyrrell, Marc W. D. *At the Cusp of the Information Age: Outplacement as a Rite of Passage in Late 20th Century Canada*. PhD dissertation, Department of Sociology and Anthropology, Carleton University, 2000; available at www.nlc-bnc.ca/obj/s4/f2/dsk2/ftp03/NQ52334.pdf section 5.3.

———. "The First Culture Turn: Ethnographic Knowledge in the Romano-Byzantine Military Tradition." Paper presented at the 2008 Inter-University Seminar on Armed Forces and Society, Royal Military College, Kingston, November 2008; available at http://marctyrrell.com/uploads/TFCT.pdf.

van Wijk, J. J. "The Value of Visualization," from *IEEE Visualization* (2005); available at www.win.tue.nl/~vanwijk/vov.pdf.

Wallace, Anthony F. C. "Revitalization Movements," *American Anthropologist* (New Series) 58, 2 (April 1956), 264–281.

Wardak, Mirwais, Idrees Zaman, and Kanishka Nawabi. "The Role and Functions of Religious Civil Society in Afghanistan: Case Studies from Sayedabad and Kunduz." *Cooperation for Peace and Unity*, July 2007; available at www.cmi.no/pdf/?file=/afghanistan/doc/Kunduz%20and%20Sayedabad%20Report%20-%20Final.pdf, 8.

Waters, Malcomb. *Modern Sociological Theory*. London: Sage Publications, 1994.

Welsch, Robert, and Kirk Endicott. *Taking Sides: Clashing Views on Controversial Issues in Cultural Anthropology*. New York: McGraw Hill, 2003.

White, Leslie A. *The Evolution of Culture: The Development of Civilization to the Fall of Rome*. Walnut Creek, CA: Left Coast Press, 2007 (originally published in 1959).

Wilson, David Sloan. "Social Semantics: Toward a Genuine Pluralism in the Study of Social Behaviour, *Journal of Evolutionary Biology* 21, No. 1 (January 2008), 368–373.

Wilson, George Grafton. *Handbook of International Law*. St. Paul, MN: West Publishing Co., 1939.

Wolf, Paul. "Pakistan: Partition and Military Succession," Pashtunistan Documents from the U.S. National Archives (Afghanistan–Pakistan Relations, Declassified Airgram of the U.S. Embassies to the Department of State from 1952 to 1973; retrieved on March 23, 2005, from www.icdc.com/~paulwolf/pakistan/pashtunistan .htm.

Wolkstein, Diane, and Samuel Noah Kramer. *Inanna, Queen of Heaven and Earth*. New York: Harper Perennial, 1983.

World Bank Watching Brief for Afghanistan. "Afghanistan's International Trade Relations with Neighboring Countries," February 2001; retrieved on March 7, 2005, from http://lnweb18.worldbank.org/SAR/sa.nsf/Attachments/8/$File/intltrade.pdf.

WorldPublicOpinion.org. "Public Opinion in the Islamic World on Terrorism, al Qaeda, and US Policies," February 25, 2009; available at www.worldpublicopinion .org/pipa/pdf/feb09/STARTII_Feb09_rpt.pdf.

Yusufzai, Rahimullah. "Analysis: Pakistan's Tribal Frontiers," *BBC News*, December 14, 2001.

———. "Pakistan's Army in the Tribal Areas," *BBC NEWS World Edition*, June 25, 2003; retrieved on February 25, 2005, from http://news.bbc.co.uk/1/hi/world/ south_asia/3020552.stm.

Zaman, Aly. "India's Increased Involvement in Afghanistan and Central Asia: Implications for Pakistan," *Islamabad Policy Research Institute (IPRI) Journal* 3, no. 2 (Summer 2003); retrieved on July 19, 2004, from www.ipripak.org/journal/ summer2003/indiaincreased.shtml.

Zinni, Anthony. Non-Traditional Military Missions: Their Nature, and the Need for Cultural Awareness and Flexible Thinking. Quantico, VA: U.S. Marine Corps War College, 1998.

INDEX

ABCT (Airborne Brigade Combat Team), 11, 215
ABP (Afghan Border Police), 185, 230–34
adversary, 4, 21–4, 37–8, 40
adviser, 189–93, 195; agricultural, 191
Afghan: Amirs, 96, 113, 153; army, 159, 161, 227, 233; Border Police (ABP), 185, 230–34; border with Pakistan, 112, 137, 161, 168; and Coalition forces, 205–6, 209; communities, 178, 195; constitution, 135; counterinsurgency environment, 186; cultural adviser, 190, 253; culture, 12, 19, 253; district government, 178, 191, 193; enablers, 190, 194; glory, 155; government, 121, 132, 136, 142–43, 152, 155, 160, 164, 189, 193, 204–205, 208, 232, 237; hinterland, 160; history, 98, 115, 130, 135, 239; identity cards, 158; information operations, 192–93; insurgency, 120, 129, 137, 253; Islamists, 134; jihad, 145, 156; journalists, 230; law, 144, 184; media, 121; military, 201; nation, 151; nation-state, 120; National Army (ANA), 149, 176, 180, 182–85, 193–95, 199, 205, 227, 230–31, 233; National Police (ANP), 179, 184–85, 195, 205–206; National Security Forces, *see* ANSF; negotiating team, 151; Parliament, 152; poetry, 230; politics, 98–99, 116–17, 120; population, 8, 14, 182, 215, 219, 253; provinces, 79, 124, 188; refugees, 142, 149, 158–60, 169, 173; security forces, 10, 177, 182, 184, 186, 195, 205, 233–34; society, 120, 122, 135, 141; state, 96, 113, 120, 137; Taliban, 128, 146, 242; territory, 150, 169; training, 13; ulema, 133, 135, 137; war with Soviet Union, 238; wars, 151, 167, 192
Afghanistan: border, 96; destabilization of, 150; enemies of, 199; geography of, 124; history of, 120; investment in, 101; landlocked, 171; modern, 9, 177, 253; National Army of, 149, 161, 176, 180, 182–85, 193–95, 199, 205, 227, 230–31, 233; National Development Strategy (ANDS) of, 132; neighboring, 167; porous border of, 168; rebuilding, 2; relations with Pakistan, 96, 140, 149, 162, 173–74, 239–40; ruled by, 113; southern Pashtun region of, 129; war-ravaged, 164; workers in, 193
Afghans, 11, 14, 98, 116, 118, 120, 122, 127, 134–35, 139–41, 150–51, 153–58, 182–86, 190–92, 194–95; average, 181; committed, 120; disenfranchised, 127; educated, 115; fellow, 135; local, 182; rural, 179; weak, 107
agriculture, 99–100, 107, 113, 118, 169, 190–92, 194, 197
Airborne Brigade Combat Team (ABCT), 11, 215
al-Qaeda, 5, 9, 57, 68–70, 116, 136, 165–68, 177, 206
all-source, cells, 39–40; intelligence, 27, 29, 40